The Vital Art of D. H. Lawrence

THE VITAL ART OF D. H. LAWRENCE

Vision and Expression

Jack Stewart

SOUTHERN ILLINOIS UNIVERSITY PRESS
Carbondale and Edwardsville

02 01 00 99   4 3 2 1

Library of Congress Cataloging-in-Publication Data

Stewart, Jack, 1935–
    The vital art of D. H. Lawrence : vision and expression / Jack
Stewart.
        p. cm.
    Includes bibliographical references (p.   ) and index.
    1. Lawrence, D. H. (David Herbert), 1885–1930—Criticism and
interpretation. I. Title.
PR6023.A93Z92397 1999   98-26124
823′.912—dc21   CIP
    ISBN 0-8093-2168-8 (cloth : alk. paper)

The paper used in this publication meets the minimum requirements of
American National Standard for Information Sciences—Permanence of
Paper for Printed Library Materials, ANSI Z39.48-1984. ♾

To my wife, Greta

and daughters, Susan and Rosalyn

CONTENTS

PLATES

ACKNOWLEDGMENTS

I wish to thank L. D. Clark and Keith Cushman for their perceptive comments, which helped me to see the shape of what I was trying to express, at a formative stage. I am indebted to both for their knowledge of Lawrence and their editorial expertise, as well as for generously taking time from various projects to advise me. I want especially to thank Michael Squires for his farseeing insights on my "finished" manuscript, which gave me encouragement as well as constructive criticism that I found invaluable for the process of revision. I might say of Squires's reading what Catherine Carswell said of Lawrence's: "He read that he might find out what the writer would be at, and, having found out, that he might expound it to the writer. . . . It was this, with his astonishing patience, his delighted recognition of any sign of vitality and his infectious insistence upon the hardest work, that made him unique among critics" (17–18). I would also like to thank James Cowan, first editor of *The D. H. Lawrence Review*, and his successors, Dennis Jackson and Charles Rossman, for their interest in and encouragement of my Lawrence studies.

Parts of the following chapters of this book are based on my previously published research. Chapter 3: "Expressionism in *The Rainbow*," *Novel* 13 (1980): 296–315. Chapter 4: "Rhetoric and Image in Lawrence's 'Moony,'" *Studies in the Humanities* 8 (1980): 33–37, and "Common Art Interests of Van Gogh and Lawrence," *Studies in the Humanities* 11 (1984): 18–32. Chapter 5: "Primitivism in *Women in Love*," *D. H. Lawrence Review* 13 (1980): 45–62. Chapter 7: "The Vital Art of Lawrence and Van Gogh," *D. H. Lawrence Review* 19 (1987): 123–48, and "Primordial Affinities: Lawrence, Van Gogh and the Miners," *Mosaic: A Journal for the Interdisciplinary Study of Literature* 24 (winter 1991): 93–113. Chapter 8: "Lawrence on Van Gogh," *D. H. Lawrence Review* 16 (1983): 1–24. Chapter 9: "Lawrence and Gauguin," *Twentieth Century Literature* 26 (1980): 385–401. I would like to express my appreciation to the editors of these journals for opening their pages to my earlier studies of Lawrence and for allowing me to use this material in the writing of this book.

For permission to reprint selections from other, previously published works, I wish to acknowledge the following: From *The Complete Letters of Vincent Van Gogh* by Vincent Van Gogh (Boston: New York Graphic Society, 1978). By permission of Little, Brown and Company in conjunction with the New York Graphic Society. All rights reserved. By permission of Little, Brown and Company and by permission of Thames and Hudson, Ltd. Paul Cézanne, *Letters*, ed. John Rewald; trans. Seymour Hacker; rev. ed. (New York: Hacker Art Books, 1984). Used by permission. "Selected Excerpts" from *The Letters of D. H. Lawrence* by D. H. Lawrence; Introduction by Aldous Huxley. Copyright 1932 by the Estate of D. H. Lawrence. Used by permission of Viking Penguin, a division of Penguin Books USA, Inc., and by permission of Laurence Pollinger, Ltd. "Introduction to These Paintings," "Art and Morality," "Christs in the Tirol," "Flowery Tuscany," "Indians and an Englishman," "Morality and the Novel," "New Mexico," "Nottingham and the Mining Countryside," "Pan in America," "Study of Thomas Hardy," "Why the Novel Matters," from *Phoenix: The Posthumous Papers of D. H. Lawrence*, by D. H. Lawrence and edited by Edward McDonald. Copyright 1936 by Frieda Lawrence, renewed © 1964 by the Estate of the late Frieda Lawrence Ravagli. Used by permission of Viking Penguin, a division of Penguin Books USA, Inc., and by permission of Laurence Pollinger, Ltd. "Making Pictures" by D. H. Lawrence, copyright © 1959, 1963, 1968 by the Estate of Frieda Lawrence Ravagli. " . . . Love Was Once a Little Boy" by D. H. Lawrence, copyright © 1925 by Centaur Press, copyright renewed © 1953 by Frieda Lawrence Ravagli. "The Novel" by D. H. Lawrence, copyright © 1959, 1963, 1968 by the Estate of Frieda Lawrence Ravagli. "À Propos of *Lady Chatterley's Lover*" by D. H. Lawrence, copyright © 1930 by Frieda Lawrence, renewed © 1958 by the Estate of Frieda Lawrence Ravagli. "Reflections on the Death of a Porcupine" by D. H. Lawrence, copyright © 1925 by Centaur Press. Copyright © renewed 1953 by Frieda Lawrence. "The Two Principles" by D. H. Lawrence, copyright © 1959, 1963, 1968 by the Estate of Frieda Lawrence Ravagli, from *Phoenix II: Uncollected Papers of D. H. Lawrence* by D. H. Lawrence, ed. Roberts and Moore. Used by permission of Viking Penguin, a division of Penguin Books USA, Inc., and by permission of Laurence Pollinger, Ltd. "Almond Blossom," by D. H. Lawrence, "Spiral Flame," by D. H. Lawrence, "New Heaven and Earth," by

D. H. Lawrence, "Pomegranates," by D. H. Lawrence, "Thought" by D. H. Lawrence, "Poetry of the Present" by D. H. Lawrence, *The Complete Poems of D. H. Lawrence*, by D. H. Lawrence, edited by V. de Sola Pinto & F. W. Roberts. Copyright © 1964, 1971 by Angelo Ravagli and C. M. Weekley, Executors of the Estate of Frieda Lawrence Ravagli. Used by permission of Viking Penguin, a division of Penguin Books USA, Inc., and by permission of Laurence Pollinger, Ltd. "Daughters of the Vicar," copyright 1922 by Thomas Seltzer, Inc., renewed © 1950 by Frieda Lawrence, and "Odour of Chrysanthemums," copyright © 1933 by the Estate of D. H. Lawrence, renewed © 1961 by Angelo Ravagli and C. M. Weekley, Executors of the Estate of Frieda Lawrence, from *The Complete Short Stories of D. H. Lawrence* by D. H. Lawrence. Used by permission of Viking Penguin, a division of Penguin Books USA, Inc., and by permission of Laurence Pollinger, Ltd.

The Vital Art of D. H. Lawrence

INTRODUCTION

For D. H. Lawrence, "real works of art are made by the whole consciousness of man working together in unison and oneness: instinct, intuition, mind, intellect all fused into one complete consciousness, and grasping what we may call a complete truth, or a complete vision . . . " ("Introduction to These Paintings" 574). Truth in art is a matter of "intuitive vision," calling on the senses and not just on the isolated, logocentric mind. So Cézanne, according to Lawrence, "could only believe in his own expression when it expressed a moment of wholeness or completeness of consciousness in himself" (575). "Expressiveness," as Susanne Langer observes, "has endless degrees. Complete artistic success would be complete articulation of an idea, and the effect would be perfect livingness of the work" (79). Substitute *being* for *idea* and here is the goal of Lawrence's vital art. Langer's theory takes on new meaning when Lawrence's verbal imagination is connected with the "vitalized space" (89) of Van Gogh, Cézanne, and Gauguin. But her rigorous formalism, in which the "life in art is a 'life' of forms" (79), does not comprehend the dynamics and roughened textures of Lawrence's art.

"Vision," as Lawrence uses the term, refers both to the faculty of visual perception and to ontological vision activated in the process of writing or painting.[1] His reflections on painting contain some vital ideas on the phenomenology of perception and imagination,[2] both in the visual arts and (by implication) in writing. In making vision and expression my focus, I follow such clues, based on Lawrence's experience of paint and canvas and his close study of "real vision paintings," such as Cézanne's and Van Gogh's. Apart from the cross-fertilization that goes on between writers and painters,[3] appreciation of painting and appreciation of literature support each other in various ways. Fictional styles are clarified when brought into contact with form languages in painting that spring from similar artistic temperaments or worldviews. The effect of placing the writer in the imaginative context of the painter is to intensify our perception of the work of each, not just as

1

technical expression belonging to the medium, but also as expressive form—
"a tremulation on the ether" of "the whole man-alive" (Lawrence, "Why the
Novel Matters" 195).

Critical disagreements about Lawrence's writing may legitimately stem
from conflicting aesthetics or ideologies. But one should recognize his aims
and the new styles of reading they demand. With a view to enriching the
experience of reading Lawrence's work, I propose to bring his vision and
expression into closer contact with parallel modes in modern art. Several
critics have previously discussed Lawrence's relations with the visual arts.[4]
The first major study was Keith Alldritt's *The Visual Imagination of D. H.
Lawrence* (1971), which is iconographic rather than iconological,[5] examining
allusions to artworks, artists, and art theory in major novels and relating
visual narration to its social and cultural frames. Illuminating as Alldritt's
study is on settings in the first two novels or on Renaissance painting and
Gothic architecture in *The Rainbow*, the limitations of realistic criteria become evident when they are brought to bear on the more extreme scenes in
Women in Love. Alldritt regards such scenes as elaborate pictorial "tableaux"
that slow down the narrative rather than as visually dynamic expressions of
the unconscious. The difference between our two readings depends on a recognition of the role of expressionism in Lawrence's style. Alldritt regards the
Arab mare scene as "manifestly pictorial," conflating the narrator's presentation with Gudrun's retrospective view of it. But I do not find a "comparative
lack of texture and complexity" in Lawrence's polarization of animal and machine; the element of "abstraction" that the critic objects to is that of expressionist drama, signifying character through symbolic action rather than the
allegorizing of "a morality play" (213–14). Expressionism is an art of excess
that highlights unconscious forces by exaggerating their physical manifesta-
tions. Here Gerald and Gudrun are *inwardly* exposed to view by the action,
as they will be progressively revealed in ritualistic scenes like "Rabbit." The
narrative, with its modernist technique of disjunction that activates a network of cross-references, exists for the sake of such scenes, rather than the
scenes subserving a socially constructed "plot." To this extent, "spatial form"
is part of Lawrence's strategy.

Alldritt finds that, in the lantern-lighting scene in "Water-Party" (*Women
in Love*, chapter 14), "the visual writing is too intense," providing "a richness in colour, light and texture which appears in no very immediate way
endemic or necessary" (214). The interlude does create a lull in the action
by means of visual elaboration and a talismanic symbolism that identifies

the sisters with contrasting designs on their lanterns. I agree that Lawrence's "importation of visual glamour" does look like "poeticising"—by contrast with temporally driven narrative action. But this impressionist and painterly scene plays its part in the visual and dramatic economy of a richly diverse chapter. Intensity, lavish color, and exaggeration are characteristics of Lawrence's style in the years between 1912 and 1917. If we are to appreciate his innovative language, we will have to appreciate his use not only of impressionism but also and more significantly of an expressionism that does not match outward reality as it appears to the uninvolved eye, but heightens and distorts it to make a subjective reality visible. Norms of realism and decorum do not apply to such writing. In this period, Lawrence's vision undergoes a vital reorientation. He is no longer confined to English culture, with its principles of realism and common sense, but draws freely on prewar European culture, with its ferment of expressive styles.

Jeffrey Meyers's *Painting and the Novel* (1975) includes iconographic studies of three paintings—Maurice Greiffenhagen's *An Idyll*, Fra Angelico's *Last Judgment*, and Mark Gertler's *The Merry-Go-Round*—in relation to their contexts in *The White Peacock*, *The Rainbow*, and *Women in Love*, respectively. Meyers relates these paintings to Lawrence's literary themes, whereas I am concerned with how his visual style reflects his ontological vision. Kim Herzinger's *D. H. Lawrence in His Time* (1982) places Lawrence "within the cultural matrix" in which his art took shape. Herzinger focuses usefully on Lawrence's early Georgian phase, then, in "The Impact of Futurism, Imagism, and Vorticism" (chapter 6), assesses his style in the formative period from 1912 to 1915. But her emphasis is cultural-historical, and she does not include extended analyses of particular novels.

Marianna Torgovnick, in *The Visual Arts, Pictorialism, and the Novel* (1985), situates Lawrence among modernist writers whose work interrelates with the visual arts. While the term "pictorialism" suggests iconography, Torgovnick deals mainly with stylistic parallels, identifying *decorative*, *biographical*, *ideological*, and *interpretive* modes. "Pictorialism" seems a relatively static concept, however, lacking a generative base in unconscious drives that interact with cultural forces to produce literary works. Torgovnick dichotomizes the *linguistic* and the *visual*, although semiotic studies show that these two modes are intricately connected. But her "double vision of the artistic model and the verbal text" (214), with the one informing the other, is certainly a fruitful approach.

Nancy Kushigian, in *Pictures and Fictions* (1990), aims "[to] place

Lawrence within a cultural context larger than the English literary tradition" (1). Adopting Torgovnick's "interpretive" tactics, she examines Lawrence's aesthetic ideas in letters and essays, relating his prewar novels to the contemporary visual arts. But she doesn't take the concept of "visual modernism" very far, stopping short of *Women in Love*. Tony Pinkney, in *D. H. Lawrence and Modernism* (1990), "focuses on Lawrence as modernist, counter-modernist and meta-modernist" (3), relating his work to a dialectics of realism and imagism, classicism and expressionism. Pinkney prefers the organicism and "Gothic modernism" of *The Rainbow*—which he relates to the expressionism of *Die Brücke* and the architecture of Gropius and the Bauhaus—to the abstractionism and classicist modernism of *Women in Love*. He reads the text of the later novel against itself, as part of a deconstructionist project of unmasking the ideological assumptions of modernist aesthetics—a method that leads him to devalue the experimental, visionary form of Lawrence's most complex novel, seeing it as a reflection of the high modernist ethos it attacks.

Anne Fernihough's *D. H. Lawrence: Aesthetics and Ideology* (1993) is fully informed by critical theory, drawing on Nietzsche, Heidegger, Adorno, Benjamin, Kristeva, Eagleton, and others, but is primarily concerned "with Lawrence as *critic* or *theorist* of art, and with models of *reading* or *interpreting* works of art and literature, not with Lawrence's novelistic, poetic, or painterly practice" (14). Robert Montgomery, in *The Visionary D. H. Lawrence: Beyond Philosophy and Art* (1994), claims to treat Lawrence as artist/philosopher, "beyond" the usual distinction of these roles. Yet his book is mostly about Lawrence's relation to Schopenhauer, Nietzsche, Heraclitus, and Boehme with no mention of Cézanne or Van Gogh. He is concerned with vision in the philosophical, poetic, or "mystical" sense. Montgomery's approach is very different from mine, in that he attempts to elucidate *ideas* in Lawrence's "poetic vision," independent of their forms of expression.[6] "Vision," as Montgomery uses the term, means speculative thought related to theosophical traditions: the apparent disjunction of categories in his subtitle turns out to signify an intended conjunction.

Leone Vivante, who is directly concerned with the conjunction of opposites in Lawrence, "maintain[s] that art is . . . at one and the same time . . . expression and immediate revelation of the spirit" (*Essays* 12). In *A Philosophy of Potentiality*, he affirms that "spontaneity is identified by Lawrence with being—with real being, intimately creative, vitally potential . . . " (56).

This vitalism is evident in *Kangaroo*, when Lawrence's protagonist says: "But I want if possible to send out a new shoot in the life of mankind—the effort man makes forever, to grow into new forms" (69).

If Lawrence sees art as an overflow of fulfilled being, Merleau-Ponty sees it as an enactment, "whereby we take up this unfinished world in an effort to complete and conceive it" (*Phenomenology* xx). His phenomenology provides grounds for interarts comparison and is attuned to the dynamic equilibrium of Lawrence's novels "by reason of the same kind of attentiveness and wonder, the same demand for awareness, the same will to seize the meaning of the world or of history as that meaning comes into being" (xxi). For this philosopher, the body is the locus of perception and sentient source of all images, visual or verbal, "which reverberates to all sounds, vibrates to all colours, and provides words with their primordial significance . . ." (236). Colors on canvas or words on a page reflect the artist's way of seeing and feeling, as well as his object. *Aisthesis*, as Heidegger reminds us, is "*sensuous apprehension*"; the artwork that "opens up a *world* and keeps it abidingly in force" is itself "a symbol" of being ("Origin" 79, 44, 20; my italics). It is valid and rewarding to compare fiction with painting, on such phenomenological and ontological grounds—always remembering the intrinsic capacities and limitations of each medium.[7] Like the poetic text and "in contrast to everyday perception," Lawrence's language "makes possible . . . a mode of perception at once more complex and more meaningful, which as aesthetic pleasure is able to rejuvenate cognitive vision or visual recognition (*aisthesis*)" (Jauss 142).

The present study focuses on Lawrence's form language in key works. His vision of nature in *The White Peacock* originates in lyrical and nostalgic qualities of nineteenth-century English landscape painting, but the shock of the modern enters the novel with Aubrey Beardsley's drawings, and, with the protagonist's move to the city, Lawrence's vision enters the orbit of urban impressionism (chapter 1). The masterful realism of *Sons and Lovers* is supplemented by impressionism, symbolism, and expressionism; to take the novel as monolithically realistic is to miss much of its richness. Reality is represented through an objective style that interacts with more subjective modes to sustain an expressive image of life (chapter 2).

Lawrence does not lose confidence in visual realism after *Sons and Lovers*, despite what some critics think, so much as surpass it through new modes of vision and expression. Appreciation of *The Rainbow* and *Women in*

Love, both written in the new key of symbolic resonance, requires reorientation to the visual dimensions of Lawrence's language. A reading that ignores these dimensions, or considers them marginal, cannot grasp the full significance of his vision. Literary norms of realism no longer apply to Lawrence's style after *Sons and Lovers*. His vision communicates the unseen along with the seen, permeating character, action, and theme. *The Rainbow* and *Women in Love* are complex masterpieces that must be read with new visual sensitivity if entire dimensions of meaning and being are not to be lost. Just as Cézanne's or Van Gogh's paintings were misjudged as clumsy efforts at representation, so Lawrence's most challenging novels have been misjudged as distorted, excessive, or unbalanced—rather than as artfully *exposing* distortion in characters and culture, while expressing unconscious states of being.

In *The Rainbow*, which is grounded in cultural and historical reality, Lawrence advances beyond realism to a style that parallels expressionism in the visual arts, with violent projection of "soul-states" and distortion of natural imagery. In a series of moonlight scenes, he dramatizes "allotropic states" in an expressionist language that has distinct affinities with the paintings of Nolde, Marc, and Kirchner; the impact of futurism is seen in Lawrence's use of electrochemical imagery (chapter 3).

The new dynamism takes various forms in *Women in Love*, including the language of bodily movement and touch. Expressionist language and imagery are examined in a sequence of scenes in *Women in Love*. The sadistic rabbit ritual is a *psychomachia* that recalls Kirchner's wartime paintings and Kokoschka's plays; the rhythms of moon-stoning and wrestling bout draw on the kinetic languages of expressionist dance and sculpture; the mystical/tactile imagery of "Excurse" probes relations of language and being in a manner related to Heidegger's ontology (chapter 4).

Drawing on African art and anthropology, I reevaluate Lawrence's construction of "primitivism" and fetishism in *Women in Love*. Birkin's empathy for African sculpture initiates a civilized/primitive, mental/sensual dialectic, giving him insight into the entropic tendencies of "African" and "Nordic" cultures and the modes of being they empower (chapter 5).

While experimenting with "The Sisters" (an embryonic version of *The Rainbow* and *Women in Love*) in Italy in 1912–14, Lawrence came in contact with futurism, which had a major impact on his style, especially when it came to expressing destructive and unconscious forces. In *Women in Love*, wrestling and winter sports are described with the "plastic dynamism" of Boccioni's sculpture, with its lines of force and interpenetrating planes, while lovers' bodies are transformed into electrical force-fields. Loerke's factory frieze reflects a *vorticist* aesthetic of streamlined stasis, but his celebration of mechanization comes straight out of Marinetti's *futurist* manifestos (chapter 6).

The poet H.D. (Hilda Doolittle) is not the only one who felt an extraordinary affinity between Lawrence's vision and Van Gogh's. Lawrence himself read Van Gogh's letters, copied one of his drawings, and made the *Sunflowers* the focus of his own attempt to conceptualize art. They shared a vision of the "incarnate cosmos" that animates Van Gogh's paintings and letters and Lawrence's letters, fiction, and travel writing. The subliminal connection between their styles in the same and different media highlights the vitalism of Lawrence's vision and expression (chapter 7).

Despite his conscious endorsement of Cézanne's art, Lawrence's expression has primordial, perceptual, and rhythmic affinities with Van Gogh's. His approval of Cézanne and secret sharing with Van Gogh reveal an inner dialectic in Lawrence's visionary art. Van Gogh's incandescent color and surging lines, which express intense states of being, must have had a powerful impact on Lawrence's sensibility. In "Morality and the Novel" (1925), the *Sunflowers* sparks an intricate meditation on the ontology of art, leading to Lawrence's manifesto on the vitalism of the novel. But in "Introduction to These Paintings" (1929), he criticizes Van Gogh's projection of himself into landscapes and praises Cézanne for bringing back solid objects after the impressionists had diffused them in a dazzling play of light. He identifies his own attempt to recover physical consciousness in art with Cézanne's attempt to paint the material essence of an apple,[8] not just its appearance to the eye. While his elective, ideological affinities are with Cézanne, his expressive, primordial affinities are clearly with Van Gogh (chapter 8).

Lawrence's use of the iconic language of Hokusai and Hiroshige has not, so far as I know, been previously recognized. From Japanese art, to which he refers in his letters, he learned to construct landscapes in swift metonymic strokes and sharply delineated shapes and planes, as he does in *Kangaroo*. This clear-cut "Japanese" design alternates with the muted tones and sensuous harmonies of Gauguin's Tahitian palette in the painterly landscapes of *The Plumed Serpent* (chapter 9).

Lawrence's sensory/emotive vision and surging verbal expression have striking affinities not only with Van Gogh but also with expressionism. The clarity and intensity of seeing that made him exclaim, "If I were a painter . . . " (*Sea and Sardinia* 97), demand that we open our critical appreciation of Lawrence's style to illumination by the visual arts. Relating his "art speech" to ways of seeing and structuring perception in modern painting and sculpture leads not only to a clearer reading of his novels but also to the heart of his ontological vision.

1

AESTHETICISM AND IMPRESSIONISM IN *THE WHITE PEACOCK*

In *The White Peacock*, Lawrence draws on a variety of sources while seeking to express a barely formed vision. His own acute, if overly harsh, assessment of the novel as "a decorated idyll running to seed in realism" (*Letters* 1: 184) suggests its hybrid form. Lawrence's iconographic models are chiefly of five kinds: (1) English landscape painting, (2) Pre-Raphaelite landscapes and portraits, (3) late Victorian allegories, (4) Beardsley's erotic drawings, and (5) the urban impressionism of Whistler and Monet. While critical consensus considers the novel to be pastoral in style,[1] impressionist elements have been largely overlooked. Taking for granted the lushness of pastoral in the earlier part of the novel, I shall focus on the impact of the modern on Lawrence's vision and style.

The aesthetic and decadent movements of the 1890s are marked by self-conscious attention to style and surface and by increasing symbiosis of the arts: forms and themes mutate and migrate, as one medium fertilizes another. In Arnold Hauser's words, "Aestheticism reaches the pinnacle of its development in the age of impressionism. Its characteristic criteria, the passive, purely contemplative attitude to life, the transitoriness and non-committing quality of experience and·hedonistic sensualism, are now the standards by which art in general is judged" (2: 883). In writing his first novel (1906–11) a decade after "the Beardsley boom," Lawrence worked toward his own vision through a sensibility saturated in English Pre-Raphaelitism,[2] Georgianism, and Aestheticism, as well as in French realism, symbolism, and impressionism.

Cyril Beardsall's awakening to new forms occurs when

> I came upon reproductions of Aubrey Beardsley's "Atalanta", and of the tail-piece to "Salomé", and others. I sat and looked and my soul leaped out upon the new thing. I was bewildered, wondering, grudging, fascinated. I looked a long time, but my mind, or my soul, would come to no state of coherence. I was fascinated and overcome, but yet full of stubbornness and resistance. (*White Peacock* 159)

Beardsall's response to Beardsley's electrifying line is an ambiguous mixture of fascination and resistance. In Nietzschean terms, the graphic images activate his attention by "definiteness of line . . . [and] *distinct[ness]* . . . the effect of works of art [being] to *excite the state that creates art*—intoxication" (Nietzsche, *Will To Power*, qtd. in Milton 187). But, as he struggles to assimilate the shock of the new, Cyril feels a restless lack of satisfaction. Lawrence underlines the significance of the experience by placing it at the beginning of a chapter entitled "The Irony of Inspired Moments." Beardsley's ambivalence toward women, simultaneously identifying with and fearing them (Heyd 113), matches a complex in Sybil/Cyril. Beardsley's illustration of Swinburne's poem "Atalanta in Calydon," which Lawrence recommended to Jessie Chambers, depicts the huntress-goddess as a powerful hermaphrodite,[3] more likely to take the initiative with men than the girl in Greiffenhagen's *Idyll*—whose passivity Lawrence complained of, while admitting his "intoxication" with the painting (*Letters* 1: 103). Beardsley's grotesque and flamboyant art sparks an "inspired moment," with ironic consequences for George Saxton. The thrill he receives from the drawings spurs his last effort to win Lettie Beardsall in the white violet scene, but his impulse comes too late.

Lawrence devotes two pages to a discussion of Beardsley's sensational illustrations to Wilde's *Salomé* (1893). The "tail-piece" is presumably *The Climax*,[4] an orgasmic, perverse Art Nouveau fantasy in which the triumphant Salomé, hair aswirl, soars aloft clutching the severed head of John the Baptist. An earlier version that accentuates the peacock motif is inscribed with the words "*J'ai Baisé ta Bouche, Iokanaan.*"[5] Ironically, the prophet was beheaded for refusing to make love to Salomé, while George loses his hold on life by failing to make love to Lettie. The drawings help him to articulate half-suppressed desires: " 'I want her more than anything.—And the more I look at these naked lines, the more I want her. It's a sort of fine sharp feeling, like these curved lines' " (*White Peacock* 160). In Beardsley's eroticized aesthetic, form becomes idea and stimulates perception;[6] according to Lord

Kenneth Clark, his genius consists in "that perfectly clear conviction, which creates its own skill, that a thing must be thus and thus and not otherwise" (qtd. in Weintraub 269). Beardsley's clear-cut form arouses a will-to-form in George: the intensity of line challenges him to give coherent outline to his own amorphous existence. Lacking a matching clarity and decisiveness, he feels pathetically that Beardsley's designs can relieve him of the need to communicate his desires to Lettie. If she looked at those tense, quivering lines, "she'd feel it clear and sharp coming through her" (*White Peacock* 160). This is doubly ironic, as, in "The Education of George," Lettie used landscape art to test her "Taurus's" sensibility and he failed the test. Now *he* wants art to arouse *her* to *his* desire. He has experienced a fusion of erotic form and feeling but doesn't know how to apply the lesson in life and so wants to substitute art for action.

An earlier chapter is entitled "Strange Blossoms and Strange New Budding." Blossoming, for Lawrence as for Nietzsche, signifies a fusion of spiritual and sensual, and Beardsley's drawings inspire George to conceive of such a consummation. But as he fails to express his impulses clearly and distinctly, the lines of his life slacken and grow blurred. "I never felt so lost. Then I began to think of her, if she'd have me—but not clear, till you showed me those pictures. I must have her if I can—and I must have something. It's rather ghostish to have the road suddenly smudged out, and all the world anywhere nowhere for you to go" (160). The question of eroticized perception is transposed from the taut lines of Beardsley's drawings to the smudged landscape of George's life. His response to vital form brings out his need to take hold of the woman who arouses his deepest impulses and give both their lives direction. His senses are sharpened and he smells violets that even Cyril cannot smell. In a scene that foreshadows Paul's petal-chewing in *Sons and Lovers*, George chews the white violets with his white teeth before spitting them out. Symbolically, he is rejecting his own destiny, for a white violet is the emblem of Lettie, as a White Peacock is the symbol of Woman.

The peacock was a favorite icon in Art Nouveau and an obsessive image of the nineties, flaunting itself in paintings and poems. Beardsley was impressed by Whistler's lavish panels for the Peacock Room at Frederick Leyland's house,[7] where "walls, woodwork, shutters and ceiling . . . [were] covered with a peacock design in blue paint and gold leaf" (Weintraub 20). He adopted the peacock as a motif in illustrating Tennyson's *Morte D'Arthur* and Wilde's *Salomé*, where it is associated with "narcissism and pride"

(Kooistra 71). One of the illustrations is *The Peacock Skirt* (Zatlin fig. 74), a marvel of rococo design, matching hairline tension with airy gracefulness and abandon. Salomé has a wreath of peacock feathers in her hair and an elaborate design of sickle moons on her skirt, while the peacock itself, symbol of female vanity, appears in the background in an aura of stipple dots. Weintraub associates "the swirling, Japanesque" *Peacock Skirt* with *À Rebours* (1884), in which Huysmans describes in glittering, jeweled language a painting of Salomé in Des Esseintes's gallery.[8] The peacock hair and long-necked bird reappear in *The Eyes of Herod*, in which Salomé exerts her seductive powers on the Tetrarch, and peacock feathers flare from her hair in the voluptuous *Stomach Dance* (Wilson, pls. 14, 15).

Lawrence introduces the peacock motif into the chapter "A Shadow in Spring," giving Annable a platform for his misogyny. It is the "vanity and screech and defilement" of the bird that particularly offend the keeper, who attributes such qualities to the aristocratic Lady Chrystabel who seduced and patronized him. Adapting Annable's symbol, Cyril suggests that his dead lady was "[a] white peacock"—just as he later calls Lettie "[a] white violet" (*White Peacock* 151, 161). Morrison observes: "The association of peacocks with Salomé's perversity in Wilde's text, and . . . the identification of peacocks with Salomé herself in Beardsley's illustrations, establish the white-peacock-woman as decadent, possessive, and deadly" (247). The novel's title iconicizes the idealizing woman's attractive/destructive duality. The bird in the novel is not actually white, "the full wealth of its tail glimmering like a stream of coloured stars," but becomes metaphorically so by association with false ideals and whitewashed corruption.

In a moment of symbiotic contact between intellectual and sensual man, Cyril is "startled . . . by the white sympathy [his own hand] expressed extended towards [Annable] in the moonlight" (151). The unsolved problem is how to unite these opposites. After they have parted, Cyril "[comes] out on the bare white road . . . [while] the big flushed face of the moon poised just above the tree-tops, very majestic, and far off—yet imminent" (152). This flushed face is an apotheosized image of the keeper, a prophet of sensuality who is about to become an icon in Cyril's memory through his sudden death. Like Whistler, Lawrence has devised a *Symphony in White,* in which many colors interact but white is the dominant motif. As Oscar Wilde writes at the height of the Aesthetic movement when Pre-Raphaelitism was shading into Art Nouveau and Symbolism, "All art is at once surface and symbol" (xxxiv).

Lawrence's dense iconography combines allusions to Pre-Raphaelite painting with traces of Whistlerian and Beardsleyan aestheticism. His iconic language, with its emphasis on ritual and symbol, shows a sensuous plasticity that foregrounds the self-consciously aesthetic quality of the novel.

But nineties aestheticism is not the whole story. Lawrence's early work takes shape in a "climate of impressionism" (Kronegger 33) that was especially pervasive in the arts between 1874 and 1914.[9] In the chapter "A New Start in Life," Cyril gives George some watercolor landscapes described in distinctly impressionist language: "I stood the four large water-colours along the wall before him. They were drawings among the waters and the fields of the Mill, grey rain and twilight, morning with the sun pouring gold into the mist, and the suspense of a midsummer noon upon the pond" (*White Peacock* 239). The substance is English landscape, such as George would recognize and appreciate, but the motifs are impressionist, showing Cyril's sensitivity to half-light, sun-in-a-mist, or sunlight reflected on water—favorite atmospheric effects of Claude Monet, Camille Pissarro, and Alfred Sisley. George's response to the paintings reveals his romantic and fatalistic sensibility: "All the glamour of our yesterdays came over him like an intoxicant, and he quivered with the wonderful beauty of life that was weaving him into the large magic of the years" (239). Hauser identifies "the feeling that every phenomenon is a fleeting and never-to-be-repeated constellation, a wave gliding away on the river of time" as the "Heraclitean outlook" of impressionism, "stressing that reality is not a being but a becoming, not a condition but a process" (2: 872). This "intoxication with life" (Hatzfeld 177–86), combined with a sense of the moment, is the essence of impressionism.

Impressionist blurring of outlines, while it depersonalizes, can paradoxically reveal the life-quality of a character by dissolving time. An image of George in all his potentiality hints at his later domestic entrapment: "The little square window above him filtered a green light from the foliage of the great horse-chestnut outside and the glimmer fell on his dark hair, and trembled across the plates . . . " (*White Peacock* 3). Lawrence modulates his style from a decorative fidelity to nature, as prescribed by Ruskin, to an atmospheric diffuseness and rendering of color interactions characteristic of impressionism: "The larch-wood was afloat with clear, lyric green, and some primroses scattered whitely on the edge, under the fringing boughs. It was a clear morning, as when the latent life of the world begins to vibrate afresh in the air. The smoke from the cottage rose blue against the trees, and thick yellow against the sky" (152). Cyril's painterly eye reveals the instantaneity of visual phenomena and the relativity of color. The freshness and lyricism of the scene matches Renoir's *Country Road* (1873), *Path in the Woods* (1874), or *The English Pear Tree* (1885),[10] while the neutral gray smoke that looks blue against dark green trees and yellow against complementary blue sky recalls Monet's experiments with luminosity, reflections, and chromatic variations. The ontological vision is of primal vitality and growth.

Cyril accompanies George and Meg to Nottingham, and in the Castle Art Gallery they see "a fine collection of Arthur Melville's paintings" (247–48). Melville (1858–1904) was a Scottish impressionist whose work Lawrence had seen in 1907. Cyril begins "to expound" the paintings but gives up because his companions aren't interested. The significance of Melville for Lawrence is made clear in a passage deleted from the text: "so [George] died without ever appreciating impressionism in painting" (*White Peacock* 388nn). Paintings by Melville that Lawrence probably appreciated include *A Cabbage Garden* (1877), which shows a worker knee-deep in plants speaking to a girl at the edge of a field; *A French Peasant* (1880), which could be compared to Bastien-Lepage's subjects although the treatment is clearly impressionist; *Audrey and Her Goats* (1884–89), a mysterious "woodland scene treated as an all-over pattern of leaves and light"; *Mediterranean Port* (1892), a dazzling harmony in indigo, gold, umber, mauve, and white; and *Autumn—Loch Lomond* (1893), a magically decorative watercolor.[11] Melville, who had studied with the impressionists at the Académie Julian in Paris, was noted for his originality. His painting was appreciated because "it was alive" (*Scottish Painting* 24).

When Cyril takes the newly married George and Meg to a performance of Bizet's *Carmen* at the Theatre Royal, the impressionist style conveys overwhelming emotional excitement that alters perceptions: "The theatre surged and roared dimly like a hoarse shell . . . " (*White Peacock* 248). The impression of the moment, symbolically encapsulating George's fate, is formed of wavelike noise, music, drama, in tumultuous rhythms. The visual scene condenses an atmosphere of social life and entertainment, as in many cabaret and theater scenes by Manet, Degas, and Renoir. Cyril and Lettie move comfortably enough in the cultivated world of theater, music, and the arts, but this world is disturbing to George, who can neither distance himself from the emotion nor control it. In the style of the Goncourts, Lawrence focuses on the subjective impact of the scene, narrowing the sense of life to emotional pulsations that obliterate all external detail. "They were both in a tumult of confused emotion. Their ears were full of the roaring passion of life, and their eyes were blinded by a spray of tears and that strange quivering laughter which burns with real pain" (248). The emotional impressionism of this overwritten passage is encoded in metaphors of a tumultuous sea, as the characters are immersed in an impersonal flood of sensation. The rational ego, which deals with phenomena selectively, dissolves in tidal waves of music and feeling.

Kronegger claims that "Flaubert and the Goncourts, Conrad and Lawrence have extended into literature the method of the French impressionist painters" (30). There are "pre-impressionist" scenes in Flaubert's *Madame Bovary* (1857), which Lawrence had read by summer 1906, and *Sentimental Education* (1869), which Lawrence's mother was reading in August 1910 while he awaited proofs of *The White Peacock* (*Letters* 1: 174–75). Ford Madox Ford (or Hueffer), Lawrence's first editor and grandson of the painter Ford Madox Brown, was a great advocate of Flaubert's technique. But Lawrence was resistant, and if he was influenced by Flaubert it must have been in matters of imagery rather than form. Kronegger writes of *L'Education Sentimentale*: "The quality of the images of light, of steam, of heat, of sound, of movement, of fog, of mist, and of the river is evocatory and atmospheric: it isolates the observer and creates the impression of vagueness and distance" (15–16). She also notes "a predominance of color over objects," "subjective impressions," and "onomatopoeic overtones"—all of which occur in Cyril's narrative style.

If the roots of Lawrence's vision are in English landscape, he consciously experiments with a variety of aesthetic sources in *The White Peacock*. Georgianism, Pre-Raphaelitism, and Aestheticism shape parts 1 and 2, but Lawrence's move to the city reoriented his sensibility toward realism and impressionism in part 3. As Jessie Chambers says, "[He] began to explore London, and to write about the lights that flowered when darkness came" (Lawrence, *Letters* 1: 87). Gordon and Forge call Monet's *Boulevard des Capucines* (1873–74; see pl. 1), with its blur of people and foliage and its bustle of rapid movement, "a supreme statement of the city as landscape" (68). Herzinger, who sees Lawrence's style in the London scenes as "a poetry of the city" parallel to the earlier "poetry of the country," calls it "pastoralization" (84). But to overemphasize the pastoral model in *The White Peacock* is to neglect the variety of styles through which Lawrence articulates his narrator's ways of seeing. While the pastoral mode affords a literary and natural framework for understanding his experience of his home countryside, close parallels with impressionism in painting mediate his experience of the city and of modernism.

Most remarkable in this first novel is the blossoming of a full-blown urban impressionism that matches Lawrence's early imagist poetry:

> The Spring came bravely even in South London, and the town was filled with magic. I never knew the sumptuous purple of evening till I saw the round arc-lamps fill with light, and roll like golden bubbles along the purple dusk of the high-road. Everywhere at night the city is filled with the magic of lamps: over the River they pour in golden patches their floating luminous oil on the restless darkness; the bright lamps float in and out of the cavern of London Bridge Station like round shining bees in and out of a black hive; in the suburbs the street-lamps glimmer with the brightness of lemons among the trees. (264)

In this highly impressionist scene, color and light, spilling from dimly perceived round shapes that repeat and reflect themselves in endless proliferation, are the essential subject. "Reality, for the impressionist, has become a vision of space, conceived as sensations of light and color" (Kronegger 48). Complementary purple and gold make a harmonious composition, as the light of the lamps dissolves outlines visible by day. Colorful luminosity saturates the otherwise void and alien space, subsuming it in aesthetic vision. The scene becomes the visual record of a moment of being, rather than an attempt to render an illusion of external objects.

With the transition from daylight to lamplight, the city comes alive, as in Camille Pissarro's *Boulevard Montmartre, Night Effect* (1897) or Whistler's *Nocturnes*.[12] All is flowing and glowing, nothing is static. Sensory elements are recombined and interwoven with metaphors and similes that add an imaginative dimension. There is a painterly sense of fluidity; the activity of light striking the observer's eye is expressed in the verbs "pour," "float," and "glimmer." The sense of life comes from a dynamic interplay of light and dark; the drama is not in external activity but in the perceptual process that transforms the scene. Lawrence sees London through impressionist eyes, as Whistler and Monet had done before him. The impressionist style is appropriate to his vision of the city at night.[13] Lamplight or sunlight-and-shadow over water was a favorite motif of Monet and Renoir, as in their parallel paintings of *La Grenouillère* (1869),[14] or in Monet's *Thames below Westminster*

(1871; see pl. 2), while Joseph Conrad used it with symbolic resonance to set the opening scene on the Thames in *Heart of Darkness*.

Urban impressionism is a response to the speed and dynamism of city life. As Hauser sees it:

> Modern technology . . . introduces an unprecedented impressionist dynamism in the whole attitude to life and it is above all this new feeling of speed and change that finds expression in impressionism. . . . Impressionism is an urban art, and not only because it discovers the landscape quality of the city and brings painting back from the country into the town, but because it sees the world through the eyes of the townsman. . . . [It] describes the changeability, the nervous rhythm, the sudden, sharp but always ephemeral impressions of city life. And precisely as such, it implies an enormous expansion of sensual perception, a new sharpening of sensibility, a new irritability. (2: 871)

Lawrence's urban impressionism comprises Cyril's vernal or nocturnal impressions and the painful "expansion" and "irritability" of George's alienated consciousness. As Hauser puts it, "the feeling of being alone and unobserved, on the one hand, and the impression of roaring traffic, incessant movement and constant variety, on the other, breed the impressionistic outlook on life in which the most subtle moods are combined with the most rapid alternation of sensations" (2: 878–79). Cyril, the narrator-artist, exemplifies this outlook. Even George has some of the hypertrophied impressionist sensibility, but he is unable to mediate it through art, let alone express it in a living relationship, and so he falls prey to alcohol, which blurs all sensations.

Cyril's impressions involve the flow of lives and faces in the London crowd:

> In the mornings I loved to move in the aimless street's procession, watching the faces come near to me, with the sudden glance of dark eyes, watching the mouths of the women blossom with talk as they passed, watching the subtle movements of the shoulders of men beneath their coats, and the naked warmth of their necks that went glowing along the street. I loved the city intensely for its movement of men and women . . . and the sudden flash of eyes and lips as they pass. Among all the faces of the street my attention roved like a bee which clambers drunkenly among blue flowers. I became intoxicated with the strange nectar which I sipped from out of the eyes of the passers-by. (*The White Peacock* 264)

Cyril cultivates aesthetic detachment toward the lives that flow around him, enjoying an ambivalent sense of closeness and estrangement. His attitude, like that of Hauser's impressionist artist, is "the expression of a fundamentally passive outlook on life, an acquiescence in the role of the spectator, of the receptive and contemplative subject, a standpoint of aloofness, waiting, non-involvement . . . " (2: 873). Immersed in the crowd, his own sense of separateness is heightened and his faculty of observation intensified to the point of voyeurism. He is the still point in the flux, the observer who is "only an eye," as Cézanne said of Monet. The narrator sees city life as animated by organic rhythms,[15] deliberately overlooking motives that lie beneath the visual surface. The "sudden glance of dark eyes" is a spontaneous reflex; "the mouths of the women blossom" floral but unheard; "the subtle movements of the shoulders of men" are so much unconscious muscular activity; "the naked warmth of their necks" suggests a desire to touch. Fantasy suffuses objects with a subjective coloring (contemplative "blue"); human beings are depersonalized as flora and fauna of an urban jungle.

In an impressionist reverie, Cyril lets country memories overlap with city perceptions, reducing people to an interplay of movements and forms. Unlike the socialist George, he focuses on the abstract *pattern* of movement—"people weaving and intermingling in the complex mesh of their intentions" (*The White Peacock* 286)—rather than on individual lives. His passivity heightens and defamiliarizes the impression of human activity, so that it seems no more than surface design. The poetic image of bees buzzing in imaginary flowers implies a way of looking through half-shut eyes that dissolves distinctions between country and city, past and present. People exist as optical phenomena, moving in and out of focus in complex interrelations. In this dance of life, seeing transcends knowing and eye preempts mind.

Lawrence was living in Croydon as Cyril is in Norwood, and the coming of spring to streets and gardens occasions a style that could be called suburban impressionism—reminding one that Monet, Renoir, Pissarro, and Sisley liked to paint in suburban gardens and villages on the outskirts of Paris. During his exile in London in the 1870s, Pissarro lived in the "charming suburb" of Lower Norwood, where he "studied the effects of fog, snow and springtime," while Sisley lived in Molesey and painted Hampton Court (Pissarro, qtd. in Blunden 92; Cogniat 26).[16] Monet, who confined himself to central London and the Thames, had earlier painted views of Hyde Park and Green Park. "Monet and I were very enthusiastic about the London landscapes," Pissarro recorded. "We also visited the museums, studying the watercolors and paintings of Turner and Constable" (Blunden 92). Monet's vision permeates Lawrence's Croydon poem "Suburbs on a Hazy Day" (*Complete Poems* 53).

In *The White Peacock*, Lawrence mixes decorative Pre-Raphaelite metaphors with more direct visual impressions: "I did not know how time was hastening by on still bright wings, till I saw the scarlet hawthorn flaunting over the road, and the lime-buds lit up like wine drops in the sun, and the pink scarves of the lime-buds pretty as louse-wort a-blossom in the gutters, and a silver-pink tangle of almond boughs against the blue sky" (264). The pictorial image of the tree matches Monet's, Pissarro's, or Van Gogh's orchards in springtime and recalls Van Gogh's *Branches of an Almond Tree in Blossom* (Tralbaut 293; see pl. 13).

George and Cyril share a brief spell in London, and "our old intimacy burned again like the fragile burning of alcohol. Closed together in the same blue flames, we discovered and watched the pageant of life in the town . . . " (*White Peacock* 281). Watching, they reject "the tyranny of old romance" and "the faded procession of old years." Cyril, as a modernist, is not content with looking back to the impressionists, who led the avant-garde in the 1870s. His outlook, at times, seems close to that of the futurists, whose manifestos had started to appear in 1909 and continued to do so with increasing vigor through 1911, the year of *The White Peacock*'s publication.

From a medley of impressions the narrator proceeds to a cacophony of sounds, which he orchestrates into an overall impression of London life, giving "The Dominant Motif of Suffering" its specifically musical overtone. The futurists also experimented with sounds, and Luigi Russolo constructed sound machines for his "Arte di Rumori." Looking for new ways to express sensory phenomena was a compulsion, not just of the futurists, who called themselves "primitive Impressionists" (Sweeney 70), but also of all modernist artists. Cyril, turning his back on "the vast pilgrimage of bygone romances" that attracted the Pre-Raphaelites, asks:

> Were we not in the midst of the bewildering pageant of modern life, with all
> its confusion of bannerets and colours, with its infinite interweaving of sounds,
> the screech of the modern toys of haste striking like keen spray, the heavy
> boom of busy mankind gathering its bread, earnestly, forming the bed of all
> other sounds; and between these two the swiftness of songs, the triumphant
> lilt of the joy of life, the hoarse oboes of privation, the shuddering drums of

tragedy, and the eternal scraping of the two deep-toned strings of despair. (*White Peacock* 281)

The opening image of this purple passage of Zolaesque modernism is the verbal equivalent of Monet's *Rue Saint-Denis, Celebrations of June 30, 1878* (see pl. 3), with its mass of colorful banners waving in wild agitation. Monet painted such scenes not as a camera would see them but as he experienced the complex excitement of the moment, "a dynamic interplay in which individual forms and identities tend to be drowned" (Seitz 108). In looking at Monet's festive canvas, one can almost see sounds—the voices of the crowd, the tramp and shuffle of feet, the vigorous flap of banners. The rhythmic interplay of colors dissolves the outlines of objects and conveys an excited *response* to the city's life.

If the energy of Lawrence's pageant and its cumulative rhetoric strike a proto-futurist note, the interweaving of sounds with sights and colors suggests the desire of Marinetti and Boccioni to "exalt the uproar" of the modern city. I am not suggesting that Lawrence, in his first novel, shows a conscious awareness of futurism; rather that the seeds of futurism, clearly derived from impressionist dynamism, were already germinating in his style. Seemingly random sounds form the "music" of modern life. There are screeching vehicles, the bass drum of work, swift songs, "hoarse oboes of privation," "shuddering drums of tragedy," and the resonant cello of despair. The city has become a concert hall where one can listen to the strident symphony of modern life.

Lawrence's city contains movement and rhythm, "the surging of the ocean of life" (*The White Peacock* 281), in a synthesis of separate impressions. George and Cyril watch a troop of Life Guards in the "green cavern" of the park. Going beyond the homoerotic pageantry of "white smooth thighs," there is an impulse toward impressionist abstraction and spatial dynamics in the scene, as individual cavalrymen, whose muscularity catches the eye in close-up, merge into a "body of men," then into a mass of color ("scarlet and silver"), and finally into a distant but vital force (a "wavering spark of red life blown along").

By way of negative contrast, destitution and squalor, the sheer indifference of a great metropolis to the human misery it spawns is described in realistic vignettes supplemented by impressionist scenes: "The shining cars were drawing tall in the distance over Westminster Bridge, a fainter, yellow light running with them on the water below. The wet streets were spilled with golden liquor of light, and on the deep blackness of the river were the restless yellow slashes of the lamps" (282). When Jessie Chambers visited him in London, Lawrence "took [her] to Waterloo Bridge and made [her] look at the human wreckage preparing to spend the night on the Embankment. He wanted [her] to see the bridges at night, with the lights of the trams reflected" (qtd. in *White Peacock* 392 nn). This atmospheric scene, with its vague movements of traffic and reflections on streets and water, is a verbal counterpart of Whistler's nocturnes, Monet's and Pissarro's boulevards,[17] or Monet's views of London bridges and Houses of Parliament,[18] the last of which were painted only a few years before Lawrence's novel appeared. The main difference lies in Lawrence's realistic emphasis on suffering,[19] whereas impressionist painters such as Whistler and Monet aimed solely at lyrical and chromatic variations.

Lawrence's characters adopt an attitude of passivity and inertia that, according to Hauser's analysis, is "the aesthetic attitude purely and simply" (2: 873). This is Cyril's attitude in London, and it is worth noting that he has the dual roles of painter and narrator, but no other visible occupation. It is also Siegmund's attitude in *The Trespasser*, when he returns by train from his island idyll with Helena to find himself plunged into London in a state of total estrangement. Immersed in the crowd at Westminster, he sees "the city sky, a lovely deep purple, and the lamps in the Square steaming out a vapour of grey-gold light" (*Trespasser* 169). Here Lawrence consciously experiments with painterly impressionism, omitting fixed focus and lapsing out from the character's anguished self-consciousness into purely visual sensations.

Siegmund's London is an impressionist nocturne, drenched in an aura of purple, gold, and gray. People and objects, multiplied, diminished, diffused, appear as flecks or patches of moving light or color against a dark background. Serpentine reflections on water and streaming traffic create hypnotic movement and a sense of disembodied dynamism. The euphoric but doomed protagonist has slipped so much into the shadows that he can see the glamorous flow of life only from an outsider's viewpoint. The dissolution of his ego leaves him helpless, a hypersensitive void in which sensations are passively registered. The momentary illumination he experiences in this fugue state depends on virtual extinction of personality: the "I" has been displaced from the center, which becomes a vortex of sensations, all the more vivid for lack of control. The irony of Siegmund's fate, like George's, is that of "[i]mpressionist protagonists [who] have sacrificed the most precious parts of their own self: lucidity and will. Their initial urge to live life fully destroys personality even as it exalts it" (Kronegger 67).

If impressionism can be seen as "the climax of self-centred aesthetic culture" (Hauser 2: 873), it is virtually inevitable that Cyril, transplanted to an urban setting in which he feels his isolation, will cultivate impressionist attitudes. His detached aestheticism is contrasted with George's emotional socialism, in a way that justifies the former and undermines the latter. With the failure of artistic and sensual counterparts to sustain a relationship, the dialectic of detachment and involvement remains unresolved. George has the moral weakness and alcoholism of Cyril's biological father, together with the physical strength and unfulfilled potential of his surrogate father, Annable: all the narrator can do is helplessly, even cynically, watch his companion's decline.

Toward the end, Cyril paints a verbal impression of the city in which the key metaphor is that of a labyrinthine poem:[20]

> In the vast cavern of the station the theatre-goers were hastening, crossing the pale grey strand, small creatures scurrying hither and thither in the space beneath the lonely lamps. As the train crawled over the river we watched the far-flung hoop of diamond lights curving slowly round and striping with bright threads the black water. [George] sat looking with heavy eyes, seeming to shrink from the enormous, unintelligible lettering of the poem of London. (*White Peacock* 286)

The painterly/poetic image illuminates the narrator's observation of the character's decline using a dramatically articulated way of seeing. Again the focus is on movement, on agitated or lazy rhythms, lamplight among shadows of the cavernous station suggesting Monet's series of paintings of the *Gare Saint-Lazare* (1877; Gordon and Forge 76–79). Just as impressionist painters frequently took high angles of vision looking down on crowds in the street and reducing figures to black strokes, Lawrence's viewpoint diminishes individuals to "small creatures scurrying hither and thither in the space beneath the lonely lamps." When the object is not seen closely and in outline, as in the cognitive mode of realism, reflections can lend it a costumed glamour, so that "the far-flung hoop of diamond lights" turns the sordid black river into something magical.

Cyril's aesthetic delight in London contrasts with George's despair. The latter's roots in the countryside go much deeper, and once uprooted he cannot adopt a safe distance. The city at night is like a vast black mirror of his own chaotic soul: "The town was too large for him, he could not take in its immense, its stupendous poetry. What did come home to him was its flagrant discords. The unintelligibility of the vast city made him apprehensive, and the crudity of its big, coarse contrasts wounded him unutterably" (*White Peacock* 286). This might be called the negative psychology of impressionism, the reverse of its hedonist sundance. Urban impressionism was a response to the swiftness, confusion, and turmoil of modern life, in which individuals could easily become disoriented, carried along by the stream, and alienated from their own inner being.

Unable to synthesize his fragmentary impressions into a poetic whole, George is struck by the meaninglessness of the scene, "its flagrant discords." "The Dominant Motif of Suffering" that he sees and hears in the city echoes his own schizophrenia and dipsomania, as well as social malaise. Bewildered with unmanageable sensations and emotions that drive him to seek oblivion in alcohol, he fails to press his life-claim on Lettie, whose shallow sophistication when they meet at her London house is symptomatic of their failure to connect: "Lettie sang, no longer Italian folk songs, but the fragmentary utterances of Debussy and Strauss. These also to George were quite meaningless . . . " (284). Kronegger observes that Debussy's mood pieces, such as "Reflections in Water," "suggest objects which have neither function nor substance . . . " (46). The fragmentary and inconsequential quality that is so frustrating to George is precious to Lettie; impressionist and romantic music helps her evade emotional reality. But George, who cannot find relief from the burden of an unfulfilled life in impressionist music, as Lettie does, or aesthetic visions like Cyril's, begins to descend the path of self-destruction.

This rather morbid and melodramatic theme—George's drift toward death in a world in which he has failed to claim his place—is emphasized by visual impressions: "In the sudden darkness I saw his pale shadow go across to the sofa in the window-space. The blinds were undrawn, and the stars looked in. He gazed out on the great bay of darkness wherein, far away and below, floated a few sparks of lamps like herring boats at sea" (*White Peacock* 287). Oceanic images emphasize the vastness of empty space amid which the individual feels a sense of angst and loneliness. One is reminded of Whistler's nocturnes and Paul's existential experience when the darkness seems to engulf him after his mother's death in *Sons and Lovers*. As George gazes out on the darkness, his desolation floods the city. The figure of the lonely drinker has some of the expressionist melancholy of Edvard Munch's *Night* (*Night in St. Cloud*) (1890), in which a hunched figure by a window is steeped in dark blue light.[21] When the painting was first exhibited, it seemed to represent "the new European aesthetic of Decadence: the cultivation of the self and a neurasthenic sensibility" (Andreas Aubert, qtd. in Varnedoe 186)—themes that relate in different ways to both the narrator and protagonist of *The White Peacock*, and to the novel's impressionist ethos.

2

FORMS OF EXPRESSION IN *SONS AND LOVERS*

Sons and Lovers has been considered a breakthrough from the shallow aestheticism of *The White Peacock* and overripe Wagnerianism of *The Trespasser* to a "triumph of realism" in which Lawrence mastered his own painful experience. But to take *Sons and Lovers* as simply "realistic" is to neglect much of the novel's richness—or to expand the concept of realism beyond recognizable limits. Critics who put a high premium on realism tend to identify the completion of Lawrence's apprenticeship with the culmination of his career and to regard subsequent departures with suspicion. Holderness theorizes a full range of stylistic development between the aesthetic experiment of *The White Peacock* and "the triumph of realism" in *Sons and Lovers*, while Kushigian condenses the entire pattern of Lawrence's early development into this one novel.[1] In proclaiming his bildungsroman his masterwork, Holderness, like Emile Delavenay in "Lawrence's Major Work," tends to regard Lawrence's post-realist writing as a falling off, rather than a breakthrough. But Lawrence's mastery of realism released him, if not from youthful obsessions, then from any further compulsion to treat them directly in fiction.

In *Sons and Lovers*, the contingent and the essential—whatever lights up the writer's imagination as real—are conveyed through an objective style that interacts with subjective modes of vision. Rather than monolithic realism, a fluid interaction of styles animates and sustains an expressive image of life. Various styles frame and then penetrate the experience of a central self: realism supplies the bedrock, impressionism the atmosphere, symbolism the significance, and expressionism the vision. While literary realism and symbolism may have little to do with interarts comparison, I discuss them here as integral components of Lawrence's style that have much to do with his evolving vision and expression. I apply a series of lenses to the novel, not in order to label or categorize, but to give a fuller view of the complex integrity of Lawrence's art in its first full flowering. Realism clings to close observation of individuals in the social contexts from which their lives derive meaning. The first part of *Sons and Lovers*, which presents a history of the coal mines, a view of the town and people, and an account of the Morels' marriage, is authentic realism. Basing the narrative on his own experience, Lawrence describes "the actual conditions of living" (*Sons and Lovers* 10), presenting individuals in family and community contexts. He renders feelings and actions with the authoritative insight of an insider and "[builds up] a real world . . . through an astonishingly detailed re-creation of a complex human environment" (Moynahan, *"Sons and Lovers"* 565). Characters are embedded in a social matrix; conflicts can be traced to economic conditions and class differences; actions are generated within a fully realized setting.

Beyond depicting the environment, realism conveys the experience of living in a given place at a given time. "Rarely," writes Alfred Kazin, "has the realistic novelist's need to *present*, to present vividly, continually, and at the highest pitch of pictorial concentration . . . reached such intense clarity of representation as it does in *Sons and Lovers*" (605). Jessie Chambers, disappointed with the first draft of "Paul Morel," urged Lawrence to get closer to reality, in the conviction that he "possessed the miraculous power of translating the raw material of life into significant form" (192). She felt that "the common round was full of mystery, awaiting interpretation" and that Lawrence, who "had the rare gift of seeing [the working class] from within," should become "an interpreter of the people to whom he belonged" (198). Lawrence's ability to express reality through sensory detail, dialogue, and physical action is a major element in the novel's success. It takes a flexible use of language to capture the movement of life at close range. But the realist writer has to detach himself from his milieu in order to see it clearly; imaginative distance, as well as intimate knowledge, is necessary.

In early 1914, Lawrence referred to *Sons and Lovers* as highly "visualised." Although he recalled his "joy in creating vivid scenes" and "accumulating objects in the powerful light of emotion," he told Edward Garnett that he would not write again in "that hard, violent style full of sensation and presentation" (*Letters* 2: 132). As he gained perspective, he saw how the "autobiographical" novel was vital to his development as a writer; in facing the challenge of mastering his experience, he had developed his powers of realistic expression. The importance of visual representation to understanding is implicit in Garnett's remark that *Sons and Lovers* is "a piece of social history on a large canvas, painted with a patient thoroughness and bold veracity which both Balzac and Flaubert might have envied" (95). Lawrence had studied Balzac with enthusiasm. After reading *Eugénie Grandet* he declared: "Balzac can lay bare the living body of the great Life better than anybody in the world. He doesn't hesitate at the last covering . . . he goes straight to the flesh; and, unlike De Maupassant or Zola, he doesn't inevitably light on a wound, or a festering sore. Balzac is magnificent and supreme; he is not mysterious nor picturesque . . . " (*Letters* 1: 91–92). Seldom does Lawrence pour out such a paean of praise to a modern writer: he clearly derived much inspiration from Balzac's "level-headed, fair, unrelenting realism."

Garnett observes that *Sons and Lovers* "restores [working-class life] to its native atmosphere of hard veracity" but considers it "marred a little by a feeling of photographic accuracy in the narrative . . . " (95). Documentation of surfaces is only one aspect of the novel's realism, however; the "expressive function" of the image in Lawrence's style should also be recognized (Van Ghent 529). Tony Pinkney relates Lawrence's concrete visualization to imagism, and "the clipped, staccato hardness of the novel's language" to "the lives of the working people themselves" (42, 44). Characterizing the modernist element in Lawrence's style as a combination of "linguistic hardness and Imagistic visualism," Pinkney suggests that *Sons and Lovers* might be called "the first Imagist novel" (48, 42). But the "linguistic hardness" is limited to dialogue and documentation, while the "Imagistic visualism" appears chiefly when objects are enlarged in close-up or diminished by distance. Neither term accurately describes the numerous impressionist or symbolic scenes that add depth or atmosphere to the narrative. Pinkney applies the imagist thesis reductively when he describes scenes like those of Mrs. Morel in the moonlit garden or Paul and Clara making love by the river as "crisply visualised episodes" (47). The "totalizing realist gaze" and the imagist/classicist "[focus] on minute details" do not form a simple dichotomy: isolating and totalizing functions complement each other, and the broad sweep is balanced by the close-up. According to Gestalt psychology, concrete particulars relate to each other within an overall vision that selects them for special attention and that they, in turn, sustain by their coherence. Several critics underline the atmospheric rather than merely documentary quality of Lawrence's style.[2] Pinkney's realist/imagist dialectic does suggest, however, that imagism may have contributed clarity and edge to Lawrence's verbal visualization.

Georg Lukács singles out the following aspects of realism: (1) closely observed, precise details and concrete phenomena of historically situated daily life; (2) understanding of social forces that underlie these phenomena and give rise to change; and (3) a human interest in life, progress, and fulfillment of the individual within the community. One difference between Lukács's theory and Lawrence's practice is that Lukács, following Marxist doctrine, sees realism as dealing with types rather than individuals, and as consequently anti-subjectivist and anti-impressionist. Alldritt offers a more balanced view of visual and social representation when he defines "the true realism of the novel . . . [as] a matter of the alertness, the creative quickness of the narrative eye, which allows the phenomenal world of miner's home, colliery, farm, countryside and industrial landscape to figure in their actual fullness and complexity of interaction, free from all authorial predisposition" (41). This perceptual immediacy, by means of which ordinary details spring into life, may be technically related to imagism.

Lawrence's description of the miner's breakfast consists of practical details yet conveys the energy, anticipation, and satisfaction of the man. It makes him real to the reader, arousing sympathy without asking for it, by combining, as Lukács would have it, the individual with the type, and the personality of Walter Morel with the physical circumstances of a miner's workday:

> He went downstairs in his shirt, and then struggled into his pit-trousers, which were left on the hearth to warm all night. There was always a fire, because Mrs. Morel raked. And the first sound in the house was the bang, bang of the poker against the raker, as Morel smashed the remainder of the coal to make the kettle, which was filled and left on the hob, finally boil. His cup and knife and fork, all he wanted except just the food, was laid ready on the table on a newspaper. Then he got his breakfast, made the tea, packed the bottom of the doors with rugs to shut out the draught, piled a big fire, and sat down to an hour of joy. He toasted his bacon on a fork and caught the drops of fat on his bread. Then he put the rasher on his thick slice of bread, and cut off chunks with a clasp knife, poured his tea into his saucer, and was happy. . . . He preferred to keep the blinds down and the candle lit, even when it was daylight. It was the habit of the mine. (*Sons and Lovers* 37–38)

The casual efficiency of the style, based on close observation, conveys to a middle-class audience the miner's love of comfort and cheerful acceptance of routine. The description of habitual practices in the historic past might seem incidental, as it does not advance the narrative; but it functions as primary realism, establishing the life-quality of the man in his independence and "all-roundness." Such descriptions emanate a genuine warmth. Morel's character may be distorted to suit the balance of relationships, but here he stands firm in his wholeness and heartiness, free from any negative insinuation. In a single paragraph, Lawrence's realism reveals in close-up the pattern of a life, and of many lives.

Lukács maintains that "[the] characters created by the great realists, once conceived in the vision of their creator, live an independent life of their own; their comings and goings, their development, their destiny is dictated by the inner dialectic of their social and individual existence" (11). Lawrence treats the outer, physical/instinctual framework of Walter Morel's character objectively, while his inner, moral self is bent to fit the Oedipal pattern of the narrative and subjected to harsh judgment: "He had denied the God in him" (*Sons and Lovers* 88). But by expressing the inner workings of Paul Morel's soul and psyche, as well as fleshing out his social and familial context, Lawrence allows the reader to understand the process that forms his protagonist's self. Rejecting his actual father and projecting a father image onto the distant pit-head, Paul dedicates himself to a quest for the unknown, or Promised Land.

Graham Holderness characterizes *Sons and Lovers* as a "triumph of realism." The concept derives from Engels's critique of Balzac as expounded by Lukács (11) and involves an imaginative response to reality that comes through *in spite of* the author's conscious intentions. Art that sets out to demonstrate preconceived ideas inevitably fails—"the novel walks off with the nail." The hardest test of all is to achieve objective realism in an autobiographical novel. The author knows his environment from the inside and may render it accurately, but does he know himself or present himself fairly? Lawrence consciously strives to see Paul Morel as a character acted upon by social and psychological forces but remains subjectively involved in the outcome of Paul's relationships and in the choices that shape his destiny. For this reason, Pinkney, who identifies the text's "realist achievement" with Paul's personal claims to normalcy, sees a breakdown of realism in the novel's second half. Yet Lawrence's portrait of the artist does achieve a high degree of subjective realism. As Merleau-Ponty points out, "involvement in a point of view . . . makes possible both the finiteness of [one's] perception and its opening out upon the complete world . . . " (*Phenomenology* 304).

For the Russian critics, Bielinski, Chernyshevski, and Dobrolyubov, "art grew out of life and creatively reproduced it" (Lukács 107). Applied to *Sons and Lovers*, this view has dual significance, depending on whether life is taken as primarily communal or personal. The miner in *Sons and Lovers* frequently commands attention *in himself* rather than in the role in which he is cast. While Lawrence later proclaimed a credo of "art for my sake" and saw the artwork as a supplement to, or overflow from, the artist's life, Lukács's emphasis is consistently objective: "artistic principles [are to be integrated] with the faithful reproduction of all the phenomena of life" (109). Lukács's aesthetic resembles Plato's theory of mimesis, with social forms replacing Platonic ideas: socialist or humanist realism, as he describes it, does not simply reflect the surfaces of life; it uncovers the causes of social conditions.

The struggle within Lawrence's narrative between subjective expression and cathartic control gives *Sons and Lovers* its scope, its ambiguity, and its power. In Merleau-Ponty's words, "[this] subject-object dialogue, this drawing together, by the subject, of the meaning diffused through the object, and, by the object, of the subject's intentions . . . arranges round the subject a world which speaks to him of himself, and gives his own thoughts their place in the world" (*Phenomenology* 132). This explains how Lawrence can write oblique autobiography in describing the environment of his childhood in "Nottingham and the Mining Countryside" (1930). In *Sons and Lovers* he sought to master the volatile subjectivity of his material by giving it form. He wanted to achieve maturity of vision and produce "a restrained, somewhat impersonal novel . . . " (*Letters* 1: 184). But, paradoxically, "[he] is an author who writes better, not worse, for incompletely detaching himself from an autobiographical situation" (Lerner 219). Lawrence achieves creative maturity in *Sons and Lovers* by setting aside cultural fantasies, like those of *The White Peacock*, which led him to impose a pastoral idyll on the mining countryside, and by coming to terms with the real environment in which he grew up. If an artist reveals the deepest emotional truth in himself, he will also reveal wider truths about his historical situation and that of his generation. The truth that he reveals, however singular, will be recognized by all whose consciousness has grown from similar roots. This is why Lawrence could claim that he had written "the tragedy of thousands of young men in England" (*Letters* 1: 477), and why Edvard Munch's expressionist drawings and woodcuts make such startlingly apt illustrations to *Sons and Lovers*.[3]

The strength of the novel's first part, which seamlessly integrates background and foreground, depends for its realization of the "underlying process of life" (Alldritt 42) on an accumulation of selected moments. As Lawrence's realism reveals the force of habit that molds character, Merleau-Ponty's phenomenology describes the perceptual process by which a fully rounded character is realized: "Seeing a figure can be only simultaneously experiencing all the atomic sensations which go to form it. Each one remains for ever what it is, a blind contact, an impression, while the whole collection of these becomes 'vision,' and forms a picture before us because we learn to pass quickly from one impression to another" (*Phenomenology* 14). The miner's preparations for the day's work, his taking a cup of tea to his convalescent wife, his sullen or ferocious labors in the mine, and the pugnacious spirit in which he asks the minister to feel his sweat-soaked singlet (*Sons and Lovers* 37–38, 41, 46) are good examples of the realism that makes a character convincing and presents an illusion of completeness through a selection of everyday details. Realism also dramatizes conflicts in relationships and reveals their social roots. Brutally realistic scenes, such as that in which Morel throws a drawer at his wife (53–55), modulate into symbolism as the action points beyond itself to deep-seated causes of dissension.

Morel's good nature, when unsullied by marital conflict, is expressed in cheerful work about the house, as when he hammers molten iron into shape or employs the children in making fuses. The task may be practical, but the sure-sighted, firmly handled description has ethical and aesthetic overtones: "He always had a beautifully sharp knife, that could cut a straw clean without hurting it" (88). Microscopic clarity of detail has microcosmic significance: "Then he set in the middle of the table a heap of gunpowder, a little pile of black grains upon the white-scrubbed board" (88). The meaning and danger of gunpowder and mining, even the relation between home and work, are compressed into this close-up that connects, as if by montage, the straw fuse and the "shot [fired to] blast the coal down." A realism that sticks to facts and matches words with lived experience can, through selective focus, suggest more than is said. Realistic observation has a metonymic function that matches the symbolic. Paul's fascinated observation and participation— "[he] loved to see the black grains trickle down a crack in his palm, into the mouth of the straw, peppering jollily downwards till the straw was full. Then he bunged up the mouth with a bit of soap . . . " (89)—show his unconscious identification of work with craftsmanship, extending to his interest in painting and the decorative arts. Morel's "lavish" encouragement shows the pleasure in manual work he passes on to his artist son.

Pinkney, relating Lawrence's exact, attentive language to its object, sees this scene as imagist. But in imagism the image/object implies a poetic mood or idea, while in realism it is grasped more directly in its social context. Seen as it appears in itself, the object is placed in metonymic relation to a character's life, which tends to give it expressive qualities. While an imagist precision adds sharpness of focus, primary realism contextualizes lives through a series of juxtaposed objects.

Paul observes his mother's work at close range, and his direct awareness is recorded with painful, almost clairvoyant intensity:

> Once, roused, he opened his eyes to see his mother standing on the hearthrug with the hot iron near her cheek, listening as it were to the heat. Her still face, with the mouth closed tight from suffering and disillusion and self-denial, and her nose the smallest bit on one side, and her blue eyes so young, quick, and warm, made his heart contract with love. (90)

The still moment and synaesthetic image express Paul's heart-wrung response to his mother, arresting and framing her very being. While phenomenology "puts essences back into existence" (Merleau-Ponty, *Phenomenology* vii), Lawrence's realism tends to extract essences from existence. In the following paragraph, the focus switches to Mrs. Morel's existence, as her brisk movements induce a glow of affection in the boy: "She spat on the iron, and a little ball of spit bounded, raced off the dark glossy surface. Then, kneeling, she rubbed the iron on the sack lining of the hearthrug, vigorously. She was warm in the ruddy firelight. . . . The room was warm, and full of the scent of hot linen" (*Sons and Lovers* 91). The realistic technique embodies being in action and signifies emotion in the motions that arise spontaneously in a concrete situation. This kind of realism, linking surfaces with essences, is strongly expressive of feeling without naming it. While Paul's respect, admiration, and love for his mother are compressed into a single moment, narrative "objectivity" highlights Mrs. Morel's virtues of persistence, efficiency, and care. Another masterly scene, in which she shows her son a dish she has bought (98–100), combines the particular (her character) with the representative (the life of the townspeople, the Friday-night market, the family budget), in a way that Lukács considers the strength of social realism.

Lawrence describes the homecoming of William's coffin with dramatic realism, concentrating on material arrangements, physical movements, and social responses. The preparations are described with controlled objectivity: "Morel and Paul went, with a candle, into the parlour. There was no gas there. The father unscrewed the top of the big, mahogany, oval table, and cleared the middle of the room. Then he arranged six chairs opposite each other, so that the coffin could stand on their beds" (168). The rigorously controlled view of the event as it slowly unfolds is heightened at the climax by an expressionist use of language: "the limbs and bowed heads of six men struggled to climb into the room, bearing the coffin that rode like sorrow on their living flesh" (169). Synecdoche ("limbs and bowed heads") gives the scene an autonomy and monumentality as in expressionist sculptures by Ernst Barlach, Wilhelm Lehmbruck, or Käthe Kollwitz,[4] while the animistic simile of sorrow riding on the "living flesh" manifests intensity of emotion at a point of extreme confrontation between life and death. The finely maintained objectivity suggests that Lawrence may, after all, have learned something from Flaubert's realism; but how much more potent this scene is, with its sympathy for human suffering, that must not be weakened or diffused by sentiment. The effect of Lawrence's narrative technique, combining objective realism with the response of a participant, is to fuse personal sorrow with a profounder sense of human fate, elevating the individual to the universal. The severe reserve placed on emotional expression—limited to dramatic utterance, as the mother chants, "Oh, my son—my son!"—give the moment its human and religious dignity.

Is realism an adequate term for such ritualization? Can it explain its power? Certainly not, if we think of Flaubert's realism, representing the commonplace and average with (in Joyce's terms) "a scrupulous meanness." The mystery of death-in-life is here obliquely expressed through an interplay of light and darkness. Candles or candlelight are mentioned five times, lamps twice; the darkness is "wide" but the night "faintly luminous"; the door "open[s] straight from the night into the room." The skill with which Lawrence combines symbolic and realistic techniques, integrating one within the other, gives the scene its reverberating power. The invisible—sorrow, fate—is made visible by expressionist means, while the cramped space, awkward movements, and overwhelming physical burden convey powerful emotion.

The homecoming scene in "Death in the Family" surpasses the social realism in which it is solidly grounded, using expressionist distortion, animism, and symbolism to project a participant's experience. Objective realism, lacking the intensity of built-in response, could not match this scene's effectiveness. While Lawrence's art heightens the sense of reality, it cannot be reduced to "realism." There is no meaning in a world untouched by consciousness, which infiltrates into objects, giving them significance: a subject-object dialectic shapes the image of reality. "Man can embody truth but he cannot know it," says Yeats (qtd. in Grant 55), or, as Paul tells Miriam, "God doesn't *know* things, he *is* things . . . " (*Sons and Lovers* 291). Realism in the novel is not so much an arrangement of facts as a realization of people, places, and actions within a structured vision of living.[5] The difference between Lawrence's expressive ritualization and conventional realism will be made clear by comparing the coffin scene, on the one hand, with Paul's activities in the surgical appliance factory, on the other.

The term "realism" is misleading if applied categorically to writing in which a subjective viewpoint animates the description of objects or a narrator imaginatively interprets them. In *Sons and Lovers*, impressionist views, injecting an aura of life into surrounding drabness, are interspersed with realistic narrative: "The sky overhead throbbed and pulsed with light. The glow sank quickly off the field, the earth and the hedges smoked dusk" (14); "The old brick wall by the Statutes ground burned scarlet, spring was a very flame of green. And the steep swoop of highroad lay, in its cool morning dust, splendid with patterns of sunshine and shadow, perfectly still" (150). An alertness to light and landscape is carried over from *The White Peacock*; but the style is swifter and more dramatic, and the narrator has an eye for more than local atmosphere. Here the focus on vital life ("a very flame of green"; "throbbed and pulsed") and its eclipse ("sank quickly"; "lay . . . perfectly still") might be taken as foreshadowing William's fate, if only in muted, metonymic fashion.[6]

While close-up scenes involving quarrels and violence are harshly realistic, distant views of landscape and environment tend to be impressionistic, providing relief from the claustrophobic domestic settings. After Morel kicks William, Mrs. Morel takes Annie and the baby to the cricket-field:

> The meadows seemed one space of ripe, evening light, whispering with the distant mill-race. . . . Before her, level and solid, spread the big green cricket-field, like the bed of a sea of light. Children played in the bluish shadow of the pavilion. Many rooks, high up, came cawing home across the softly woven sky. They stooped in a long curve down into the golden glow, concentrating, cawing, wheeling like black flakes on a slow vortex . . . (49)

As often happens when impressionist passages are interspersed in realist contexts, symbolic overtones are sounded, as in the figure of the vortex. "The

problem," as Merleau-Ponty puts it, "is to understand these strange relationships which are woven between the parts of the landscape, or between it and
me as incarnate subject, and through which an object perceived can concen-
trate in itself a whole scene or become the *imago* of a whole segment of life"
(*Phenomenology* 52).

The sense of being there, experiencing the world through the character's
eyes and ears, is built up with sensory touches, amplified by simile and
metaphor: "Mrs. Morel could hear the chock of the ball . . . could see the
white forms of men shifting silently over the green, upon which already the
under-shadows were smouldering. Away at the grange, one side of the haystacks was lit up, the other sides blue-grey. A wagon of sheaves rocked small
across the melting yellow light" (*Sons and Lovers* 49–50). The impression of
animated peacefulness and privilege, in which white-clad men replace black,
is a relief from the domestic battleground that Mrs. Morel has momentarily
escaped. The division of light on the haystacks, recalling Monet's motif,[7] and
the light dissolving over the sheaves show an awareness of chromatic variations. Impressionist vision, endowing objects with complementary colored
shadows and highlights, modulates into symbolism through a parallel intuitive process that endows Mrs. Morel's second son with a prophetic aura:

> [She] watched the sun sink from the glistening sky, leaving a soft flower-blue
> overhead, while the western space went red, as if all the fire had swum down
> there, leaving the bell cast flawless blue. The mountain-ash berries across the
> field stood fierily out from the dark leaves, for a moment. A few shocks of corn
> in a corner of the fallow stood up as if alive: she imagined them bowing: per-
> haps her son would be a Joseph. (50)

Although the passage is predominantly visual, a metaphorical pattern
runs through it, connecting refinement (the purity of a bell cast in fire) with
upright and outstanding qualities (sheaves animated by light). Inner and
outer vision converge, as Mrs. Morel's consciousness, playing over the field
with the sunset, projects her desires onto objects. While the text presents the
visual field before her, her mind subsumes the natural in the biblical, forming a symbol. Paul is seen to have inherited this symbol-forming capacity
when he links the steam and flame of the pit-head with the pillars of cloud
and fire in Exodus. The illuminated corn-shocks suggest a symbolic analogy,
while the psychological process, harmonizing imagination and environment,
reveals the mother's ambition for her son. Symbols arise naturally from the
real world, as the characters' responses trigger associated images from the

unconscious. Lawrence, like Paul, goes beyond impressionism to symbolism, "[painting] rather definite figures that had a certain luminous quality . . . [and fitting these] into a landscape, in . . . true proportion" (345).

While Paul is recovering from an attack of bronchitis, his perceptions are slowed down and intensified. This convalescent phase, combined with the Oedipal situation that makes him so sensitive to his mother's feelings, stimulates his development as an artist. In reverie, he transforms objects around him, fusing sensory images with memories or fantasies. Despite his professed enthusiasm for the "life [and] warmth" of the working class (298), his view of the miners is mostly distanced and diminished. Lying in bed, he likes "[to] watch the miners troop home, small, black figures trailing slowly in gangs across the white field. Then the night came up in dark blue vapor from the snow" (92). Although Lawrence gives a wealth of factual data about the miners' working conditions, impressionist perspectives are frequently applied to the distant but ever-present mines. Subsuming details in atmospheric views—"Down in the great trough of twilight, tiny clusters of lights burned where the pits were" (85)—paradoxically conveys a more pervasive sense of living conditions.

As Paul convalesces and cultivates powers of observation, he becomes fascinated by the ephemeral in nature: "The snowflakes, suddenly arriving on the window pane, clung there a moment like swallows, then were gone, and a drop of water was crawling down the glass" (92). Images of snowflakes and water show Paul transforming his perceptions into impressions. As he contemplates the phenomena of metamorphosis, he himself is growing up and changing. The connection, to such a mind, of things small and large, near and far, vertical and horizontal appears in a glimpse "across the valley, [of] the little black train crawl[ing] doubtfully over the great whiteness" (92), just as the water drop crawls down the windowpane. The black-and-white schema recalls the "Japanese" patterning of Van Gogh's sketches: Kazin finds the "miniature" of horses feeding in the snow and miners trooping home "exquisite as a Japanese watercolor" (608). The effect of symmetry in disparate things reveals a mind in the act of comparing and ordering its impressions.

Interspersed with highly realistic accounts of work in the factory are impressionist views that provide distance and poetic relief from the daily grind:

> From the train going home at night, he used to watch the lights of the town, sprinkled thick on the hills, fusing together in a blaze in the valleys. . . . Draw-

ing further off, there was a patch of lights at Bulwell, like myriad petals shaken to the ground from the shed stars; and beyond was the red glare of the furnaces, playing like hot breath on the clouds. (*Sons and Lovers* 140)

For all its similes and metaphors, the scene is not merely decorative: Paul's viewpoint dramatizes a conflict between fantasy and reality. His artist's eye selects and arranges groups of lights in varying configurations and intensities, while his poetic imagination, playing off near against far, adds decorative or apocalyptic images.

Paul develops his capacity for looking when he goes on excursions with his mother. In one emblematic scene,

Mother and son stood on the road to watch. Along the ridge of the great pit-hill crawled a little group in silhouette against the sky, a horse, a small truck, and a man. They climbed the incline against the heavens: at the end the man tipped the wagon; there was an undue rattle as the waste fell down the sheer slope of the enormous bank. (152)

The group forms a Hardyesque silhouette that highlights a moment in successive generations of working lives. Paul "sketch[es] rapidly" a scene that would certainly have attracted Van Gogh, who sketched similar scenes in the coalfields of the Borinage. As an embryonic artist, Paul finds aesthetic form in industrial landscapes. His animistic image of the pit—"Look how it heaps together, like something alive, almost—a big creature that you don't know. . . . And all the trucks standing waiting, like a string of beasts to be fed . . . " (152)—is worthy of Zola's voracious "Le Voreux."[8] The act of sketching sharpens Paul's appetite for the function and life of things. Looking with his mother stimulates his keenest awareness; he seems to see an image of his father's life, from which she has averted her eyes, shadowed forth in the trucks: "But I like the feel of *men* on things, while they're alive. There's a feel of men about trucks, because they've been handled with men's hands, all of them" (152). Paul's viewpoint expresses a vitalism in which material things are significant in proportion to the will and energy invested in them.

The scene from the grounds of Nottingham Castle, which Paul visits with Clara, is a painter's view of the industrial landscape,[9] arranged in planes to emphasize variety and distance and fusing natural and man-made forms in a synthetic vision:

Away beyond the boulevard, the thin stripes of the metals showed upon the railway track, whose margin was crowded with little stacks of timber, beside which smoking toy engines fussed. Then the silver string of the canal lay at random among the black heaps. Beyond, the dwellings, very dense on the river flats, looked like black, poisonous herbage, in thick rows and crowded beds, stretching right away, broken now and then by taller plants, right to where the river glistened in a hieroglyph across the country. . . . Great stretches of country, darkened with trees and faintly brightened with corn-land, spread towards the haze, where the hills rose blue beyond grey. (313)

This panorama dramatizes the act of looking, as the eye moves in leisurely fashion, contrasting line and mass, foreground and distance, clarity and haze. As Paul broods over it, the landscape loses its decorative detail and is submerged in symbolic vision. A powerful projection transmutes the texture of his vision from impressionist to expressionist: "All that remained was a vast, dark matrix of sorrow and tragedy . . . a dark mass of struggle and pain" (316). Paul sees before him what he feels inside himself and his community: the landscape, with its symmetrical design blurred and darkened, shifts into the somber register of his soul. His eyes merge natural, industrial, social, and sexual strata in a Munch-like vision of desolation.

Paul explains his painting to Miriam in terms of impressionism. He tells her that one of his sketches seems true to life "because there is scarcely any shadow in it—it's more shimmery—as if I'd painted the shimmering protoplasm in the leaves and everywhere, and not the stiffness of the shape. . . . Only this shimmeriness is the real living. The shape is a dead crust. The shimmer is inside really" (183). Intuitively, he has described the essential aim of impressionism: to paint the dance of life perceived by the eye and not the dead shapes conceived by the mind. As Edmond Duranty put it in *La Nouvelle Peinture* (1876), impressionists aimed "to render the trembling of leaves, the shimmer of water and the vibration of air drenched with light. . . " (qtd. in Blunden 142). Paul struggles to express in words the vision that inspires his painting—a "struggle for verbal consciousness [that] should not be left out in art" (Lawrence, "Foreword," 486). At this stage of his apprenticeship, he clearly identifies the search for "real living" with impressionism, but for him the source of light is inside the leaves, a vital incandescence rather than a diffusely shed light. His insight into the life of matter emerges in the exchange with Miriam, and significantly his words "[give] her a feeling of life again, and vivif[y] things which had meant nothing to her" (*Sons and Lovers* 183).

The vitalizing effect of impressionism eventually had its impact on a resistant public; now anyone can see a poppy field or a lily pond the way Monet painted them. As Georges Grappe said in *L'Art et le Beau*, for the impressionists "[it] is light that is all-powerful, that magnifies forms, brings out their beauty, renews their luster, metamorphoses their appearance, displaces their contours and quickens them": ultimately "all the forms [dissolve] in light" (qtd. in Blunden 211).[10] In "Introduction to These Paintings" (1929), Lawrence looked back on his earlier enthusiasm for the impressionists:

> Let us say what we will, but the real grand thrill of modern French art was the discovery of light. . . . No matter how Cézanne may have reacted from the impressionists, it was they, with their deliriously joyful discovery of light and "free" colour, who really opened his eyes. Probably the most joyous moment in the whole history of painting was the moment when the incipient impressionists discovered light, and with it, colour. . . . They escaped from the tyranny of solidity and the menace of mass-form. They escaped . . . from the dark procreative body which so haunts a man, they escaped into the open air, *plein air* and *plein soleil*: light and almost ecstasy. (*Phoenix* 563)

But after his apprenticeship phase, reflected in Paul's perceptions, Lawrence was no longer content with the impressionist dance of light without substance. Like Cézanne, he wanted to bring back objects and the body in all their solidity and integrity.

Another day Paul paints some trees in the sunset and exclaims to Miriam: "Now look at them and tell me, are they pine trunks or are they red coals, standing-up pieces of fire in that darkness. There's God's burning bush, for you, that burned not away" (*Sons and Lovers* 183). With biblical myth and Blakean rhetoric, Paul projects his own sexual, religious, and aesthetic passion into the trees, so that the "dead crust" of shape is transfigured and the pine trunks vibrate with subjective intensity. As with the shimmering leaves, it is an epiphany, "a sudden spiritual manifestation." Impressionist vitalism takes on expressionist force,[11] as in Van Gogh's *Pine Trees with Setting Sun* (1889), which Ronald Pickvance describes as "[p]owerfully conceived with an almost brutal coloristic and symbolic imagery . . . " (149; pl. 34). In Paul's symbolic vision, black trunks reddened by the setting sun signify a miracle of immanence, of matter *alive* and constantly transformed by the life-force as well as by perception. Blake meant something similar when he affirmed that the sun was not a golden guinea in the sky but a host of heavenly angels singing "Hosanna!"

Paul's vitalism makes Miriam see the pine trunks, that might have "meant nothing to her," as "wonderful" and "distinct." Once her perceptions are awakened, she in turn stimulates Paul in his struggle to express creative impulses. Her spirit flares up like the tree trunks in the sunset in response to his painter's vision; but to him she lacks the "ordinary," "fidgety" life-quality of leaves in a breeze, as in the "shivering foliage" of Monet's *Poplars*, painted with "a long, fidgety stroke . . . " (Lassaigne 92). The novel, combining Paul's point of view with an omniscient narrator's, contrasts the life-quality in the two characters, going considerably deeper than realism could do.

Paul's mother and Miriam stimulate his development in complementary ways. His mother sits passively reading while he sketches:

> And he, with all his soul's intensity directing his pencil, could feel her warmth inside him like strength. . . . He was conscious only when stimulated. A sketch finished, he always wanted to take it to Miriam. Then he was stimulated into knowledge of the work he had produced unconsciously. In contact with Miriam, he gained insight, his vision went deeper. From his mother he drew the life warmth, the strength to produce; Miriam urged this warmth into intensity like a white light. (*Sons and Lovers* 190)

He speaks, out of "the white intensity of his search," about Michelangelo, and "[it] felt to her as if she were fingering the very quivering tissue, the very protoplasm of life, as she heard him" (232). Miriam has clearly absorbed Paul's lesson about protoplasm in the leaves and is now penetrating to a similar essence in him. Later, as Paul talks of his hopes and fears, "his whole soul seemed to lie bare before her. She felt as if she watched the very quivering stuff of life in him" (289–90).

Paul has awakened a vital awareness of life in Miriam, just as Cyril and Lettie awakened it in George and the young Lawrence did in his friends. Paul's "white intensity" becomes Miriam's; it represents an exclusively spiritual quality they stimulate in each other. Responding to her yearning for "mystic participation," Paul quickens this vital sense in the girl, then steals it back for his art.

> He saw her crouched voluptuously before his work, and his heart beat quickly. . . . There was for him the most intense pleasure in talking about his work to Miriam. All his passion, all his wild blood went into this intercourse with her, when he talked and conceived his work. She brought forth to him his imaginations. She did not understand, any more than a woman understands when she conceives a child in her womb. But this was life for her, and for him. (241)

Sexual energy is sublimated into artistic conception and gestation. But having served as a threshing-floor for Paul's ideas, Miriam cannot also serve in the Demeter role that Clara fills.

Lawrence increasingly supplements the novel's realism and impressionism with symbolism. Just as Renoir in *The Bathers* (1884–87) and Cézanne in *Women Bathers* (1898–1905) show classical tendencies supplanting impressionism,[12] so Paul progresses to more organic yet vital forms of art:

> He loved to paint large figures, full of light, but not merely made up of lights and cast shadows, like the impressionists; rather definite figures that had a certain luminous quality, like some of Michael Angelo's people. And these he fitted into a landscape, in what he thought true proportion. (345)

Paul's painting mirrors Lawrence's fiction. Lawrence also fits characters into landscapes with which they interact naturally and symbolically, and Paul's development prefigures his use of Renaissance models for concepts of organic character and form in *The Rainbow*.

In *Sons and Lovers*, Lawrence seeks to express psychological and spiritual meanings that lie beneath vividly realized material surfaces. Examples of such symbolism are the madonna lily scene, the sun baptism, the swing, Miriam's stroking the daffodils, Paul's feeling the blood-heat of eggs in a nest, his scattering cowslips on Clara's hair, the cherry-picking, the red carnations, the "baptism of fire," and the pit-head image. Paul tells Clara:

> I like the rows of trucks, and the headstocks, and the steam in the daytime and the lights at night.—When I was a boy, I always thought a pillar of cloud by day and a pillar of fire by night was a pit, with its steam, and its lights and the burning bank—and I thought the Lord was always at the pit-top. (364)

He applies the Exodus symbol of God's guidance to his father's work and his own experience of being-in-the-world. The convergence of concrete reality and mythic symbol yields intimations of the unconscious, uniting fatherhood and godhead. Such symbol-formation shows a religious imagination at work, forging links between matter and spirit, finite and infinite. The same psycho-mythic process appears in a scene of children fighting around a lamppost at night, in which the boy's experience of hatred, terror, guilt, and revenge is illuminated by an apocalyptic symbol from the Book of Revelation: "Paul . . . [saw] a big red moon lift itself up, slowly, between the waste road over the hill-top; steadily, like a great bird. And he thought of the bible, that the moon should be turned to blood" (101).

Realistic and symbolic images depend alike upon concrete verisimilitude and sensory power. Van Gogh believed that "all reality is symbolic," objective forms evoking subjective responses, while Rudolf Arnheim maintains that "genuine culture [involves] the constant awareness of the symbolic meaning expressed in a concrete happening, the sensing of the universal in the particular" (*Art and Visual Perception* 454). As Lawrence seeks meaning among things and patterns in events, his imagination forges symbols from reality.[13] Concentration on things produces images whose meaning, embedded in the object yet associated with a character, must be grasped in context rather than extrapolated. Images of lilies, roses, carnations, trucks, or pithead are saturated with a significance that flows through things from human lives. This homeophoric function accounts for the density of texture in symbolic scenes that are just as "full of sensation and presentation" as scenes of "hard, violent" realism.[14] "[The] categories of 'being' and 'meaning' coincide" (Neumann 175), as consciousness actively transforms objects of perception. Interactions between characters and places generate phenomenal images that function as symbols.

The episode in which Mrs. Morel is thrust outdoors by her drunken spouse is the first of a series of intense moonlight scenes in *Sons and Lovers*, *The Rainbow*, and *Women in Love*. Perfume, glistening leaves, vibrating moonlight, distant sounds, and swooning sensations merge in a mélange of impressions detached from mental control. The "mixing-pot" of Mrs. Morel's experience modulates into a symbolic cluster that points beyond the moment; thrown back on nature in a moment of personal crisis, her being is rhythmically intermingled with night, moth, phlox, and roses. She is immersed in the bath of moonlight, the "tall white lilies . . . reeling" with her emotion. These flowers preside ominously over the prelude to Paul's birth, when "the child boiled within her" (*Sons and Lovers* 34, 33).

Rather than simply representing a hostile Life-Force, as Van Ghent suggests,[15] the lilies are a complex symbol. As an extension of Mrs. Morel, they symbolize spirituality intensified to the point of reification in opposition to the overbearing sensuality of her husband. The ambiguity of the symbol makes it all the more powerful and disturbing: the lilies' whiteness and fragrance are associated with the woman's aura, their pollen with the indifferent Life-Force that makes her its vessel. Odors are mixed; the lilies are slightly sickening, while "the raw, strong scent" of the phlox is invigorating. The "fresh scent" of the white roses associated with "morning-time and sunshine" is an ironically displaced Apollonian symbol of Mrs. Morel's conscious identity. Keith Sagar sees the scene as "a false epiphany," ushering Paul "not into a rich unknown, but into an all-encompassing mother-love" and suggests that "[the] blanched white light symbolizes the possession of his soul by women . . . " (*Life into Art* 96–97). While I agree with Sagar's interpretation of "whiteness," I do not think that these images, suspended in a richly ambiguous matrix, can be read univocally from Paul's point of view. Such homeophoric symbols give the atmosphere and dynamics of experience, rather than specific foreknowledge of a character's destiny.

In the scene in which Miriam takes Paul to see her white rose-bush, a mysterious effect is created by impressionist means: "In the old oak-wood a mist was rising and he hesitated, wondering whether one whiteness were a strand of fog or only campion flowers, pallid in a cloud" (*Sons and Lovers* 195). The symbolic ritual that follows is centered on communion, holiness, and worship. Pausing at the threshold of the dark wood, "they saw the sky in front, like mother-of-pearl," an image that hints at the source of Paul's inhibition. His uneasiness is partly fear of annoying his mother by being out late with Miriam; Mrs. Morel's jealous judgment of the girl as "one of those who will want to suck a man's soul out till he has none of his own left" (196) projects her own possessiveness while expressing his fears. Paul's unconscious identification of Miriam with his mother casts a dark shadow over his feelings.

The white rose-bush is the counterpart of the fiery red pine-trunks, "God's burning bush," that Paul made Miriam see through his eyes. In these scenes of projection and empathy, each tries to initiate the other into his or her own vision, which is immanent in some form of nature. Now it is Miriam's turn to initiate Paul, and her iconic rose-bush—incandescent with spiritual power as his pine-trunks were with sensual—emanates a spellbinding *mana* of beauty and spirituality: "In bosses of ivory and in large splashed stars the roses gleamed on the darkness of foliage and stems and grass. . . . Point after point, the steady roses shone out to them, seeming to kindle something in their souls. The dusk came like smoke around, and still did not put out the roses" (195). The ritual involves looking at and responding to an object that remains magically illuminated while its devotees are immersed in twilight. A strong sense of the numinous can be inhaled along with the "streaming scent" of honeysuckle. But it is excessive, unbalanced, overpowering—and before it Paul feels unmanned.

The scene symbolizes the threat of spiritual sublimation to Paul's precarious sexual being. But does he read Miriam's look correctly? "She was pale and expectant with wonder, her lips were parted, and her dark eyes lay open to him. His look seemed to travel down into her. Her soul quivered. It was the communion she wanted. He turned aside, as if pained" (195–96). The dialogic principle is sufficiently at work here to leave some doubt as to what Miriam expects and why Paul turns aside. At a conscious level, the sexual undertow of the phrasing foregrounds sublimation. Yet however heavy with virginal spirituality the scene may be, it remains profoundly erotic; Miriam's sensitivity lies vulnerably exposed, like an offering to her lover.

Paul recoils because he hates (fears) Miriam's capacity for spiritual loving as "too intimate." He laments that she "make[s] [him] so spiritual" (226), but the spirituality she arouses is his own. Miriam is identified with the talismanic roses, and her spiritual/sensual duality is suggested in a centripetal/centrifugal image: "She looked at her roses. They were white, some incurved and holy, others expanded in an ecstasy" (196). The narrator overdetermines the meaning of the scene, in order to justify Paul's reaction, by referring to Miriam's "worship" of the flowers (196). Anxious about the spiritual magnetism she has projected into "her" rose-bush, he interprets her desires arbitrarily. The formal and dramatic impetus of the narrative tilts such scenes toward a monologic reading that coincides with Paul's point of view—his fear of, and rebellion against, female spirituality, traceable to his mother's domination. Every detail fits, and the meaning is manifest; but the subtext subtly allows some of the ambiguity of undetermined experience to seep through. The monologic voice leaves an impression of subjectivity, not only in Paul's experience but also in the narrator's interpretation of it.

The haunting power of the scene derives from Lawrence's symbolism, which maintains "the trembling instability of the balance." The mingled sensory and psychological imagery creates an ambiguity that hovers over the source of the emotion. Miriam's "satisf[action] with the holiness of the night" is clearly attributed to her by external omniscience. As Paul reviews the encounter, he needs to believe that Miriam is satisfied with what dissatisfies him. Because his point of view is privileged, one knows what he feels; but who knows exactly what she feels? Her feelings are as yet unformed and depend largely on his responses. Paul's inhibition and sublimation, his penchant for the mystical, appear quite explicitly in a scene in the church at Alfreton, where he responds along with Miriam to the Pre-Raphaelite religious atmosphere and "[all] his latent mysticism quiver[s] into life" (203).

A scene in Paul's garden—referring back to Mrs. Morel's experience in the moonlight—contrasts the scent of madonna lilies with that of carnations and irises (337–38). It is the prelude to Paul's breaking-off with Miriam and becoming reconciled with his mother. The garden presents a spiritual/sensual complex, in which images are "patterned" according to psychosomatic responses. As Merleau-Ponty observes, "my body is not only an object among all other objects, a nexus of sensible qualities among others, but an object which is *sensitive* to all the rest, which reverberates to all sounds, vibrates to all colours, and provides words with their primordial significance . . . " (*Phenomenology* 236). The tension of Paul's triangular relationship with his mother and Miriam has heightened his perceptions, as he intuitively seeks a way out. Lawrence's animism is powerful: the maternal aura that pervades and subdues Paul's consciousness seeks him out "stealthily," and "the air all round seem[s] to stir with scent, as if it were alive." The "dim white fence of lilies" is a barely visible barrier, its intoxicating aroma a living presence. All this correlates with the seductive attraction and deep-seated fear of all-absorbing mother-love.

The "keen perfume" of the carnations "[comes] sharply across the rocking, heavy scent of the lilies," evoking crosscurrents of loyalty in Paul. His sympathy for his embittered and exhausted mother is projected onto the lilies that "flagged all loose, as if they were panting"; yet their scent "[makes] him drunk," suggesting loss of control. He is still under the regressive spell of "the great flowers" when "like a shock he [catches] another perfume, something raw and coarse." There is no conflict between this sensual perfume and the spiritual perfume of the lilies, because Paul knows that his mother would rather condone a purely sensual relationship with Clara than a spiritual one with Miriam.

The raw, coarse perfume that attacks Paul's senses stimulates him to hunt around in the dark until "he [finds] the purple iris, touch[es] their fleshy throats, and their dark, grasping hands" (338). The search moves from scent and dim vision to touch and possession, foreshadowing his "baptism of fire" with Clara. Anthropomorphic imagery embodies the female object of desire in "fleshy throats" and "dark grasping hands," male phallicism in the stiffness of the stalks. The fleshy irises are associated with Clara, whose full throat and large hands, with their "almost coarse, opaque and white [skin], with fine golden hairs" attract Paul's artistic and sensual attention, while "her faint natural perfume . . . [drives] him wild with hunger"(*Sons and Lovers* 270, 375). He is obsessed with Clara's physique and, at one point, actually identifies with her "white, heavy arms, her throat, her moving bosom" (375). Clara stimulates in him "that thickening and quickening of his blood, that peculiar concentration in the breast, as if something were alive there, a new self or a new centre of consciousness . . . " (294).

The whole fragrance scene brilliantly yet unobtrusively epitomizes Paul's oscillation between three centers of consciousness. Having pondered the knot of his relationships in vain, he abruptly cuts it, gravitating spiritually toward his mother and physically toward Clara. He chews the petals of a carnation and spits them into the fire, sacrificing Miriam's love to his mother's will. Delicate pinks then give way to passionate reds, and Clara's scarlet petals, sprinkled on the earth "like splashed drops of blood," counterpoint Miriam's "pure white" roses with their "large splashed stars" (355, 195). Contrasting images reflect the *structure* of Paul's relationships rather than functioning as separate symbols.

A distinction of Lawrence's style is his power to link sensation and emotion with underlying forces. As language reaches out toward the unconscious, "individuality fade[s], and a primal stratum emerge[s], intoxicated, image-laden, Panic" (Benn, *Selected Writings* 42). It is significant that Lawrence's writing of the final version of the novel (July–November 1912) coincided not only with his experience of passionate love with Frieda, with whom he had eloped to Germany in May, but also with the high point of European expressionism.

Expressionism in the arts (1905–20) was a revolutionary tendency that called for a complete break (*Aufbruch*) with the immediate past and a return to simpler, more primitive ways of living. Dissatisfied with civilization as they knew it, the expressionists wanted to prepare the way for a new humanity. They claimed the priority of personal experience over reason and convention, demanding the right to express visions that sprang from the unconscious, no matter how irrational or startling. Northern expressionism (originating in Dresden and Berlin) retained the human image, distorting it to bring out spiritual qualities or depersonalizing it as an element of nature or the city. Southern expressionism (centered in Munich) substituted animal forms or lyrical abstractions for human images, aiming at spiritual essences. Rejecting impressionism as superficial phenomenalism, expressionists "wanted . . . to look behind the outward appearance and to penetrate the forces which move the world" (Buchheim 21).[16] Expressionist art springs from inner necessity projected into outward forms. It is presentational rather than representational (Vajda 48), confronting the viewer with the artist's vision and aiming, by distortion, to shock him into awareness of hidden truths, sensations, and desires that have a universal basis.

Lawrence's lyrical description of Paul's and Clara's lovemaking employs expressionist elements of depersonalization, disorientation, animism, and universalism: "The naked hunger and inevitability of his loving her, something strong and blind and ruthless in its primitiveness, made the hour almost terrible to her. . . . They had met, and included in their meeting the thrust of the manifold grass stems, the cry of the peewit, the wheel of the stars" (*Sons and Lovers* 397–98). The human sounds and movements of lovers participate mystically in those of nature—there is an expressionist engagement with primal energies that breaks down isolated individuality. Paul's sense of oneness with the blindly thrusting grass stems is an erotic realization of transpersonal energies that obliterates personal love for Clara. Sexual and creative become one.

From such transports Paul gains a keener sense of physical reality and of the vital force that "rolls through all things" (Wordsworth, "Tintern Abbey"). The rhythmic rhetoric does not "symbolize" anything so much as manifest a universal dynamic. Submerging erotic sensation in sublimely simple images of nature and kinetic rhythms, Lawrence strives to express a preverbal experience through what Kirchner calls "the religious sensuality of art" (Grohmann 84)—"If so great a magnificent power could overwhelm them, identify them altogether with itself, so that they knew they were only grains in the tremendous heave that lifted every grass-blade its little height, and every tree, and living thing, then why fret about themselves: they could let themselves be carried by life" (398). The intensity, expansiveness, ritualism, mythicism, universality, extremism, pantheism, and vitalism all look toward Lawrence's mastery of a fully charged expressionist language in *The Rainbow*. The sexual rhythm that obliterates ego-consciousness is "a pulsation in little of the rhythm at life's Source" (Cheney 323). But because the experience is transcendent, the participants are only vessels of the life-force, who do not meet as persons. The expressionist style marks a wide difference between ecstatic, impersonal states and normal, everyday experience, the province of realism.

Expressionist overtones add resonance to impressions of the Lincolnshire coast: "As they . . . looked round at the endless monotony of levels, the land a little darker than the sky, the sea sounding small beyond the sand-hills, his heart filled strong with the sweeping relentlessness of life" (*Sons and Lovers* 400). The bare landscape and exposure to empty space strike a lyrical, exultant note. But as Paul watches Clara, she "grew smaller, lost proportion, seemed only like a large white bird toiling forward" (402). The receding and diminishing figure is the negative side of cosmic vision: Paul sees Clara as dwarfed and dehumanized by surrounding immensity—unlike Kirchner's bathers who are integrated with their seaside or forest environments.[17] Distance invites a dangerous indifference to identity: "She represents something," thinks Paul, "like a bubble of foam represents the sea. But what is *she*! It's not her I care for—" (402). He is not in love with an individual, but with an archetype. Clara looms large only when the perspective switches back to close-up and he watches her drying her breasts: then, as Woman, she seems "even bigger than the morning and the sea" (402). Expressionist language links Paul's sensations with cosmic rhythms, as "[he becomes], not a man with a mind, but a great instinct" (408). In the swelling rhythms and images of Lawrence's vitalist manifesto, Paul achieves a "subtle inter-relatedness" with the cosmos (*Phoenix* 528), recalling the Taoist belief "that the artist . . . was brought into direct relation with the creative power indwelling in the world . . . " (Lawrence Binyon, *The Flight of the Dragon* [1911], qtd. in Cheney 124). The harmony of physical impulses, freed from mental control, with the source of all life typifies a primitivizing strain in expressionism.

As Paul glances around before encountering Baxter Dawes, he sees "the houses [standing] on the brim of the dip, black against the sky, like wild beasts glaring curiously with yellow eyes down into the darkness" (*Sons and Lovers* 409). The image is a grotesque projection of fear and aggression. In the fight that follows, the primitive autonomy of instinctual life is stressed: "He felt his whole body unsheath itself like a claw. . . . Tighter and tighter grew his body, like a screw that is gradually increasing in pressure, till something breaks" (409–10). But he relents and takes a brutal beating. He returns to his mother and, shortly after he recovers, his life is overshadowed by her illness. Subsequent images of fatality and apocalypse suggest the dark world of suffering and death in Edvard Munch's paintings and woodcuts.

The furnaces flared in a red blotch over Bulwell, the black clouds were like a low ceiling. As he went along the ten miles of high-road, he felt as if he were walking out of life, between the black levels of the sky and the earth. But at the end was only the sick room. If he walked and walked for ever—there was only that place to come to. (434)

Through expressionist projection of Paul's feelings, surrounding space is transformed into a rigid diagram. Monotonous, compulsive motion offers no escape from this dark, horizonless landscape, whose oppressive parallels signify claustrophobia and nightmare.

After his mother's death and the final parting with Miriam, Paul is left alone with nothing. His existential struggle against the "deathward drag" is projected onto blank space, as Lawrence makes his existence the core of being in an alien world: "Whatever spot he stood on, there he stood alone. From his breast, from his mouth sprang the endless space—and it was there behind him, everywhere. . . . There was no Time, only Space" (464). The language is expressionist, with staccato sentence-forms, broken syntax, poetic parallelisms, exclamations, and monumental abstractions. Paul's despair is universalized, becoming an apocalyptic vision of the void, like Marlow's vision of "triumphant darkness" at the end of *Heart of Darkness*. Emotionally tied to his dead mother, Paul is responding to a deep-seated death wish. He stands like cosmic man, alone at the center of a derelict world, suffering the anguish of alienation. He is divided between the pull of his dead mother's spirit, "gone abroad into the night," and his own body, stuck fast in the physical world.

> On every side the immense dark silence seemed pressing him, so tiny a speck, into extinction, and yet, almost nothing, he could not be extinct. Night, in which everything was lost, went reaching out, beyond stars and sun. Stars and sun, a few bright grains, went spinning round for terror and holding each other in embrace, there in a darkness that outpassed them all and left them tiny and daunted. So much, and himself, infinitesimal, at the core a nothingness, and yet not nothing. (464)

The extrasensory perception, distortion of spatial relationships, and profoundly religious reaching out to the cosmos match the ethos of Van Gogh's *Starry Night* (1889),[18] in which stars and moon become spinning suns and constellations plunging waves. Expressionist form-language is marked by dynamism—"the backward-forward design, the poised or coiled tension path, the thrust and return and contrapuntal variations of the plastic elements" (Cheney 58). In Lawrence's night vision, as in Van Gogh's field of gyrating forces, "the pressure of feeling . . . forces the bounds of the visible and determines the fantastic projections . . . " (Schapiro, *Van Gogh* 100). The artist's desire "to express his aspiration towards infinity in nature" produces visual apocalypse;[19] the centripetal pressure of space breaks down his enclosed identity, making way for an oceanic inflow and outflow of Being. In Lawrence's vision, the "few bright grains" of stars in the vast darkness and the rapturous "embrace" of opposites may be unconscious symbols of conception and gestation, as that infinitesimal "speck" of being, the self, struggles to be born from the womb of night. In a Manichean conflict Paul's desire to *be* narrowly overcomes his desire not to be, and the novel ends with his sudden conversion to the life-force, in an act of self-overcoming.

So exhaustively did Lawrence employ realistic methods, among others, in *Sons and Lovers*, that he surpassed the limits of realism and concluded: "I have to write differently" (*Letters* 2: 142). The novel is a triumph of *art* ("art for life's sake," or "art for my sake," as Lawrence would say), in which an emerging modernist consciousness interrelates various forms of expression. The graphic realism on which Lawrence's vision is founded is supplemented by impressionist, symbolist, and expressionist language that deepens the image of experience and amplifies major themes. *Sons and Lovers* marks the watershed between Lawrence's apprenticeship to nineteenth-century traditions of realism and his achievement of a unique and innovative style, shaped by expressionism, primitivism, and futurism, in *The Rainbow* and *Women in Love*.

3

VISION AND EXPRESSION
IN *THE RAINBOW*

Lawrence draws on sources as diverse as Renaissance art, English landscape painting, French impressionism, German expressionism, and Italian futurism, transforming all into the textures of his own vision. "Influence" is too crude a concept for his response to the zeitgeist, and evidence of his knowledge of expressionist painting is scant, if intriguing. On 4 September 1913, he wrote to Ernest Collings: "I was in Munich the other day, at a great Exhibition of pictures and sculpture—German Spanish Italian Russian Swedish and so on. . . . The Germans are vigorous, and brutal, and get simply amazing technical effects . . . " (*Letters* 2: 69)—clearly a description of expressionism. The exhibition would be the huge Gesamtausstellung, which ran from August to September 1913 in Munich,[1] featuring paintings by Heckel, Kirchner, Pechstein, and Schmidt-Rottluff as well as Gauguin, Munch, and Van Gogh. Although he found the Munich pictures "shrill and restless" (*Phoenix* 82), Lawrence uses expressionist elements in abundance in *The Rainbow*. According to the journal *Der Sturm*, expressionism was "an attitude to life, an attitude moreover of the senses, not of the mind" (qtd. in Hodin, *Oskar Kokoschka* 104), which suggests its appeal to Lawrence. Certainly a religious impetus generates the expressionist desire to create a new spiritual order. "Thus the whole of space," says Kasimir Edschmid, "becomes vision for the Expressionist artist" (qtd. in Sotriffer 6). Even such a formally oriented painter as Lyonel Feininger saw his work as a struggle to express the unconscious: "From deep within rises an almost painful urge for the realization of inner experiences, an overwhelming longing, an unearthly nostalgia overcomes me at times, to bring them to light . . . " (qtd. in Myers 208). This statement bears a striking resemblance to Lawrence's "Foreword to *Women in Love*": "The creative, spontaneous soul sends forth its promptings of desire and aspiration in us. . . . This struggle for verbal consciousness should not be left out in art. . . . *It is the passionate struggle into conscious being*" (485–86).

Expressionism involves empathy *and* abstraction, reaching through the personal to the archetypal. The artist aspires to a prophetic role, "surrender[ing] [him]self to the swelling force of existence . . . [and] be[ing] entirely imbued with the utter profundity of a personal divinity" (Alfred Kubin, qtd. in Buchheim 12). So Lawrence, composing "The Sisters," feels "there is something deep evolving itself out in me. And it is *hard* to express a new thing, in sincerity. . . . [But] my novels must be written from the depth of my religious experience" (*Letters* 2: 165). Expressionism is marked by intensity, concentration, convulsion, exaggeration. Emil Nolde's style, for instance, inspired by late Monet, Van Gogh, and Oceanic art, is remarkable for fervid excitement that dissolves forms into sweeping lines and glowing colors, presenting a direct image of ecstatic experience, as in *Candle Dancers* (woodcut 1917; see pl. 4) or *Tropical Sunset* (1914).[2] Herbert Read observes that Lawrence, as a painter, was "an expressionist" and compares him to Nolde or Soutine (63–64), while Edward Lucie-Smith relates his later paintings to Kirchner's (227). Canvases like *Red Willow Trees* (1927) and *Dance Sketch* (1928) support such claims, although Lawrence's paintings illustrate preconceived visions and lack the mastery of expression and sensitivity to the medium he has with words.

Lawrence shared the expressionist drive toward Being; for him the novel is a cathartic, exploratory, prophetic form. His dialogic discourse relates to the dual thrust of expressionism, in which subject and object are mutually transformed.[3] Such organic completeness contrasts with the modernist aesthetic of clinical detachment. Art is to be valued not as an entity in itself but as an expression of the artist's struggle to live more abundantly. The excitement of the act of composition gives the rhythms of Lawrence's writing an expressionist quality. While the art of Joyce and Woolf aims at a "luminous silent stasis," that of Lawrence and Van Gogh is dynamic. As Tuchman notes, "[the] expressionist [brush stroke] . . . implies the gesture of the artist in the painting act—a gesture of body movement. . . . Thus Van Gogh's stroke seems to burn into the canvas with savage but deliberate forcefulness" (Introduction n.p.).

This impulse to cut deep is akin to that of the expressionists, who revived the art of the woodcut with its primitive discipline, polarized contrasts, and capacity to grasp "[the] irrational, the mystical, the transcendental" (Buchheim 27). "I don't care so much about what the woman *feels*," Lawrence writes. "I only care about what the woman *is*—what she *is*—inhumanly, physiologically, materially . . . what she *is* as a phenomenon (or as representing some greater, inhuman will) . . . " (*Letters* 2: 183). The "old stable ego" is exposed as a literary convention, comparable to illusionist realism in painting. "There is another ego," he proclaims, "according to whose action the individual is unrecognisable, and passes through . . . allotropic states"—as the main characters of *The Rainbow* and *Women in Love* pass through ritual scenes that expose the activity of their unconscious.

Max Wildi calls the latter part of *The Rainbow* (1915) "the first example of expressionist writing within the covers of a Lawrence novel" (243); in his view, Lawrence shares "the [expressionist] impulse to present, directly and indirectly, states of the individual soul; to project a powerful, spontaneous, often explosive inward life into the universe . . . " (258).[4] Henry Schvey draws some interesting (if rather loose) parallels with Kokoschka and lists Lawrence's expressionist characteristics as "the break with realism, the concern with the elemental in man . . . and the conception of art as visionary or religious experience . . . " (127). Recently Tony Pinkney has maintained that "*The Rainbow* may be Britain's first (and best) Expressionist [novel]," its blend of modernism and medievalism matching that of German expressionism (75).[5] Yet the extent to which expressionist vision and style pervade *The Rainbow* has still to be fully recognized.

In his famous letter to Garnett, Lawrence uses the futurist manifestos of Marinetti as an aid to self-discovery. Writing in Italy, he called *The Rainbow* "a bit futuristic—quite unconsciously so" (*Letters* 2: 180). The ferment of futurism—its creative energy as well as its destruction of obsolete forms— appealed to him. But the futurists idealized war, despised woman, and worshiped the machine, thus reflecting the disintegration of European society. Lawrence blames them for abstracting scientific phenomena from human life, whereas he wants to express being directly as it undergoes formative changes. He had recently traveled through Germany (May–August 1912) at a time when expressionism was burgeoning and when relationship with a woman he loved and contact with a foreign culture were shaping his genius. Frieda not only introduced him to Freud's ideas but, in addition, she was intimate with Otto Gross,[6] whose erotic philosophy and struggle against his father had a profound impact on literary expressionism, as well as with the circle of Ludwig Klages and Alfred Schuler, whose ideas on blood and sun struck a responsive chord in Lawrence. "Gross's theory of the necessary opposition between the ego and the non-ego" (Green 71) influenced expressionism and became a keystone of Lawrence's philosophy. *The Rainbow* is dedicated to Frieda's sister Else von Richthofen, who had had a child by Gross in 1907, whose husband, Edgar Jaffe, owned a painting by Franz Marc, and whose struggle for intellectual emancipation is one side of Ursula's character, as Frieda's *Lebensphilosophie* is another.

In the first expressionist scenes of *The Rainbow*, Lawrence attempts to convey unconscious processes in the courtship of Lydia Lensky and Tom Brangwen with a shift from realism to expressionism that intensifies, distorts, and thickens the texture of the language.[7] This is not just a matter of individual passages (the microlevel) but of an entire rhythm of attraction and repulsion.[8] Preparations for courtship are realistically described; then the technique becomes oblique, as mood, atmosphere, and feeling are expressed in a few verbal brush strokes: "as grey twilight was falling, he went across to the orchard to gather the daffodils. The wind was roaring in the appletrees, the yellow flowers swayed violently up and down, he heard even the fine whisper of their spears as he stooped to break the flattened, brittle stems . . . " (*The Rainbow* 41). The reader is projected immediately into the character's world and feels the tension that heightens his sensitivity to color, movement, sound, and touch. The rhythmic imagery is a key to Tom's agitated inner state, which contrasts ironically with his stiff, formal manner. The recurring image of the daffodils, combined with contrasts between darkness and light, outside and inside, has a nonlogical, expressionist force that "make[s] the invisible visible."[9] The man stands outside a window in the dark, looking in at an intimate cameo that seems to exclude him: "The mother's face was dark and still, and he saw, with a pang, that she was away back in the life that had been. The child's hair gleamed like spun glass, her face was illuminated till it seemed like wax lit up from the inside. The wind boomed strongly" (42). The monumental simplicity of the scene, merging space with time, has the starkness and emotional relief of an expressionist woodcut or sculpture.

Brangwen is immobilized, spellbound, listening with such acute sensitivity that he can hear "the slight crunch of the rockers." The images that follow are discordant, abrupt, surreal, suggesting disorientation. His gaze switches from the child's "black and dilated" eyes to "the clouds which packed in great, alarming haste across the dark sky" (42). The sense of psychological distance is enhanced by images of sound, silence, and space, while the character's inner pulsation is projected onto the hurrying clouds. He stands still, yet emotionally he is rushing toward a confrontation with the unknown, his universe changing around him. Strangeness, awkwardness, and compulsion characterize the scene. Lawrence controls the focus with a painter's sensibility, objectifying the emotion, which has no immediate outlet. Ezra Pound defines an image as "an intellectual and emotional complex in an instant of time" (qtd. in Pratt 18). Just so, "the gripped fist of flowers" (*The Rainbow* 43) stands out forcefully as a symbol of the man at a crucial moment. It is not so much a characterizing image as an expression of emotional upsurge leading to growth and change.

Chapter one closes with an expressionist rendering of the chaos of passion, fear, and desire in Tom as he opens himself to the unknown. The turbulence of his soul is projected onto the violence of the elements, with image patterns creating discords. Lawrence does verbally what Van Gogh does pictorially in *The Starry Night* (see pl. 5): he superimposes an image of man's soul upon the cosmos. This is not anthropomorphism but an act of visionary transformation:

> He went out into the wind. Big holes were blown into the sky, the moonlight blew about. Sometimes a high moon, liquid-brilliant, scudded across a hollow space and took cover under electric, brown-iridescent cloud-edges. Then there was a blot of cloud, and shadow. . . . And all the sky was teeming and tearing along, a vast disorder of flying shapes and darknesses and ragged fumes of light and a great brown circling halo, then the terror of a moon running liquid-brilliant into the open for a moment, hurting the eyes before she plunged under cover of cloud again. (48)

Synesthesia, movement, chiaroscuro create an atmosphere of turmoil projected into visual forms that have the hallucinatory strangeness of a dream. The objective scene is distorted and saturated with feeling as Lawrence reaches through character to grasp the substance of emotion and express it spatially.

Expressionist imagery pervades *The Rainbow*, giving many scenes a preternatural intensity. Thus Lydia's look and Tom's response are described with bizarre force: "Her eyes, with a blackness of memory struggling with passion, primitive and electric away at the back of them, rejected him and absorbed him at once" (47). Here Lawrence dramatizes the shock and recoil of contrary impulses. Along with its promise of renewed life, the lovers' embrace carries a threat of annihilation, recalling Edvard Munch's *The Kiss*, in which the faces of two lovers are absorbed into one blank.[10] The Lawrentian male must struggle to preserve a core of integral being; he desires union with the unknown yet fears absorption into Woman:

> Then again, what was agony to him . . . she leaned forward a little, and with a strange, primeval suggestion of embrace, held him her mouth. It was ugly-beautiful, and he could not bear it. He put his mouth on hers, and slowly, slowly the response came, gathering force and passion, till it seemed to him she was thundering at him. . . . He drew away, white, unbreathing. Only, in his blue eyes, was something of himself concentrated. And in her eyes was a little smile upon a black void. (*The Rainbow* 47)

It is the woman's prerogative to accept or reject the man who comes to her in fear and desire to seek his fulfillment. Woman, in *The Rainbow*, is creator and destroyer; sex becomes apocalyptic. Munch expresses male ambivalence toward woman in his *Madonna* (1893–94; see pl. 6), in which an archetypal female is shown at the moment of conception. Her ecstasy brings the soul of man into being, giving birth to life and death simultaneously. Munch underlines the theme by painting a trail of sperm around the red frame and a skeletal embryo in one corner. Lawrence's Madonna has "a little smile upon a black void," Munch's a blood-red halo.

Lydia's existence, rooted in nature, participates in natural rhythms, "laps[ing] again to stupor and indifference," then "opening, unfolding, asking, as a flower opens in full request under the sun . . . " (54). Their mutual responses are vital and unconscious, the style grotesque and abrupt. At first Tom oscillates between "elemental" unconsciousness and everyday reality. But as his knowledge of Lydia deepens, it stabilizes his experience: "[He knows] she [is] his woman, he [knows] her essence, that it [is] his to possess. And he seem[s] to live thus . . . in contact with the unknown . . . " (58). He gives himself fully to passion, as the motif of the flood shows:

> She lapsed into a sort of sombre exclusion, a curious communion with mysterious powers, a sort of mystic, dark state. . . . Then suddenly, out of nowhere, there was connection between them again. . . . The tension, the bond, burst, and the passionate flood broke forward into a tremendous, magnificent rush, so that he felt he could snap off the trees as he passed, and create the world afresh. (60)

Tom's pent-up energy overflows, distorting and re-creating the image of the world. External reality bows to the power of his being. He *is* life ("the zest of life was strong in him" [70]), for his being is momentarily identified with the energies that create and sustain life. Individual personality is annulled. His power is a gift, a possession, not something attained by the will.

Lawrence's use of biblical metaphor to spiritualize marital sexuality has an expressionist edge: "[T]heir flesh was one rock from which the life gushed, out of her who was smitten and rent, from him who quivered and yielded" (71). Depersonalization points to primitivism and the "utter sensuality" of the fetish in *Women in Love*. *The Rainbow*, however, emphasizes the solidarity of man and wife: "She looked at him as a woman in childbirth looks at the man who begot the child in her; an impersonal look, in the extreme hour, female to male" (77). Religious expressionism appears in the emphasis on suprapersonal absolutes and infinites of passion. Tom affirms this spiritual dimension while Lydia is in labor: "The swift, unseen threshing of the night upon him silenced him and he was overcome. He turned away indoors, humbly. There was the infinite world, eternal, unchanging, as well as the world of life" (77). Expressionism breaks through personal experience to seize the archetype. Tom must curb his passion, yet he has touched an absolute of experience: "For she was Woman to him, all other women were her shadows" (79).

The rhythms of desire and rejection in marriage culminate, in the last pages of "Childhood of Anna Lensky" (chapter 3), in a ritual of spiritual transfiguration. The sequence begins with short sentences, cryptically expressing Tom's struggle to yield himself to the unknown. "He knew she spoke a foreign language. The fear was like bliss in his heart. . . . He wanted to go" (89–90). The inward struggle is played out in tensely interlocking main clauses, slowed down by participial and infinitive phrases, without extenuation or subordination. Tom must enter the unknown, accepting intimate connection with the otherness that overawes him. Initiation leads to transfiguration, as the two selves come together as one—the miracle that Tom will proclaim at Anna's wedding: "His blood beat up in waves of desire. . . . If he could come really within the blazing kernel of darkness, if really he could be destroyed, burnt away till he lit with her in one consummation, that were supreme, supreme" (90).

The physical encounter is encoded in abstractions and metaphors that, combined with pulsing rhythms, express an inward, emotional reality. The flood motif is present ("he began to flow towards her") in conjunction with flame imagery and daring parallels with the Gospels ("losing himself to find her, to find himself in her"). The style is expressively alive. Sexual imagery is fused with spiritual so that one cannot talk about two separate kinds of experience; rather, the two become one, as the lovers do. Oceanic rhythms give the language its momentum, and erotic urgency has the force of spiritual quest. The risks of writing this way are enormous, but the expressionist seeks out such challenges. Through rhythmic parallelism, with participial phrases suggesting abandonment, infinitives purpose, impulse, desire, and fulfillment, Lawrence achieves a complex mimesis of tension and release, centered on the "mystic oxymoron"[11] of a "blazing kernel of darkness," in which opposition is dissolved and a marriage of light and dark consummated.

In that mystic nucleus, erotic experience is subsumed in religious initiation: "It was the entry into another circle of existence, it was the baptism to another life, it was the complete confirmation" (90). So intense and value laden is the experience that the two lovers are visually transformed into religious icons, facing each other in floodlit open doorways as in panels of a Fra Angelico painting. While Lawrence draws his iconography from the Renaissance,[12] style and theme are in the mystical vein of expressionism ("it was the transfiguration, the glorification, the admission" [91]).

In the next generation, Will Brangwen's inner conflict is put in expressionist focus: "And the youth went home with the stars in heaven whirling fiercely about the blackness of his head, and his heart fierce . . . " (108). His potentiality, locked inside him, is projected against a vast backdrop of space, and the abstraction recalls Van Gogh's spiritual portraiture.[13] Will, who has been carving his phoenix, is immersed in a darkness unmarried to light. His inner being is portrayed in nonrepresentational, phenomenal imagery: "He seemed to be hidden in a tense, electric darkness, in which his soul, his life was intensely active . . . " (108). After Anna has declared her love for him, biblical and expressionist imagery converge in Will's reborn awareness: "The veils had ripped and issued him naked into endless space. . . . The walls had thrust him out, and given him a vast space to walk in. Whither, through this darkness of infinite space, was he walking blindly? . . . The hand of the Hidden Almighty, burning bright, had thrust out of the darkness and gripped him" (112). Responding to this claim on him, Will carves his Creation panel, symbolizing a process of self-creation with Eve as his tentative, half-emerged Anima: "With trembling passion, fine as a breath of air, he sent the chisel over her belly, her hard, unripe, small belly. She was a stiff little figure, with sharp lines, in the throes and torture and ecstasy of her creation" (112–13). In the midst of his struggle with Anna, Will chops up the icon and throws it on the fire, sacrificing his spiritual drive to her conquering fecundity.

Their marital conflict is described in a dramatic realism with heavily expressionist overtones: "Everything glowed intensely about them, the world had put off its clothes and was awful, with new, primal nakedness" (156). Anna celebrates the victory of her womb over Will's spirit in a spontaneous fertility rite in which the "rhythmic exulting" of the dance enacts a primitive religious sensibility, as in Nolde's more wildly gestural paintings, *Maria Egyptiaca* and *Candle Dancers* (1912).

> [She] swayed backwards and forwards, like a full ear of corn, pale in the dusky afternoon, threading before the firelight, dancing his non-existence, dancing herself to the Lord, to exultation. . . . Her fine limbs lifted and lifted, her hair was sticking out all fierce, and her belly, big, strange, terrifying, uplifted to the Lord. Her face was rapt and beautiful, she danced exulting before her Lord, and knew no man. (*The Rainbow* 170–71)

The content of the ritual is symbolic and archetypal, with Anna impersonating a harvest goddess; the dance is expressionist, celebrating the victorious self-sufficiency of her pregnant body. Like many expressionist painters, Lawrence conveys the power of dance as an emotive language of gesture. As Haftmann writes: "What Nolde looked for in dancing was above all a rapt, total surrender to bodily expression; in this most primitive aspect of the dance, man himself appeared to him as a primeval being" (*Emile Nolde*, facing pl. 12). In "New Mexico," Lawrence later describes the religion of primitive dances as "an uncontrollable sensual experience, even more so than love: I use sensual to mean an experience deep down in the senses, inexplicable and inscrutable" (144). This is exactly what Kirchner meant when he said: "[R]eligious sensuality in art is an instinct of nature. . . . It can be developed and cultivated but can never be schematized . . . " (qtd. in Grohmann 24). *Religious sensuality*—of which Anna's dance before the Lord is a supreme example—is a key to allotropic expressionism in *The Rainbow*.

As Will and Anna approach the spiritual womb of the cathedral, he becomes aware of his own life, suspended at a point of "transitation" ("the action of passing, passage" [OED]) between the darkness before birth and the darkness after death. Entering the cathedral, he "enter[s] the twilight of both darknesses, the hush of the two-fold silence, where dawn was sunset, and the beginning and the end were one" (*The Rainbow* 187). Will becomes aware that extremes of being contain contraries; in his epiphany in the cathedral, he participates in a mystic marriage of light and darkness. The luminous language is fraught with oxymorons and opposites coupled in Taoistic embrace: "east and west," "dawn and sunset," beginning and end, "coloured darkness," "jewelled gloom," "music upon silence," "light upon darkness," "fecundity upon death," "the root and the flower," " 'before' and 'after.' " Will's visionary rite of passage recalls Wordsworth's crossing of the Alps:

> Tumult and peace, the darkness and the light—
> Were all like workings of one mind, the features
> Of the same face, blossoms upon one tree;
> Characters of the great Apocalypse,
> The types and symbols of Eternity,
> Of first, and last, and midst, and without end.
>
> (*Prelude*, Book 6, ll. 635–40)

Apocalyptic symbolism in "The Cathedral" is crossed with primitivism and expressionism. Through projection and empathy, Will fuses his spiritual drive with architectural forms in a kind of Gothic animism. Most remarkable are the concentration and vitalism of the language, that make the passage not just a mystical excursus but also a ritual enactment, moving in intensifying stages toward the spiritual climax of "one-ing."[14] The excitement and driving rhythms stem from attraction and interpenetration of mutually implicated opposites.

Spiritually, Will achieves oneness with the Cathedral, his soul "at the apex of the arch, clinched in the timeless ecstasy, consummated" (*The Rainbow* 188). But the cultural form is a limitation, and his inspiration is undercut by Anna's skepticism. Against the centrifugal drive of her being toward open sky, his drive is revealed as centripetal, falling back on itself, enclosed within inorganic form. While his vision has intensity, the ironic framing shows it to be incomplete, solipsistic, spiritually onanistic. Will's spirit needs to be married to Anna's sensual drive, or erotic energy will be displaced and inspiration remain unfruitful. His vision of oneness is the substanceless pattern, or ghost, of the Rainbow fusion of spirit and senses, Gothic and Norman, vertical and horizontal, heaven and earth, within a fulfilled form of living. The "third thing" that emerges from this spiritual/material dialectic is radiance—the reader's sense of vital creative vision. Through cumulative phrasing, incremental repetition, and oxymoronic images, Lawrence's language conveys simultaneous but opposing impulses of movement and poise, flow and concentration, kinesis and stasis. It is dynamic, expressing tension of opposites ("clinched") rather than resolution ("consummated"). The kinetic emphasis falls on *desire* for harmony rather than its achievement. Abstraction and empathy are well matched, but assertion of the ideal outdoes realization. The "perfect, swooning consummation, the timeless ecstasy" cannot be sustained in time, especially when body and spirit are sundered as in Will's and Anna's marriage. The very intensity of Will's striving hints at willful sublimation; not surprisingly, Anna resents his stealing fire from their marriage. His vision lacks substance, because it depends upon the "neutrality" of conflicting drives rather than their "consummation" in a genuine marriage of opposites.

Expressionist dynamism and abstraction—the colorful cornucopia of symbols and pulsing, mimetic rhythms—deepen the reader's experience. There is a sense, in "The Cathedral," of dim symbols, momentarily illuminated, overarching and overshadowing individual existence. The passage is an attempt to express the "inner necessity" of Will's spirit, that of a religious artist, in which "coloured darkness" produces "spiritual vibration,"[15] and its structural symmetries and luminous images recall the dreamlike style of *Der Blaue Reiter* (Marc, Macke, Kandinsky, and Feininger). "The Cathedral" combines symbolism with expressionism; ideas come alive and the tension of Will's being is expressed in inspired vision. Lawrence's empathy with spiritual dynamics does not, of course, mean that his vision is limited by the character's, as Anna's conflicting viewpoint shows. But expressionism reveals the conflict and yearning for fulfillment in Will in a way that realism could never do. Lawrence's style projects Will's inner being into the interplay between abstract "form-harmony" (Kandinsky) and concrete sensuousness. Here expressionism, animating symbolism, conveys an "abstract-whole" (Lawrence, *Letters* 2: 263) that could not be suggested by the most faithful mimesis. Will's sublime, all-encompassing experience is objectively placed as the phenomenon of a being in transit. His spirit animates stone, transforming it into a symbol of aspiration. But, for Anna, "God burned no more in that bush" (*The Rainbow* 188). Will and Anna represent dialectically opposed spiritual and material drives, and the novel presents the "trembling instability of the balance."

The three moon scenes mark a retrogression from equilibrium through disequilibrium to disintegration. The first ritualizes the courtship of Will and Anna, relating their experience to primordial rhythms of sex and fertility until they *become* those rhythms. Expressionism prefers to deal with archetypes—of suffering, sickness, death, passion, puberty, jealousy, anxiety, ecstasy—rather than with individuals; for Lawrence, the hero of any great novel is "[not] any of the characters, but some unnamed and nameless flame behind them all" ("The Novel" 182). The problem for him, as for Munch, was to develop a system of expression strong enough to penetrate the personal unconscious and unite it with the archetypal.

Spontaneous impulses incorporate human life in cycles of seed time and harvest.[16] In a scene that glows with transcendent livingness, like Munch's *White Night* (1901),[17] an impressionist space, hallucinatingly divided into moonlight and shadow, prostrate and erect, is set for the "coming and going" of lovers—a "pulsing, frictional to-and-fro, which works up to culmination" (Lawrence, "Foreword"). Animism takes on sacramental overtones and the magical aura intensifies: "The air was all hoary silver. . . . Trees stood vaguely at their distance, as if waiting, like heralds, for the signal to approach. In this space of vague crystal her heart seemed like a bell ringing" (*The Rainbow* 113). Anna, initiate in the symbolic action, is responding to an "inhuman will" that seeks expression through her. In offering herself to the Moon, she resembles a priestess of Astarte performing fertility rites. Will is a passive instrument of the life-force, who serves her "dutifully," until "a low, deep-sounding will in him" (114)—not his own—begins to "vibrate." As in a primitive ritual, the rhythm of his being is transmuted into impersonal rhythms. He no longer draws on his limited ego; like Paul with Clara in *Sons and Lovers*, he vibrates in unison with the source of all energy: "There was only the moving to and fro in the moonlight, engrossed, the swinging in the silence, that was marked only by the splash of sheaves, and silence, and a splash of sheaves" (115). Movement becomes meaning; the verbal rhythms are not simply mimetic but express a fully charged state of being. The intensity and rapture of the scene—"How can we know the dancer from the dance?"—derive from a visionary expressionism that merges human and cosmic.

The reenactment of such rites in language recalls the rhythmic brush-work of Van Gogh's late paintings. Van Gogh "longed for the night atmosphere, the stars, and moonlight," says A. M. Hammacher; "in this way his links with the primeval, nocturnal life forces gained symbolic expression" (*Genius* 83). Paintings like *The Starry Night* and *Road with Cypress and Star* are remarkable for their lunar and spiral symbolism.[18] According to Hammacher, "the spiral is a primeval symbol of movement, which does not belong to sun-worshiping but to the sphere of the moon. It is the eternal cycle, which reveals itself in the fertility of woman, in agrarian life, and in the four seasons. . . . [The] image of the stars at night and of the harvests . . . had gained a hold on [Van Gogh's] creativity" (160). Similarly, Lawrence's creative impulses were galvanized almost to madness by the moon. Jessie Chambers recalls that "some dark power seemed to take possession of Lawrence, and when the final beauty of the moonrise broke upon us, something seemed to explode inside him"; on another occasion, he seemed "[to have] become dehumanized" (127–28). Jessie was aware of an inner conflict in Lawrence, parallel to the split in Ursula between Dionysian being and personal ego. In Lawrence, as in Van Gogh, the systole and diastole of creativity seem to have involved "a struggle against destructive forces" and to have led to an "almost demonic expressiveness" (Hammacher, *Genius* 122, 159).

"In their yearning for spiritualization," says Weisstein, "the Expressionists clung to essences without ridding themselves of the phenomenal world" (Introduction 24); conversely, Lawrence sought the essence in the phenomenon. Anna, who sees "the moonlight flash question on [Will's] face" (*The Rainbow* 115), responds to the moon rather than a man, while he embraces darkness rather than a woman: "All the moonlight upon her, all the darkness within her! All the night in his arms, darkness and shine, he possessed of it all! All the night for him now, to unfold, to venture within, all the mystery to be entered, all the discovery to be made" (116). This is more than eroticism: it is what Alois Riegl (cited in Hodin, *Kokoschka* 205) calls the "profound religious excitement" of expressionism. "He looked through her hair at the moon, which seemed to swim liquid-bright" (*The Rainbow* 116),[19] connecting with the earlier scene in which Tom is struck by "the terror of a moon running *liquid-brilliant* into the open for a moment . . . " (48 [my italics]). Exposure to moonlight, a symbol of the anima (Ben-Ephraim 223–25), becomes more devastating in successive phases, culminating in Anton's destruction as a sexual being. It is space, rhythm, and the unknown, rather than personal psychology, that make the dynamics of such scenes.

The second moonlight scene, between Anton and Ursula, is remarkable for its intensity, matching Van Gogh's tormented visions:

> The darkness seemed to breathe like the sides of some great beast, the haystacks loomed half-revealed, a crowd of them, a dark, fecund lair just behind. Waves of delirious darkness ran through her soul. . . . She wanted to reach and be amongst the flashing stars. . . . She was mad to be gone. . . . The darkness was passionate and breathing with immense, unperceived heaving. It was waiting to receive her in her flight. . . . She must leap from the known into the unknown. Her hands and feet beat like a madness, her breast strained as if in bonds. (*The Rainbow* 294–95)

Expressionism such as this subjectivizes and transforms the image of experience. Franz Marc, while affirming that expressionists "wrest [their form] from nature," which "glows in [their] paintings," points out that "there is something which is not quite nature but rather the mastery and interpretation of nature: art. . . . The bridge across to the realm of the spirit, the necromancy of humanity" (qtd. in Dube, *The Expressionists* 132). At times the dislocation of normal perception resembles hallucination or madness, Rimbaud's "dérèglement de tous les sens." Such almost schizophrenic intensity, bordering on dream or nightmare, is characteristic of expressionism.

The flood motif is pervasive. Inward and outward rhythms—Ursula's excitement, the music and motion—merge in waves, as separate identities submerge in "the deep underwater of the dance" (*The Rainbow* 295). Depersonalization is the prelude to transpersonal experience; primitive animism breaks down the subject/object barrier and sensation is intensified to a state bordering on trance or delirium. The lovers become "one dual movement, dancing on the slippery grass. . . . It was a glaucous, intertwining, delicious flux and contest in flux. They were both absorbed into a profound silence, into a deep, fluid, underwater energy . . . " (295). Despite the insidious threat of absorption, normal consciousness is transformed into rapturous being; Lawrence's supple expressionist prose conveys currents that are felt but seldom expressed.

Lawrence's focus shifts from characters to phenomena; personal subjects disappear, absorbed in a groundswell of sensation. The image of the flood is linked with a rhythmic fluctuation of consciousness and the unconscious, while the motile sensation of the dance, at once religious, sexual, and emotional, becomes a metaphor of being.

> There was a wonderful rocking of the darkness, slowly, a great, slow swinging of the whole night, with the music playing lightly on the surface, making the strange, ecstatic rippling on the surface of the dance, but underneath only one great flood heaving slowly backwards to the verge of oblivion, slowly forward to the other verge, the heart sweeping along each time, and tightening with anguish as the limit was reached, and the movement, at crisis, turned and swept back. (295–96)

Outside of the expressionist dance of Mary Wigman, the closest analogies to such verbal/biological rhythms are the plastic rhythms of Van Gogh,[20] Munch, Kirchner, or Nolde. From dance rhythms expressed as an oscillation of surface and depth, Lawrence abstracts "universal movement." A high level of abstraction from phenomena of motion is characteristic of expressionism—Kirchner "needed to invent a technique of grasping everything while it was in motion" (qtd. in Dube, *The Expressionists* 38)—as it is of futurism. The main distinction is that futurism tends to focus on mechanical phenomena such as the speed of machines, while expressionism focuses on emotive movement and gesture. Violent intensity is common to both, but expressionism focuses on human sensation and emotion, futurism on electromagnetic dynamism abstracted from human beings or machines. The deeper affinities of Lawrence's art are with expressionism, although there are futurist overtones in the antinatural, metallic imagery of his moonlight scenes.

Out of the deep, trancelike rhythm, a "moon-conscious[ness]" develops in Ursula. As in some cult of Astarte, her magnetized senses seem to expand in erotic awareness. In this aroused state, she gives herself ritually to a nonhuman source of energy:

> She turned, and saw a great white moon looking at her over the hill. And her breast opened to it, she was cleaved like a transparent jewel to its light. She stood filled with the full moon, offering herself. Her two breasts opened to make way for it, her body opened wide like a quivering anemone, a soft, dilated invitation touched by the moon. She wanted the moon to fill in to her, she wanted more, more communion with the moon, consummation. (*The Rainbow* 296).

The moon is the transcendent force of Eros that transforms sexual into spiritual energy, luring Ursula with promises of fulfillment. Immersed in moon-

light like floodwater, she surrenders to its transforming power and is identified with its *mana*: "There was a fierce, white, cold passion in her heart"
(297). She tries to go toward the moon, but Skrebensky, who cannot share
in this pantheist communion, holds her back. A contest develops between
the ecstatic energy of moonlight and inhibiting darkness.

In her quest for "pure being," Ursula becomes "a pillar of salt" to her
lover, who cannot transcend the narrow bounds of his ego. The struggle ex-
acerbates the neurotic will that prevents his letting go, as Tom let go with
Lydia. The visual world around the lovers is distorted by the intensity of
their emotion, "the great new stacks of corn glistening and gleaming transfigured, silvery and present under the night-blue sky, throwing dark, substantial shadows. . . . She, like glimmering gossamer, seemed to burn among
them, as they rose like cold fires to the silvery-bluish air" (298). In this
moonlit arena, Skrebensky faces the fires of transfiguration, among which
Ursula is a silvery flame. The symbolic scene is a painter's composition in
blue and silver that looks beyond Monet's *Haystacks* to the contorted burning world of Van Gogh's *Starry Night* (see pl. 5) or the eerie glow of Munch's
Starlit Night or *White Night*.[21]

Such scenes show a tendency to expressionist abstraction as man and
woman merge into polarized forces of light and darkness: "She seemed a
beam of gleaming power. . . . [He was] a shadow which she wanted to dissi-
pate, destroy as the moonlight destroys a darkness . . . " (298). The tension
that oversensitizes Skrebensky, so that "[the] stack stung him keenly with a
thousand cold, sharp flames," hardens Ursula into "salt, compact brilliance"
(298). The struggle that follows is expressed in a cluster of corroding, dissolving, crystallizing, annihilating images that suggest the slow but violent
interaction of chemical agents. Lawrence brings futurist vision to bear on
spiritual expressionism: as Haftmann says of a Nolde painting, "Nature is
never seen like this, but it may be experienced like this" (*Emil Nolde*, facing
pl. 37).

Futurist elements are marked in the stackyard scene,[22] which is so non-
natural that when Ursula comes back to "daylight consciousness" she thinks
she has been "possessed." Destructiveness, aimed at the dead weight of
the past, and depersonalization were futurist tendencies that appealed to
Lawrence. Birkin's analysis of Aphrodite, born in "the flood of destructive creation" (*Women in Love* 172) is relevant to the flood imagery that runs
through *The Rainbow*. Destruction itself can be creative when it dissolves

"the world's corruption" and allows "new, clean, naked bodies [to] issue to a new germination . . . " (458–59).

Ursula's allotropic states contain imagery of "that which is physic—non-human, in humanity" (*Letters* 2: 182), and Lawrence uses futurist imagery negatively to describe the process that reduces Skrebensky to a hollow core. His sexual drive is revealed as "limited mechanical energy . . . mere purpose of self-preservation and self-assertion," as in the lowest forms of sentient matter. Hidden in the darkness of the senses, he cannot stand the glare of transforming moonlight; Ursula, on the contrary, reaches for a consummation that would be "a supreme, gleaming triumph of infinity" (*The Rainbow* 409). Like the futurists, Lawrence uses "the phenomena of the science of physics," in the form of metallic, chemical, or electrical imagery, to describe what she "*is* as a phenomenon." The imagery of "soft iron," "corrosive salt," and crystallization (299) suggests chemical reduction: there could be no more dehumanized image of sexual "love." Ursula, "cold as the moon and burning as a fierce salt," must pass through such purgatorial fires before she can transcend her sexual will-to-power.

Lawrence's style takes on apocalyptic overtones in the third and final moon scene (441–45). Once more Ursula undergoes a strange allotropic state; this time she casts off Skrebensky and destroys the incubus of personal self. The rhetoric is hypnotic and futuristic, with incremental repetition of chemical/physiological images—"electric fire," "salt burning," "incandescent," "metallic"—while the state of being borders on Dionysian frenzy.[23]

Heightened sensitivity to sight, touch, and sound signifies an extremity of sensation, while imagery of the "non-human in humanity" parallels futurist dynamism:

> The silk, slipping fierily on the hidden, yet revealed roundness and firmness of her body, her loins, seemed to run in him like fire, make his brain burn like brimstone. . . . [The] electric fire of the silk under his hands upon her limbs . . . flew over her, as he drew nearer and nearer to discovery. She vibrated like a jet of electric, firm fluid in response. (442)

The language plunges into futurist physiology to abstract a chemico-erotic essence from human sensuality.

Lawrence's rendering of "allotropic states" brings a new note of transpersonality to the novel form. "Then a yearning for something unknown came over her. . . . The salt bitter passion of the sea . . . tantalis[ed] her with vast suggestions of fulfilment" (443). Skrebensky is only a feeble "personification" of Ursula's desires, for she is reaching for infinity. Lawrence forces the verbal medium to convey an experience that is irrational, ecstatic, and wordless. As Paul Klee writes: "The chosen artists are those who dig down close to the secret source where the primal law feeds the forces of development. What artist would not like to live where the central organ of all space-time motion . . . activates all functions? In the womb of nature, in the primal ground of creation, where the secret key to all things lies hidden?" (93). The power of the unconscious irradiates Lawrence's language, as forces in nature interpenetrate human lives: "There was a great whiteness confronting her, the moon was incandescent as a round furnace door, out of which came the high blast of moonlight, over the sea-ward half of the world, a dazzling, terrifying glare of white light" (*The Rainbow* 443). The biblical symbol of the furnace harks back to "Anna Victrix," where Anna offered up the infant Ursula as a living sacrifice to fires of regeneration (181). Now Ursula "seem[s] to melt into the white glare, towards the moon" (444), while Skrebensky is consumed and turned to ash.[24] There is utter disequilibrium between her moon-conscious being and his self-conscious, alienated ego.

In their final embrace, Ursula is metamorphosed into Woman-as-harpy (444). The sexual anxieties expressed in this scene find graphic illustration in Munch's *Vampire* (1895), which shows a woman crouched over a man's neck; in *Lovers in the Waves* (1896; see pl. 7), in which a man is entangled in a woman's hair; and in the horrendous *Harpy* (1900).[25] Here Lawrence accentuates sexual neurosis: "The fight, the struggle for consummation was terrible. It lasted till it was agony to his soul, till he succumbed, till he gave way as if dead, and lay with his face buried partly in her hair partly in the sand, motionless . . . " (445). This is followed by an image as stark as any of Munch's:

> He felt as if the knife were being pushed into his already dead body. With head strained back, he watched, drawn tense, for some minutes, watched the unaltering, rigid face like metal in the moonlight, the fixed, unseeing eyes, in which slowly the water gathered, shook with glittering moonlight, then, surcharged, brimmed over and ran trickling, a tear with its burden of moonlight, into the darkness, to fall in the sand. (445)

The frozen, microcosmic visual detail is so intense and dehumanizing as to approach the grotesque, although it is psychologically justified by Skrebensky's transfixed state.

The frictional intensity of moon-consciousness is balanced against the physical flow of blood-consciousness. Anton returns from Africa inoculated with a primitive sensuality. The emphasis is on "darkness" as a vital force and the word (or its variant) occurs some sixty-seven times in seven pages (412–18). Rhetorical patterns express rhythms and impulses of blood-consciousness, culminating in the couple's first sexual union; the key terms, "darkness," "vibration," "fecund," "nucleus," "potent," pullulate with associations that form a verbal force field.

After "The Cathedral" (a kind of religious watershed), Lawrence increasingly takes his images from biology and physics; at the same time, his "futuristic" emphasis on molecular and nuclear activity redirects Marinetti's "intuitive physiology of matter" toward human beings. The lovers are the sentient "nucleus" of a teeming world of matter; in a kind of reciprocal rapture, the "nucleolating darkness" comes to consciousness in them. Reacting to Dr. Frankstone's argument that life is only matter, Ursula examines a microorganism in the laboratory, sees "the gleam of its nucleus," and reflects on "the will which nodalise[s]" its functions (408). Her wonder at "the incalculable physical and chemical activities nodalised in this shadowy moving speck" recalls Paul Morel's realization of his own nuclear self as "one tiny upright speck of flesh . . . [that] yet . . . could not be extinct" (*Sons and Lovers* 464). Skrebensky cannot share Ursula's vision of self as "a oneness with the infinite," because he has accepted a socially constructed and limited identity. In such hollow men, the spirit materializes; in Lawrence and the expressionists, matter is spiritualized.[26]

Franz Marc, like Lawrence, sought to immerse himself in a religion of nature, whose medium would be the " '*Animalization*' of art." "I try to intensify my sensitivity," he wrote, "for the organic rhythm of all things; I seek pantheist empathy with the vibration and flow of the blood of nature—in the trees, in the animals, in the air" (qtd. in Selz 201). Motifs of animalization, vibration, and darkness strike a strongly expressionist note in *The Rainbow*, in which Lawrence seeks empathy with "the blood of nature" in the ebb and flow of human relationships. Animalism, primitivism, and pantheism pervade Skrebensky's post-African courtship: "He burned up, he caught fire and became splendid, royal, something like a tiger. . . . She became proud and erect, like a flower putting itself forth. . . . She was no mere Ursula Brangwen. She was Woman, she was the whole of Woman in the human order. All-containing, universal, how should she be limited to individuality?" (411–12). This expansion of being is a hallmark of expressionism. While

Skrebensky draws strength from an influx of blood-consciousness, he is no longer perceived as an individual but as "a voice out of the darkness" or "a dark, powerful vibration" (413, 418). Having no "intrinsic being," he becomes a mere channel of the life-force: "Gradually he transferred to her the hot, fecund darkness that possessed his own blood" (413). The language modulates into pure expressionism, as darkness, vibration, and fecundity become the true subject.

Lawrence sets off the expressionist world of darkness and desire against the "realistic" world of trains, trams, and city lights. To Ursula, who goes about in "sensual subconsciousness," "her eyes dilated and shining like the eyes of a wild animal," being is "a dark, blind, eager wave urging blindly forward . . . " (415). An invisible world of blood-consciousness underlies the visible world. Motifs of vibration and darkness culminate in an expressionist rendering of the sex act that spiritualizes the physical: "She was caught up, entangled in the powerful vibration of the night. The man, what was he?—a dark, powerful vibration that encompassed her. She passed away as on a dark wind, far, far away, into the pristine darkness of paradise, into the original immortality" (418). This transcendence of personal and particular puts Ursula in touch with her "permanent self" beyond daytime consciousness.

Lawrence's style expresses an animated universe of desire and procreation, with patterns of images overlapping, clustering, dissolving, re-forming in the rhythms of blood-consciousness, until the lovers become "one stream, one dark fecundity" (414). Movement within a still frame is created by wavelike series of verb phrases that give a sense of inner pulsation. This volatile restlessness is typical of expressionism, which has been called "a passionate way of looking upon the world and living it fully, an intoxicant of the spirit" (Hadermann 111). Lawrence's "to-and-fro" style works toward a mystic state of equilibrium. The analogy with painting is significant: "From a point of stability in the established picture plane, [the expressionist] creates his plastic rhythm, backward and forward, with the materials of volume, plane, color, and texture. Usually there is a dominant path of movement varied with oscillations in smaller measure . . . " (Cheney 132). So Lawrence's wavelike rhythms culminate in "one fecund nucleus of the fluid darkness" (*The Rainbow* 414), overlapping Tom and Lydia's "blazing kernel of darkness." Such verbal cross-references are not just compulsive repetition but emphasize the wavelike generational structure of the novel as a whole.

Complementing and interacting with the flow of darkness as part of the rainbow vision, Lawrence describes dawn flooding up over the horizon after the lovers have spent a night on the Downs (431). The language is more than an impressionist kaleidoscope; it presents a symbolic transformation of darkness into light, expressionistically rendered through successive colors, clusters of verb and participial phrases, and the whole *movement* of the long sentence, modulating from tension to expansion to diffusion, followed by short declarative units, dramatizing the movement of light. The sun is a living presence, like the "living darkness." It is the source of all light, life, and energy, animistically perceived as by a Mithraic sun-worshiper. The religious sense of nonhuman energy, opposed to mechanical activity, is expressed in images of regeneration: "[E]verything was newly washed into being, in a flood of new, golden creation" (431). The scene has its closest analogy in Van Gogh's painting *The Sower* (1888; see pl. 8), which shows the round disk of the setting sun flooding earth and sky with its rays. According to Frank Elgar, Van Gogh in Arles "was undertaking a rite such as the ancient sun-worshippers performed in their communion with the principle of light. . . . In every source of light he saw the [sun]," and it became a symbol of his own "impetuous creative force" (121). Like Van Gogh and Nolde, who "believe[d] in the sun and the moon, for [he felt] their influence" (qtd. in Haftmann 12), Lawrence believed passionately in sun and moon as vital forces.[27]

The novel ends with two apocalyptic scenes: Ursula's confrontation with the horses and her vision of the rainbow. Lawrence draws on instinctual animism to project Ursula's fears, first onto the forest and then onto the horses. To her disordered sensibility, the trees take on a magical, phallic presence as if threatening to enclose her (*The Rainbow* 450–51). A "small, living seed of fear" in her heart distorts the shapes around her. The horses are the stimulus that draws forth the latent content of her unconscious; these menacing creatures present a fusion of psychological and natural, subjective and archetypal forces:

> In a sort of lightning of knowledge their movement travelled through her. . . . She was aware of their breasts gripped, clenched narrow in a hold that never relaxed, she was aware of their red nostrils flaming with long endurance, and of their haunches, so rounded, so massive, pressing, pressing, pressing to burst the grip upon their breasts, pressing forever till they went mad, running against the walls of time, and never bursting free. Their great haunches were smoothed and darkened with rain. But the darkness and wetness of rain could not put out the hard, urgent, massive fire that was locked within these flanks, never, never. (452)

So strong are the inner tension, fear, and passion projected onto the horses, that they become figures of nightmare or hallucination.[28] The barrier between sensory perception and unconscious imagery has broken down. Vivid images and incantatory rhythms become the medium of an intense, disordered state of being: "She was aware of the great flash of hoofs, a bluish, iridescent flash surrounding a hollow of darkness" (452). Expressionism and futurist dynamism are virtually indistinguishable in such explosions of unconscious force.[29]

Ursula's irrational state is lucid as a dream. She does not have to look at the horses: they materialize in all their horror and splendor in her psyche. The vision is nonnatural in focus, with enlargement and illumination of the most terrifying detail, the hooves. Ursula obviously fears destruction by the forces unleashed upon or within her. Since the expressionist style renders a subjective response, it is impossible to measure the degree, if any, of objective menace. The horses are a traumatic embodiment of all the social and sexual pressures on Ursula,[30] now pregnant with Skrebensky's child, and a vengeful reflex of her own apocalyptic yearnings. The expressionist style emphasizes force, mass, weight, speed, and oscillations of light and dark to convey emotion springing from the unconscious. There is a clash of concentrating and dissolving wills, and of opposing elements of fire and water. Only by desperate effort does Ursula finally evade the encircling horses. But the shock is cathartic, and she reaches the ground of her being, beyond all change.

The final apocalyptic vision of the Rainbow, despite critical cavilling over closure, is a superb piece of rhetoric that carries the full onus of Lawrence's biblical, psychological, and social prophecy, subordinating expressionism to more explicit symbolism. Ursula's vision can, however, be related to the expressionist quest for dynamic spiritual experience: "In everything she saw she grasped and groped to find the creation of the living God, instead of the old, hard barren form of bygone living" (458). This search for a vital creation is Lawrence's quest, in that "one bright book of life," the novel. His development of a form of expressionism, painfully evolved from inner necessity rather than borrowed from outer sources, led him to exult in *The Rainbow* as a "voyage of discovery towards the real and eternal and unknown land" (*Letters* 2: 362).

Plate 1. Claude Monet, *Boulevard des Capucines* (1873–74). Oil on canvas. The Nelson-Atkins Museum of Art, Kansas City, Missouri. (Purchase: The Kenneth A. and Helen F. Spencer Foundation Acquisition Fund).

Plate 2. Claude Monet, *Thames below Westminster* (1871). Oil on canvas. The National Gallery Picture Library, London.

Plate 3. Claude Monet, Rue *Saint-Denis, Celebrations of June 30, 1878* (1878). Oil on canvas. © Rouen, Musée des Beaux-Arts. Photo Didier Tragin/Catherine Lancien.

Plate 4. Emil Nolde, *Candle Dancers* (1917). Woodcut on paper. Schiefler-Mosel Nr. 127. © Nolde-Stiftung (Nolde-Foundation) Seebüll.

Plate 5. Vincent van Gogh, *The Starry Night* (June 1889).
Oil on canvas. The Museum of Modern Art, New York.
Acquired through the Lillie P. Bliss Bequest. Photograph
© 1997 The Museum of Modern Art, New York.

Plate 6. Edvard Munch,
Madonna (Conception) (1895–
1902). Colored lithograph.
Kupferstichkabinett, Staatliche
Museen zu Berlin PK. (State
Museum, Berlin.)

Plate 7. Edvard Munch, *Lovers in the Waves* (1896). Lithograph. © 1998
The Munch Museum/The Munch-Ellingsen Group/Artists Rights Society
(ARS), New York.

Plate 8. Vincent van Gogh, *The Sower* (June 1888). Oil on canvas.
Collection Kröller-Müller Museum, Otterlo, The Netherlands.

Plate 9. Ernst Ludwig Kirchner, *Winter Moon Land-
scape* (1919). Oil on canvas. Copyright (for works by
E. L. Kirchner) by Ingeborg and Dr. Wolfgang Henze-
Ketterer, Wichtrach/Bern.

Plate 10. Karl Schmidt-Rottluff, *Woman with Her Hair Undone* (1913). Woodcut. © Karl Schmidt-Rottluff 1997/ VIS*ART Copyright Inc.

Plate 11. Umberto Boccioni, *Muscular Dynamism* (1913). Pastel and charcoal. The Museum of Modern Art, New York. Purchase. Photograph © 1997 The Museum of Modern Art, New York.

Plate 12. Vincent van Gogh, *Sketch of Langlois Bridge* (March 1888). Pen and ink. Owner anonymous. Reprinted from *The Complete Letters of Vincent Van Gogh*. 2nd ed. Vol. 3. Boston: New York Graphic Soc., 1978. 477.

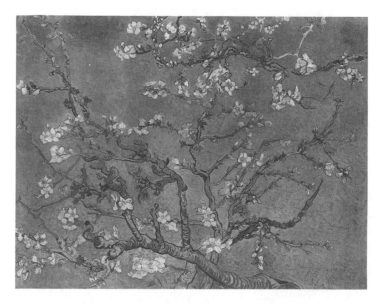

Plate 13. Vincent van Gogh, *Branches of an Almond Tree in Blossom* (February 1890). Oil on canvas. Amsterdam, Van Gogh Museum (Vincent van Gogh Foundation/F671).

Plate 14. Vincent van Gogh, *Landscape with Olive Trees* (October 1889). Oil on canvas. From the collection of Mrs. John Hay Whitney.

Plate 15. Vincent van Gogh, *Road with Cypress and Star* (May 1890). Oil on canvas. Collection Kröller-Müller Museum, Otterlo, The Netherlands.

Plate 16. Paul Cézanne, *Still Life with Fruit Dish* (1879–80). Oil on canvas. Private collection. Photo by Malcolm Varon, N.Y.C. © 1997.

Plate 17. Vincent van Gogh, *Japonaiserie: The Flowering Plum Tree* (1886–88). Copy after Hiroshige. Oil on canvas. Amsterdam, Van Gogh Museum (Vincent van Gogh Foundation/F371).

Plate 18. Ando Hiroshige,
Mountain Stream in Snow.
Reprinted from Edward F.
Strange, *Hiroshige's Woodblock
Prints: A Guide.* New York:
Dover, 1983. Pl. B.

Plate 19. Ando Hiroshige, *Sakanoshita: The Throwing-Away-the Brush Peak.*
Reprinted from Edward F. Strange, *Hiroshige's Woodblock Prints: A Guide.*
New York: Dover, 1983. Plate F.

Plate 20. Katsushika Hokusai, *The Coast of Seven Leagues in Soshu Province*. Colored print. Designed entirely in shades of blue. Copyright The Trustees of the British Museum, British Museum Press.

Plate 21. Paul Gauguin, *Nave nave Mahana* (1896). Oil on canvas. Musée des Beaux-Arts de Lyon.

Plate 22. Paul Gauguin, *The Brooding Woman* (1891). Oil on canvas. Worcester Art Museum, Worcester, Massachusetts, Museum purchase.

Plate 23. Paul Gauguin, *Tahitian Women Bathing* (1892). Oil on canvas. The Metropolitan Museum of Art, Robert Lehman Collection, 1975.

4

EXPRESSIONISM IN
WOMEN IN LOVE

Expressionism distorts, disintegrates, and disrupts the image of reality, in its desire to reach the "Hinterland der Seele" (Frieda's phrase, in Lawrence, *Letters* 2: 151). In an attempt to define it, Edward F. Rothschild wrote:

> The object is distorted, disintegrated, or disrupted by the participating, self-projecting, dynamic "transcendent subject." . . . This is why the expressionistic idiom is explosive, fantastic, violent, centrifugal, or centripetal; its colors bizarre or eerie; its composition dynamic; its texture rough and varied; its rhythms eccentric; its imagery confused or dissociative; its mood electric, thunderous, prestidigitative, or nervous. (51)

If impressionism offers "a corner of nature viewed through a temperament" (Zola), the explosive temper of expressionism threatens to obliterate and reconstruct the image of man and nature. The artist is involved in a dynamic interaction with the world, striving to break through its resistant surface to reach a core of reality. For Franz Marc, "[e]verything has appearance and essence, shell and kernel, mask and truth. . . . [The] goal of art is to reveal unearthly life dwelling behind everything, to break the mirror of life so that we may look being (*Sein*) in the face" (qtd. in Levine 14). Expressionism is an existential engagement with the physical/social world that simultaneously seeks a primordial ground of being.

Interrelations between the arts were especially close for the expressionists and their forerunners. Van Gogh wrote brilliant letters that parallel paintings; Munch achieved literary expression in lyrical accounts of experience that inspired images like *The Scream* (1893); Kubin, Kokoschka, and Barlach wrote novels or plays, while Kandinsky, Marc, Macke, and Kirchner wrote philosophical, theoretical, or critical works. Lawrence himself was a visually oriented writer who was keenly attuned to touch, motion, and rhythm and for whom writing was a kinetic as well as mental process ("Why the Novel Matters" 193).

Visnja Sepčić justly claims that *Women in Love* is "one of the greatest texts [of European Expressionism]" and that "Lawrence's . . . compulsion to sound the subterranean forces in the psyche, the turbulent, inarticulate energies which are to be found under the bland veneer of civilization . . . manifest[s] profound kinship with the aesthetics of Expressionism" ("'Women in Love' [I]" 404, 409). While Lawrence's language of the unconscious clearly has expressionist overtones, the futurist elements in his style show signs of conscious adaptation. A distinction can be made between the religious drive toward revelation of being, which is expressionist in spirit, and the consciously dehumanizing use of physical or electrical imagery, as in futurism.

I shall focus on a series of scenes—in "Coal-Dust," "Water-Party," "Rabbit," "Moony," "Gladiatorial," and "Excurse"—that convey symbolic rituals in expressionist language, and consider some interrelations with painting and dance. Torgovnick (like Alldritt) calls such scenes "tableaux" (204), emphasizing their framed, pictorial quality; I prefer to call them "symbolic rituals" in order to emphasize the structuring of action by unconscious forces, revealing the essence of character in spontaneous bodily movements and gestures.

In "Coal-Dust," Gerald's brutal treatment of his Arab mare triggers mechanical reactions. The scene is immediate and alarming, but it also functions as unconscious ritual to symbolize an inner tension of senses and will, the incipient sadomasochism of Gerald and Gudrun, and the friction of the organic and mechanical in the whole culture. Gerald's violation of the mare's instincts acts out what he inflicts on himself. He is expert at dominating more sensitive creatures, because his perverted will-to-power (*Wille-zur-Macht*) has led him to control his own impulses with iron will. This "pure mechanical organization," which turns vital currents against themselves, can be seen in sexual, social, and industrial spheres. Gudrun's complicity comes in the form of voyeurism. She looks at Gerald "with black-dilated, spell-bound eyes," and after his "gleaming," "unstained" will has left the mare quivering and bloodstained, she screams out, "I should think you're proud" (*Women in Love* 111, 112).

In Lawrence's expressionist style, violent actions are the manifestation of psychic contents. "By means of daring imaginative stylization," writes Sepčić, "which projects the core of the character's personality outwards, [such scenes] show how the mimetic principle . . . can be transcended . . . [or] incorporated in a new unity wherein the real and the imaginative, the literal and the symbolic, the mimetic and the abstract mix freely" ("'Women in Love' [I]" 440). Frictional sounds from the passing train penetrate deeply into "the wheeling mare['s]" consciousness; as the metaphor shows, mechanical rhythms infiltrate organic being. The expressionist method doesn't simply describe the experience as it appears to the eye but also presents a proprioceptive, muscular image. Prolongation of sound and motion through repetition and laborious rhythm has a grinding effect that evokes the impulse to recoil.

Gerald forces the malleable mare to confront an "inorganic principle" that would reduce and kill its spontaneous being. Expressionist concentration combines sensory and metaphoric, "the trucks rebounding on the iron buffers, striking like horrible cymbals, clashing nearer and nearer in frightful strident concussions" (111). "Compulsion" and "repulsion" are deadlocked, as Gerald attempts to reduce spontaneous impulses to controlled responses: "He bit himself down on the mare like a keen edge biting home, and *forced* her round. . . . It was a repulsive sight. But he held on her unrelaxed, with an almost mechanical relentlessness, keen as a sword pressing in to her. Both man and horse were sweating with violence. Yet he seemed calm as a ray of cold sunshine" (111). The image of "cold sunshine" signifies the unnatural will that chills blood-consciousness; it is an aspect of the Nordic motif that links Gerald's vital aura at the start, "a glisten like cold sunshine refracted through crystals of ice," with his ultimate materialization into a block of ice (14, 477–80). This is the trajectory of the Nordic will-to-power that manifests itself in the Arab mare scene and "Gladiatorial," in which the act of wrestling allows Birkin to see the "a northern kind of beauty, like light refracted from snow" (273), that is an expression of Gerald's inner being. In the conflict between horse and rider, impulse and will are brought into violent confrontation in a sequence that has the inevitability of ritual or dream: "Meanwhile the eternal trucks were rumbling on . . . like a disgusting dream that has no end. The connecting chains were grinding and squeaking as the tension varied, the mare pawed and struck away mechanically now . . . the man closed round her, and brought her down, almost as if she were part of his own physique" (111–12). Man and mare form a "centaur" figure of senses and will, interlocked in strife.

Visually, the scene has a glaring, emblematic quality. As Gudrun suddenly "[sees] the trickles of blood on the sides of the mare" and "the bright spurs . . . pressing relentlesly" on the wound, she yields up her overwrought consciousness to orgasmic sensation: "The world reeled and passed into nothingness for Gudrun, she could not know any more" (112). Yet the experience fortifies her will to see life, in all its sensuality or cruelty, from an oblique, aesthetic angle: "The guard's-van came up, and passed slowly, the guard staring out in his transition on the spectacle in the road. And, through the man in the closed wagon Gudrun could see the whole scene spectacularly, isolated and momentary, like a vision isolated in eternity" (112). Gudrun's way of seeing expresses a will-to-power in modernist art that arrests and fixes the flux of phenomena in a timeless "moment of being." Brutal and shocking as the scene is, it points to a reality beyond realism. This transposition of vision into hallucination and of violence into ritual is characteristic of expressionism. Paul Hadermann writes:

> The Expressionist space, scoured with vibrations, trepidations, spasms, or a grand lyric breath, is that of the encounter of the total self with the entire world. . . . The painters as well as the poets are fond of the panoramic or bird's eye view in the most dynamic sense of the term. The juxtaposition of objects is not static but operates according to the magnetic field of a subjective vision . . . (134)

While Gudrun's modernist perspective imposes an unnatural stasis on the scene, Lawrence's dynamic and encompassing vision focuses on that point of fusion in time and space where chaotic motion becomes pattern and violent action reveals unconscious forces in external forms. Expressionist ritual pushes underlying issues to a crisis, "mak[ing] the invisible visible."

Gerald's will yields nothing to the rebellious senses; freedom and spontaneity are stopped cold; this way lies entropy. Ursula is appalled, but Gudrun is aroused. Leaping forward and flinging open the gates, she signals her acceptance of Gerald's sadistic will. Their look of recognition has the nonrational impact of a sign in fairy tale and is punctuated by the dancing and drumming of hooves. As man and mare bound up the lane, Gudrun sinks into masochistic reverie:

> [She] was as if numbed in her mind by the sense of indomitable soft weight of the man, bearing down into the living body of the horse: the strong, indomitable thighs of the blond man clenching the palpitating body of the mare into pure control; a sort of soft white magnetic domination from the loins and

thighs and calves, enclosing and encompassing the mare heavily into unutterable subordination, soft blood-subordination, terrible. (113)

Gudrun's desire to yield up her hypertrophied will, her "nostalgia" for "soft blood-subordination," and her unconscious identification with the mare are expressionistically rendered in wavelike pulsations of parallel phrasing that simulate her masochistic blood-consciousness.[1]

In "Coal-Dust," Lawrence explores parallel disruptions of nature by industry and of being by will. As attention switches to the environment, incongruous conjunctions of the organic and mechanical are glimpsed in hens pecking around a rusty boiler or wagtails flying among trucks. (Gudrun has made painted carvings of wagtails that Gerald mistakes for "savage carving" [94].) A sophisticated focus on ugliness and garish contrast produces intense visual vibrations: "the figures of the two women seemed to glitter in progress over the wide bay of the railway crossing, white and orange and yellow and rose glittering in motion across a hot world silted with coal-dust" (114). Reduction of the women's figures to bright patches and frictional discords suggests an expressionist perception of space and color, as in Kirchner's *Girl with Japanese Parasol* (c. 1909) or *Fränzi in a Carved Chair* (1910), Heckel's *Brickyard in Dangast* (1907) or *Fränzi with a Doll* (1910), Max Pechstein's *River Landscape* (c. 1907) or Schmidt-Rottluff's more monumental *Estate in Dangast* (1910).[2]

Gudrun's *nostalgie de la boue*, her fascination with degradation, finds its correlative in the mining countryside:

The heavy gold glamour of approaching sunset lay over all the colliery district, and the ugliness overlaid with beauty was like a narcotic to the senses. On the roads silted with black dust, the rich light fell more warmly, more heavily; over all the amorphous squalor a kind of magic was cast, from the glowing close of day.

"It has a foul kind of beauty, this place," said Gudrun, evidently suffering from fascination. (115)

The underground mass-man dominates, and his blood-consciousness and raw sensuality spread over the district: "[The broad dialect] seemed to envelop Gudrun in a laborer's caress, there was in the whole atmosphere a resonance of physical men, a glamorous thickness of labour and maleness surcharged in the air" (115). Sepčić, who emphasizes the sexuality of Gudrun's response, sees the "Coal-Dust" countryside as "a stylized Expressionist landscape" and analyzes its aesthetics in terms of surface and depths:

> The outlines of this landscape are surcharged with the subjective vision which bulges forth. . . . Lawrence is all the time pushing beyond the phenomenal while his landscape slants into the realm of the visionary. . . . This landscape, whose lines quiver with the passion of creative apprehension . . . bears a strong similarity to both the thematic and the formal approach of Expressionist paintings. . . . ("'Women in Love' [I]" 425, 429)

Like Loerke and the futurists, Gudrun is attracted to the dehumanizing force of the machine that generates a perverted sensuality: "In [the miners'] voices she could hear the voluptuous resonance of darkness, the strong, dangerous underworld, mindless, inhuman. They sounded also like strange machines, heavy, oiled. The voluptuousness was like that of machinery, cold and iron" (115). The willing victim of entropy is first narcotized, like that sacrifice to male tribal power, the Woman Who Rode Away, in one of Lawrence's most "regressive" fables.[3] Gudrun "seemed to move through a wave of disruptive force, that was given off from the presence of thousands of vigorous, underworld, half-automatised colliers, and which went to the brain and the heart, awaking a fatal desire, and a fatal callousness" (115–16). Aware of the alienation and misery of the men's lives, she still has "a nostalgia for the place." Like Dr. Fergusson in Lawrence's "The Horse-Dealer's Daughter," she is seeking a drug for overacute consciousness in inchoate sensuality, instead of trying, like Birkin, to sustain a delicate balance "between the senses and the outspoken mind" (253).

Gudrun loves what she hates (the squalor of the district and the brutalized miners) and hates what she loves (the Industrial Magnate and his male power). Her consciousness vibrates frictionally against that of the miners: it is not the men who attract her (she would gladly have them killed for looking at her) but their willing submission to the machine. Their voices arouse an atavistic, "almost demoniacal" desire to relapse. In her "nostalgia" for a subterranean blood-consciousness attuned to mechanical rhythms, Gudrun betrays the organic principle of life and "beat[s] her wings like a new Daphne, turning not into a tree but a machine" (116). The mythic image emblematizes the metamorphosis of spiritual energy into mechanical forms in modern art. The critique of Gudrun's regressive desires is extended to her electrician boyfriend, Palmer, "[who] was polarised by the men. Individually he detested and despised them. In the mass they fascinated him, as machinery fascinated him" (117). Lawrence's own fears of sinking into a male homoerotic morass and his need to free himself through creative work are reflected in his treatment of Gudrun and Palmer.

During the garden-/water-party, the sisters escape to an island, and Gudrun, wishing to relieve her tension, asks Ursula to sing while she does Dalcroze exercises:

> Gudrun, looking as if some invisible chain weighed on her hands and feet, began slowly to dance in the eurythmic manner, pulsing and fluttering rhythmically with her feet, making slower, regular gestures with her hands and arms . . . her feet all the time beating and running to the measure of the song, as if it were some strange incantation, her white, rapt form drifting here and there in a strange impulsive rhapsody . . . (166)

Emile Jaques-Dalcroze, who invented the eurythmic method of self-expressive dance, defines rhythm as "the natural force which incites and vivifies, unifies and repeats our acts and wills . . . " (v). Eurythmics expresses the unconscious in consciously orchestrated bodily movements, aiming at "equilibrium," "inner harmony," and liberation from inhibition. Eurythmic exercises combine spontaneity with concentration, "harmonising the functions of the body with those of the mind . . . " (6). Eurythmics and expressionism are historically connected. The expressionists of *Die Brücke* flourished in Dresden, 1905–11, and Kirchner and Nolde sketched at the dance studios and concerts of Mary Wigman,[4] who studied eurythmics with Jaques-Dalcroze at Hellerau, near Dresden, before going on (at Nolde's suggestion) to pioneer expressive dance with Rudolf von Laban at Ascona (1913–14).[5] Late in the novel, Gudrun, having decided to throw in her lot with Loerke in Dresden, reflects: "It will be amusing to go to these eurythmic displays. . . . It *will* be amusing to take part in German Bohemian life" (464).

In *Women in Love* dance is a supplementary form of art speech.[6] In its capacity to express inner being and preverbal feeling, dance is affiliated with expressionism in literature and painting. If "many dancers are highly articulate and lean toward poetic verbalization," as Sorrell claims, Lawrence conversely sees the possibilities of expressing allotropic states through verbalizations of bodily movement and dance. Eurythmics is an apt mode of expression for Gudrun in her state of inner tension. The angular movements of her improvised dance, its intensity and contortion, suggest that she feels inwardly "contravened" and is desperately trying, through ritualized gestures, to break free. The aim of eurythmics is "to influence the mind by . . . instinctive rhythmic movements and the body through the centres of volition . . . to permeate the subconscious forces with conscious forces, and *vice versa*" (Jaques-Dalcroze 7). As Gudrun's energy is entropically arrested, it is logical, if ironic, that she should resort to eurythmics. Her dance looks unnatural or perverse, because her movements are the bodily expression of a divided will. The eurythmic goal of "[mastering] one's body, in all its relations with the intellect and with the senses, [and so breaking] down the oppositions which paralyse the free development of one's powers of imagination and creation" (36) is imperfectly realized in her dance.

The compulsive tautness of Gudrun's movements contrasts with the casual drift of Ursula's song and the mocking looseness of Birkin's dance. Her ambivalence is manifest in the civilized/primitive contradictions of her dance, with its "unconscious ritualistic suggestion" (*Women in Love* 166). The "living plastic" (Jaques-Dalcroze 10) of her "white form" is "clutched in pure, mindless, tossing rhythm, and a will set powerful in a kind of hypnotic influence" (*Women in Love* 166). Her mixture of "confidence and diffidence" (8) provides the tension and motivation of her dance. Jaques-Dalcroze wanted to stimulate Dionysiac energies but, at the same time, to control them with an Apollonian will-to-order. His aim was bodily/mental equilibrium, but the effect of trying to combine the "spontaneous and deliberate" could be tense formalism, with the mechanical imposed upon the living. Gudrun feels a compulsive need to be rapt out of the grip of mental consciousness by a surrender to sensationalism, yet she cannot abandon her will: hence the shuddering, drifting movements of her dance, in which somatic states seek expression. It is natural that Lawrence, with his vital interest in allotropic states, should find a parallel medium in dance, the "language of the body in motion," which he incorporates into the expressionist language of the novel.[7]

Gudrun's fateful dance, aimed at overcoming constricted consciousness, culminates in releasing her destructive will in a symbolic act. Confronted by the menacing cattle,

> [she] went in a strange, palpitating dance . . . lifting her body towards them as if in a spell, her feet pulsing as if in some little frenzy of unconscious sensation, her arms, her wrists, her hands stretching and heaving and falling and reaching and reaching and falling, her breasts lifted and shaken . . . her throat exposed as in some voluptuous ecstasy . . . whilst she drifted imperceptibly nearer, an uncanny white figure . . . [that] ebbed upon them, in the slow, hyp-

notising convulsion of the dance. She could feel them just in front of her, it was as if she had the electric pulse from their breasts running into her hands. (167–68)

This rhythmic yet mechanical nexus recalls the blood pulse of the cows that "beat into the pulse of the hands of the men" in *The Rainbow* (10), while the "voluptuous ecstasy" of the dance reprises Hermione's "consummation of voluptuous ecstasy" in striking Birkin (*Women in Love* 117). Gudrun manipulates animal magnetism in a ritualistic acting-out of female power that draws Gerald to her and ultimately destroys him. The totemic herd is his, but he is hers. In a series of rushes, she puts the bullocks to flight, ritually proving the repulsive power of her will over masculine brute force. Her eurythmic self-expression puts her in touch with an "unconquerable desire for deep violence" against the male sex (170).

In the sinister "Rabbit" scene, animal impulses are expressed in electrical/mechanical images with futurist overtones. Expressionist and futurist elements mingle in Lawrence's style, but Hadermann points to perceptual elements in the plastic arts that make a distinction possible.[8] While expressionism releases repressed emotions and attempts to penetrate to a hidden core of reality, futurism moves in the opposite direction, transmuting vital energy into electromagnetic lines of force. Both styles involve dynamism and distortion, but expressionism is intentional, humanizing, and subjective, whereas futurism is mechanical, dehumanizing, and objective. A ritualistic scene like "Rabbit" is essentially expressionist in its "violent projection of soul states" (Weisstein, Introduction 16); at the same time, Lawrence uses futurist imagery to dramatize the magnetism and automatism of obsessive drives.

The demonic "wonder" and "mystery" of the rabbit are invoked in German and French as well as English, for all Europe is involved in this heart of darkness. Gudrun hauls the creature out of its hutch, "and in another instant it was in mid-air, lunging wildly, its body flying like a spring coiled and released, as it lashed out. . . . Gudrun held the black-and-white tempest at arms' length, averting her face. But the rabbit was magically strong . . . " (*Women in Love* 240). Her response exposes raw impulses, in a way characteristic of expressionism:

Gudrun stood for a moment astounded by the thunder-storm that had sprung into being in her grip. Then her colour came up, a heavy rage came over her like a cloud. She stood shaken as a house in a storm, and utterly overcome. Her heart was arrested with fury at the mindlessness and the bestial stupidity of this struggle, her wrists were badly scored by the claws of the beast, a heavy cruelty welled up in her. (240)

Lawrence's phenomenology of the unconscious becomes dramatic, as violence occludes the mind. "Gudrun saw Gerald's body tighten, saw a sharp blindness come into his eyes" (241). The writhing rabbit is an extension of human sensuality, contorted by the will. The terrified, vicious creature embodies the couple's tension, fear, and twisted craving for sensation. A vicious blood-lust is projected onto "Bismarck," just as pent-up psychosexual forces were projected into the mass destruction of World War I.

This compulsion to express what is hidden in the psyche was at the heart of European expressionism in the prewar and wartime period when Lawrence was writing *Women in Love* (1913–17).[9] Kirchner, particularly, sensed the blood-lust in the air and in the streets. Apparently suffering from schizophrenia and paranoia after his breakdown during military training, he painted himself in uniform, gesticulating with a bloody stump in place of a hand; he also depicted lurid sex-crime and murder. Kokoschka, who had been left for dead on the battlefield, came back to Vienna with a severe head wound and was deeply disturbed by the war between the sexes. He lived with a life-size doll he had made, had a passionate affair with Alma Mahler, and wrote and produced a play, *Murder Hope of Women*, that started a riot (1917).[10] Violent currents were in the air. Freud, in *Civilization and Its Discontents* (1930), later speculated that repression and sublimation had led to the sanctioned blood-letting of the war, which Lawrence exposes to savage irony in "England, My England" (1921). In his *Letters*, Lawrence speaks of soldiers, whose frustrated sexuality becomes blood-lust and "atrocity" (1: 469). The rabbit's name, "Bismarck," implies a connection between blood and iron, sex-lust and war; it is an apt name for a fetishistic medium of violence and suffering, linking the Industrial Magnate with the Iron Chancellor.

As the contortions of Gudrun's dance act out inner tensions, so the sadomasochistic frenzy of "Rabbit" is an expressionist acting-out of latent violence and "interdestructivity" in her relationship with Gerald. Their reciprocal will-to-power is fueled by a Faustian will-to-know, to exploit and possess unconscious impulses, and thus ultimately to kill "the body of life." The rabbit, like the mare, becomes the embodiment of physical impulses forced into grotesque convulsions by the will:

The long, demon-like beast lashed out again, spread on the air as if it were flying, looking something like a dragon, then closing up again, inconceivably powerful and explosive. The man's body, strung to its efforts, vibrated strongly. Then a sudden sharp, white-edged wrath came up in him. Swift as lightning he drew back and brought his free hand down like a hawk on the neck of the rabbit. (*Women in Love* 241)

Demon/dragon images suggest the power of the repressed when suddenly unleashed; "white-edged" signifies Nordic will-to-power.

The impact of the scene derives from a combination of graphic realism with symbolism and expressionism. The focus moves from realistic visual detail ("all its belly flashed white in a whirlwind of paws") to nonrepresentational phenomena: "And he saw her eyes black as night in her pallid face. . . . He looked at her, and the whitish, electric gleam in his face intensified" (241). Gudrun's demonic look recalls her "black-dilated, spell-bound eyes" as Gerald dominates the mare and her "dark, dilated, inchoate eyes" just before she strikes him after conquering the cattle (113, 170). The sadistic rabbit ritual reveals the unconscious as a seething chaos of lust and cruelty just below the polished social surface. Gerald and Gudrun are plunged into this horrifying abyss as into a tide of blood. They willingly lapse out of sophisticated consciousness into demonized sensation, not really believing in the civilized orders of art and industry they sustain. In "Rabbit" the dark underside of repressive culture, with its potential for demonic and hysterical outbursts, is laid bare. The sensuality is acrid and strained, compared with the light intellectual badinage of Birkin and Ursula in "Mino." As in the Arab mare scene, Gudrun identifies masochistically with the victim as well as sadistically with the tormentor. Conspiring with destructive forces in themselves and in their culture, the couple experience "mutual hellish recognition" (242). Their struggle with the rabbit arouses a sexual/sadistic will-to-power that frightens even Gerald, the "God of the Machine." The sense of a Faustian bond with powers of evil—"There was a league between them, abhorrent to them both" (242)—is strong as they gloat over each other's wounds: "[It] was as if he had had knowledge of her in the long red rent of her forearm . . . [that] seemed torn across his own brain, tearing the surface of his ultimate consciousness, letting through the forever unconscious, unthinkable red ether of the beyond, the obscene beyond" (242).

Occult knowledge overwhelms Gerald, shattering his iron control. The metaphorical expression of soul-states is concentrated and revealing: Gerald identifies carnal knowledge with violation and sex with suffering. Ironically, some membrane of consciousness seems to be torn in him, rupturing his mental defenses; the consequent hemorrhage drowns his will in an up-surge of primitive instincts. As in some weird, totemic rite, the couple are initiated into demonic sensuality—their sadomasochistic bond sealed in the blood of a beast, their exultation in each other's wounds a mockery of blood-brotherhood. Gudrun acknowledges the destructive exploitation of impulses with a look of "shocking nonchalance"[11] that strikes Gerald like another blow across the face or a vicious scratch from the rabbit's claws. The expo-sure of raw emotion recalls Kokoschka's expressionist drama, in which "nerves and veins" were painted on the actors; here violence is displaced onto the rabbit, increasing the sophisticated perversity of the scene.

The symbolic action of "Moony" is so powerful that the reader experi-ences it immediately and sensuously, as it were, rather than cognitively. Were it not for Birkin's curse on Cybele, the female sex-principle that enslaves men, the symbolic meaning might remain obscure although the effect would be equally vivid.[12] Lawrence's language is steeped in the luminosity of a dream. As Sepčić observes, Lawrence "[uses] expressive elements akin to the realm of somnambulism, hypnotic trance, incantatory rituals . . . [and] hallucinatory vision . . . " ("'Women in Love' [I]" 441). The rhetoric of the moon-stoning is alive with movement, vibration, oscillation. In "Moony," as in Munch's paintings, visionary concentration and psychic projection transcend personal causes and unite the individual with the archetype. Lawrence penetrates the primordial with a highly conscious form of "art-speech." It is the content and form of this expressionist language that I wish to examine.

Ursula's "luminousness of supreme repudiation" (*Women in Love* 244) is a quality of female will associated with the moon and with Cybele. In her hard, bright radiance, she is asserting a self-centered will-to-integration, while Birkin is asserting a contrary will-to-disintegration aimed at the "in-sistent female ego." Before these psychic forces, locked in mutual antago-nism, can come into "star equilibrium," a rhythmic surging together and asunder of light and darkness must arouse the total potential of each being. Equilibrium for the lovers is symbolized by the mandala-condition of mystic rose or full-orbed moon-on-dark-water, a polarized balance of upper and lower centers. To achieve harmonious "freedom together," each must tran-scend the limiting ego while retaining "free proud singleness," and each must break down the other's ego while accepting "the permanent connection with others, and with the other" (254). Paradisal unity, as distinct from "horrible fusion of two beings" (309), can be achieved only through polarized inter-subjectivity. This blissful state cannot be attained through the assertion of will but only through "a magnificent gift and give again" (320).

After Birkin throws the first stone into the pool, "Ursula [is] aware of the bright moon leaping and swaying, all distorted, in her eyes. It seemed to shoot out arms of fire like a cuttle-fish, like a luminous polyp, palpitating strongly before her" (246). These images recall the moonlit lantern scene in "Water-Party," in which Ursula's second lantern seems to give her "the heavens above, and the waters under the earth"—a symbol of creation from Genesis—whereas Gudrun's second lantern, which she is ominously "dying to see," has "a great white cuttle-fish flowing in white soft streams all over it . . . [with] a face that stared straight from the heart of the light, very fixed and coldly intent" (175). Fixity and intensity are qualities of Gudrun's life-denying art expressed in her dance and here associated with the evil eye.

Birkin's moon-madness recalls Ursula's identification with the "incandescent," "corrosive" moon in *The Rainbow*. In "Moony," however, she is identified with the moon's inviolable completeness, which he is savagely attacking. The psychic identification of characters with natural forces, invoked through a pattern of action at once formal and dynamic, marks this scene as expressionist ritual. Jane Ellen Harrison, in a book that "fascinate[d]" Lawrence (*Letters* 2: 90), maintains that "ritual *makes . . . a bridge between real life and art*, a bridge over which in primitive times it would seem man must pass" (135). Ritual is the bridge between the unconscious, that strives to retain its hidden integrity, and art-speech, which is "*the passionate struggle into conscious being.*" The effect of rhythmic rhetoric and overlapping images is to make the "Moony" almost scene too dazzling to contemplate. While kaleidoscopic images activate the visual sense beyond thought, incantatory rhythms spellbind the imagination. The irrational power of the scene depends on an expressionist use of language capable of producing a profound emotive response without surrendering any fixed idea. The whole is greater than the sum of the parts, as Lawrence makes visual, tactile, and aural imagery resonate beyond semantic or referential functions.

Maud Bodkin describes the interactions between Lawrence's characters as "dreams of attraction and repulsion, negation and reassertion of impulse . . . " (293). This apocalyptic process of mutual self-destruction and re-creation is enacted in a threefold pattern, the main phases of which comprise a centrifugal-centripetal rhythm of dispersal and renewal. The structure of these pulsations may be clarified by isolating verbal or participial phrases. First there is the outward, disintegrative movement, in which "the moon had exploded on the water, and was *flying asunder* . . . [and the] furthest waves of light, *fleeing out*, seemed to be *clamouring against the shore for escape*. . . ." In answer to this outward movement, a contrary undertow moves back toward the center, with the moon's image "getting stronger . . . *re-asserting itself* . . . in triumphant reassumption" (*Women in Love* 247 [my italics]). This dual process is repeated and the conflict between light and darkness intensified, with "the broken lights *scattered in explosion* over her face, *dazzling her*," until the reverse pulsation starts and "they were *flickering their way to the centre* . . . the heart of the rose *intertwining vigorously* and blindly . . . in a pulse and an effort of return" (247 [my italics]). The interaction rhythmically "[works] up to culmination" in the third and final phase, in which a mandalalike harmony is almost completely restored. First comes the impulse toward fragmentation and dispersion; then the resurgence toward integration, the moon's image "trying to recover from its convulsion, to get over the disfigurement and the agitation, *to be whole and composed, at peace*" (248 [my italics]).

The repeated "action and reaction" of this psychic ritual, reminding one that "nothing can be sole or whole / That has not been rent" (Yeats), is a consummate example of the "pulsing, frictional to-and-fro" that is the instinctual basis of Lawrence's style. In a real sense, the expressionist style is a manifestation in language of the psychic rhythms of the writer's being. The rhythmic expansion and intensification of the moon-stoning falls symmetrically into three stages, generating a metonymic "ripple," in which "each clause or phrase takes its impetus from an item in the preceding one . . . " (Lodge 163). Expressionist rhythms project inner tensions in successive disruptions and reintegrations of the moon's image on the mirror-like surface of the pool. The complex ritual succeeds in linking man and woman, dark water and moonlight, in a mysterious homology. The process of diffusion and re-fusion is internalized in the psyche of celebrant and witness: Birkin and Ursula, coming together in search of wholeness, are initiated into sacred mysteries, just as Gerald and Gudrun are "implicated with each other in abhorrent mysteries" of cruelty and disintegration.

In the trancelike state that comes of gazing into the watery kaleidoscope,

"Ursula was dazed, her mind was all gone. She felt she had fallen to the ground and was spilled out, like water on the earth" (*Women in Love* 248)—a dream-identification that fulfills her impulsive prophecy in *The Rainbow*: "'If I were the moon, I know where I would fall down'" (331). After the intensity of the ritual, she, like the fallen moon, remains "[m]otionless and spent," although "she [is] aware . . . [that the] ebbing flakes of light . . . [are] gathering a heart again, they [are] coming once more into being" (*Women in Love* 248). And so is Ursula, as she recovers from her withdrawal into gloomy isolation and recenters her energies on Birkin. Empathy binds the invisible allotropy of her being to his ritualized act. As Birkin's moon-stoning enacts tension/release, joining/sundering, spilling out/becoming whole in the couple's relationship, so Lawrence's linguistic enactment of archetypal impulses unites the author's unconscious with the characters', while activating the reader's imagination with its brilliant play of visual forms. This is plastic dynamism in action.

Polarized themes of integration/disintegration and creation/destruction symbolize not only the psychodrama of the characters but also the upheaval of their historical period. The interplay of white fire and dark water makes a microcosm of the pool. Birkin ritually enacts the disintegration of European society he had prophesied in "An Island" and "Water-Party." Meanwhile Ursula identifies with the lunar will-to-harmony, which is either a sublime form of Eros ("the goodness, the holiness, the desire for creation and productive happiness") or a more or less sublimated will-to-power and separate selfhood. To read the moon-stoning as an objective correlative of the war going on bitterly in the background requires only a slight shift of focus from metonymy to metaphor, bringing out a dense cluster of battleground images: "a burst of sound," "a burst of brilliant light," "exploded," "flying asunder," "dangerous fire," "fires all broken," "fleeing in clamorous confusion," "battling," "forcing their way in," "fleeing out," "clamouring against the shore for escape," "writhing and striving and not even now broken open," "strange, violent pangs," "blind effort," "triumphant reassumption," "broken lights scattered in explosion over her face," "the second shot," "a battlefield of broken lights and shadows" (278–79). Lawrence unites the personal unconscious with the archetypal and the individual psyche with its historical field of action.

The closest visual analogues to Lawrence's verbal expression are to be found in German expressionist painting. In Kirchner's *Winter Moon Land-*

scape (1919; see pl. 9), Donald E. Gordon notes that "the subject, almost apocalyptical in mood, betrays the subjective quality of Kirchner's personal interpretation" and goes on to consider the expressionist dimension of the painting:

> No matter how awe inspiring the moonlit landscape appeared to [Kirchner] early that morning, these letters . . . [reveal] the process by which a peaceful subject is empathically animated with the daemonic overtones of a world in which people can dance amidst machine-gun fire. An Alpine mountain is not conceived with romantic pantheism, as it would have been in the previous century, but as a neutral screen on which are projected the frightening shock-waves of a crazed continent. (*Ernst Ludwig Kirchner: A Retrospective* 26–28)

Similarly, the stoning of the pool is an apocalyptic ritual, in which the old order of civilization is challenged and destroyed in shadow-play only to be replaced by new forms, which in their turn are destroyed and remade. Birkin's dreamlike action has symbolic ramifications: while consciously defying Cybele, he is unconsciously enacting the decline, fall, and "eternal return" of cultures. At this stage he is still caught in the dialectical ebb and flow of civilized and "primitive," ego and id, self and other. Later he envisions a resolution of his personal dilemma in "Paradisal entry." Although this happy state is not achieved until "Excurse," the way is made clear in "Moony," in which the dual intensities of ritual and reflection lead to illumination.

The machine-man is a typical figure in the expressionist plays of Georg Kaiser and Ernst Toller. At the beginning of "Gladiatorial," the Industrial Magnate finds himself "in an agony of inertia, like a machine that is without power"; the question is "where does his *go* go to..[?]" (*Women in Love* 266, 48). He can express being only in doing, or in exerting power over others— which is why he would like to hit someone, even Birkin. Like the Nordic culture he represents, Gerald is suffering from entropy; his will has been geared to the machine and all spontaneity drained out, until the mechanized will itself stalls. Success has not led to fulfillment; lost in an existential void, Gerald desperately needs a catalyst to revive his will to live.

The wrestling scene turns on varieties of energy, suggested by kinetic imagery with futurist overtones. An expressionist element is the nontactile, nonvisual awareness of physical presence. As Merleau-Ponty insists, "existence comes into its own in the body. This incarnate significance is the central phenomenon of which body and mind, sign and significance are abstract moments" (*Phenomenology* 166). As Gudrun and Winifred set out to "do" Bismarck and plumb his "mystery," so Birkin attempts to penetrate the mysterious organization of Gerald's physical being. The wrestling involves an interaction of diverse temperaments; Gerald's *angst* and *ennui*, his longing for extreme sensation, encounter the frustration and anger in Birkin who, temporarily rejected by Ursula, is yearning for salvational *Blutbrüderschaft*. In the vitalized motility of the wrestling, each exists for the other as "incarnate subject" (Merleau-Ponty).

The essential homeostasis of each man is represented by a language of intuition that draws on physics. In depicting "spontaneous gesture born of muscular imagination, passion and fantasy," the wrestling eurythmically reveals "the origin of the motor faculties" (Jaques-Dalcroze 70) in deeper layers of being than the mind.

> [Gerald] seemed to stand with a proper, rich weight on the face of the earth, whilst Birkin seemed to have the centre of gravitation in his own middle. And Gerald had a rich, frictional kind of strength, rather mechanical, but sudden and invincible, whereas Birkin was abstract as to be almost intangible. He impinged invisibly upon the other man, scarcely seeming to touch him, like a garment, and then suddenly piercing in a tense fine grip that seemed to penetrate into the very quick of Gerald's being. (*Women in Love* 269–70)

Their strengths are complementary; each needs, and is struggling to gain, some input from the other. The "physical junction of two bodies" implies a spiritual conjunction of opposites. At the high point of tension, the two wrestlers are "clinched into oneness," as Will Brangwen's soul is conversely "clinched" into solitary ecstasy in the apex of the cathedral. Will, spiritually, and Birkin, intuitively, seek "the meeting, the clasp, the close embrace . . . the perfect, swooning consummation" (*Rainbow* 187) of oneness.

In "Gladiatorial,"

> [the two men] seemed to drive their white flesh deeper and deeper against each other, as if they would break into a oneness. . . . [Birkin] seemed to penetrate into Gerald's more solid, more diffuse bulk, to interfuse his body through the body of the other, as if to bring it subtly into subjection, always seizing with some rapid necromantic foreknowledge every motion of the other flesh, converting and counteracting it. . . . It was as if Birkin's whole physical intelligence interpenetrated into Gerald's body, as if his fine, sublimated energy entered into the flesh of the fuller man, like some potency, casting a fine net, a prison,

through the muscles into the very depths of Gerald's physical being. (*Women in Love* 270)

Birkin's "white magic" combines a hint of the occult with sheer "physical intelligence." The strong inhibition against homosexuality, combined with an equally strong urge to retain and transmute the homoerotic, produces a high charge of "sublimated energy." Birkin's desire to anticipate Gerald's impulses with "rapid necromantic foreknowledge" resembles Gudrun's desire to seize on his physical/sexual essence (194, 332). Like his bullocks, Gerald represents potent but inert male substance that more intelligent agents can manipulate for good or ill. The dynamism of his "living, radio-active body" is revealed through a wrestler's or lover's touch. The narrator's fascination with Gerald's "plastic," "fully moulded" contours is subtly related to Gudrun's thirst to *know* "his mystical plastic form" (332)—although their salvational and exploitative motives are sharply contrasted.

An element of poetic abstraction appears in "Gladiatorial." Identities submerge in impersonal "junction," while minds drop out of sight along with heads to be transcended by an image of pure motion, like that of expressionist dance:

> So they wrestled swiftly, rapturously, intent and mindless at last, two essential white figures ever working into a tighter, closer oneness of struggle, with a strange, octopus-like knotting and flashing of limbs. . . . Often, in the white interlaced knot of violent living being that swayed silently, there was no head to be seen, only the swift, tight limbs, the solid white backs, the physical junction of two bodies clinched into oneness. (270)

The act of wrestling reveals the potential oneness of physical and intellectual opposites. As in Wigman's whirlwind dances, the wrestlers, "turning around [their] own axis," enter a "vortex of rotation" (Wigman 39), in which each loses himself in instinctual motion in order to find himself again.[13] The swooning exhaustion that Birkin feels after the bout is described in apocalyptic images: "The earth seemed to tilt and sway, and a complete darkness was coming over his mind" (*Women in Love* 271). Through the lens of expressionist language, a casual wrestling bout in a well-upholstered library turns into an exploration of occult phenomena and a struggle to reach "the very depths of . . . physical being."

The physical rite of "Gladiatorial" is matched by the mystical rite of "Excurse"—the distinction being blurred by oxymorons such as "physical intelligence" and "deepest physical mind." An invisible realm looms behind Birkin's and Ursula's acts, and the clusters of metaphorical and metaphysical terms have made much of the chapter seem overwritten and unreadable, even to champions of Lawrence like F. R. Leavis.[14] Some critics think the rhetoric of the strange rite of touch, with its "current of passional electric energy . . . released from the darkest poles of the body" (314) is simply a smokescreen for anal sexuality. But Lawrence's propensity to advance simultaneously on physical and metaphysical fronts is well known. His expressionist language spiritualizes the body and embodies the spirit. Thomas H. Miles has interpreted the scene in terms of Kundalini, which is plausible, given Lawrence's interest in theosophy and yoga. The "mystically-physically satisfying" relations of Birkin and Ursula are expressed in electrical imagery of passionate impulses circulating through the bloodstream—as Jaques-Dalcroze uses similar imagery to describe the energy stimulated by eurythmics.[15]

Lawrence's language projects beyond the text into the inner space of being, transmuting tactile into spiritual. Through a cluster of words and phrases whose sexual specificity is subtly subsumed in mystical overtones, and a concentrated use of parallelism, fusion, abstraction, and negation, Lawrence expands the horizons of expression. More than in most texts, "the significance carried into the reader's mind exceeds language and thought as already constituted and is magically thrown into relief during the linguistic incantation . . . " (Merleau-Ponty, *Phenomenology* 401). The heavily freighted phrasing points toward otherness and silence, creating a fruitful impasse within the verbal medium: "Quenched, inhuman, his fingers upon her unrevealed nudity were the fingers of silence upon silence, the body of mysterious night upon the body of mysterious night, the night masculine and feminine, never to be seen with the eye, or known with the mind, only known as a palpable revelation of living otherness" (320). While "vital, sensual reality . . . can never be transmuted into mind content," Lawrence's metaphors conversely (or perversely) invite the reader to transmute verbal into sensual/ spiritual experience. Language becomes an occult phenomenon, a vehicle of the physical sublime that transcends cognition. Alan Friedman says that Lawrence "dredges up for us as much of his familiar darkness as he can irradiate by a medium—the web of words—of all media the most inappropriate to that subject" (245). Everyday meaning is erased, as words point toward tactile, kinesthetic, and emotional experience. The urge to communicate an inner vision, at the cost of dislocating and overloading the medium, is essentially expressionist.[16]

The language of "Excurse" expands implications rather than contracting meaning to fixed points. But Lawrence's attempt to express an erotic ontology does not lead to the stammering and fragmentation typical of some forms of literary expressionism. The biblical/expressionist rhetoric that seemed to reach its apogee in "The Cathedral" culminates in "Excurse," where "accession into being" is achieved through rites of touch.[17] Whereas Will's spiritual experience was one-dimensional and narcissistic, Birkin and Ursula reach mutual fulfillment. Theirs is a *via mystica* of the erotic body, rather than a lonely flight of the disembodied spirit. Lawrence's fusion of opposites points to a "primordial silence" (Merleau-Ponty, *Phenomenology* 184) that transcends the self. In this dialectics of language and being,[18] Lawrence devises a rhetoric of paradox and adumbration that "can inform . . . the flow of our sympathetic consciousness . . . [and] reveal the most secret places of life . . . " (*Lady Chatterley's Lover* 104).

In "Excurse" the concealed becomes unconcealed. A dialectics of mind and sense, speech and touch lies behind the cumulative paradoxes of this chapter. Here Lawrence taps a vein that links words with touch and touch with being. Sandra Fraleigh observes: "Our world of sensation is continuous with being, and therefore with language, as language also grows out of our experienced body" (331). Lawrence might not agree with Stefan George's line, cited and expounded by Heidegger in "The Nature of Language," "Where word breaks off no thing may be," although that line points to the textual, as distinct from ontological, horizon of the novel. Lawrence's expressionist language connects the verbal with the "unthinkable," the "palpable" with the "untranslatable," the temporal with the "immemorial," the expressive with the "unutterable," breaking down binary distinctions. It is not surprising that rationalist critics are horrified by this excess and accuse the writer of intolerable jargon. Lawrence does defy the limits of logic, making one ponder the ontological implications of Heidegger's supplement to George: "An 'is' arises where the word breaks up" ("The Nature of Language" 108). The stylistic enterprise of "Excurse" is an expressionist breaking-through (*Aufbruch*) of the referential functions of language to reveal an experience of Being.

A fertile interrelation between the arts is part of the expressionist ethos, in which painting stimulates writing to seek plastic equivalents for scene and action that push against the boundaries of language. Novelistic language borrows from the visual arts to transmute or transcend its own forms of expression. In *Women in Love*, expressionist language is not just optical or kinetic but reveals the vital or conflicted life behind surfaces,[19] expressing allotropic states of being to an extent never previously attempted.

Unusual states of consciousness that cannot be rationally described are the special province of expressionism, as in Gudrun's compulsive and compelling dance or Gerald's and Gudrun's mutual recognition of demonized impulses. Such scenes contain a symptomatology of the unconscious, gathering up and condensing diffuse or latent tendencies into the nexus of a "spontaneous" act. Ritual scenes expose inner necessities through outward actions that radiate psychic significance, as in the visual imagery of "Moony." Lawrence's language is so flexibly expressive that it can present the muscular sensation of a terrified horse or the will-to-power of a man or woman acting or looking. His rhetoric is so dynamically visualized that it can project unconscious desires and conflicts onto landscapes, like the mining countryside, that resonate with intensity. Lawrence uses expressionist language as a tool to penetrate human action, reflection, and being, linking characters with their culture. The expressionist artist is hypersensitive to the etiology of his times, as Lawrence and Kirchner were to psychic cross-currents and shock waves of war. He exposes forces that underlie visible phenomena at a given historical moment and challenges readers with an alternative vision of creation or corruption.

5

"PRIMITIVISM" IN
WOMEN IN LOVE

As Joseph Masheck observes, tribal art was "a vital inspiration" to the expressionists (93). The grotesque distortions of facial features and anatomy seemed to European artists to speak a language of "raw" emotion and to embody feelings long suppressed in their own culture. These forms had the power to shock but also to liberate, by articulating unconscious drives and forces beyond the ego. The image of African art in *Women in Love* can best be understood in the context of Lawrence's "primitivism" by clarifying his concept of the "fetish" and by exploring the interplay of unconscious ritual and conscious reflection in Birkin's response to the African sculptures he sees at Halliday's apartment.

Lawrence has been considered a representative primitivist, but the nature and value of "primitivism" in general, and of his "primitivism" in particular, have been the subject of wide disagreement. Over the last twenty years there has been much critical discussion of the term,[1] with alternatives such as "African [or] Oceanic art" and "tribal art" proposed. The exhibition "'Primitivism' in 20th Century Art" at the Museum of Modern Art in 1984 stirred up a fruitful controversy. The debate ranged between poles of formalism and functionalism, art critics relating tribal masks and sculptures to modern European art, anthropologists to tribal religions and customs. Art historians, following Vlaminck, Derain, Picasso, Apollinaire, Brancusi, and Modigliani, assert that such objects should be studied for the abstract formal principles that have catalyzed change in modern art; anthropologists insist that objects commissioned for religious ceremonies or as reliquary figures can be understood only in tribal contexts. The reception of tribal objects in Europe and America is now seen to have political and cultural overtones that intrude on any "pure" aesthetic judgment.

If the terms "primitive" and "primitivism" are still to be used, it must be with a sharpened awareness of historical circumstances. Frank Willett underlines the problem of the "protean" term *primitive*: "Its basic sense is 'primary in time', and by extension undeveloped, simple, crude, unsophisticated. But so-called 'primitive' art is none of these things . . . " (27). Robert Goldwater insists that "primitive art" is a laudatory term, implying "vitality, intensity, and formal inventiveness" ("Judgments" 25), but Willett regards the concept of "primitivism" as an ethnocentric relic of nineteenth-century British anthropology.

"In view of its long evolution," argues Warren Robbins, "it would be more correct to consider African sculpture as a *classical* rather than a *primitive* art" (6).[2] Elsy Leuzinger agrees:

> [T]he classical style in its pure form in no sense deserves to be dismissed with the word 'primitive.' . . . The classical styles are far from being spontaneous, naive, crude or unskilled. . . . [They] display skilled planning and conceptual force: They are beautiful in their simplicity, overcome technical difficulties with care and patience, and form a new, logical and tense unity on the basis of an idea. (19)

Birkin, who is aware of the classical unity of African art, tells Gerald: "There are centuries and hundreds of centuries of development in a straight line behind that carving; it is an awful pitch of culture, of a definite sort" (*Women in Love* 79). Leuzinger's view that their "faith experience" gives these works "an almost magical radiance" may seem idealized, compared with Birkin's conclusion that African degeneracy matches Nordic. But, as Michel Leiris and Jacqueline Delange point out: "Today none of these [African] peoples can be regarded as 'primitive' and it is recognized that many have a highly developed sense of values" (33).

"Primitivism" reflects a longing for cultural alternatives. Tribal objects, ripped out of context, were tangible but unknown entities upon which the Western mind could project its dissident fantasies.[3] "Primitive" is a loaded term, alluding to tendencies in European modernism rather than to indigenous realities of African or Oceanic art. While the cubists were stimulated by the formal properties of African art, abstracting and alienating forms from their sources, the expressionists were excited by the raw power and savagely direct expression of emotion they saw in these forms. The Dark

Continent and its "fetishes" came to represent what was desired or feared but deemed lost or repressed in civilization; African masks and carvings struck viewers as grotesque, violent, or "expressionistic."

If African art spoke to modern artists at the beginning of the twentieth century, it was in an unknown language and ambiguous tones. The penumbra of mystery surrounding the "primitive" provided a void into which imagination could rush, with its urge to annex new territory. Western artists composed "*an image of the primitive*" to suit their own needs (Torgovnick, *Gone Primitive* 9). But sophisticated responses that willfully ignore the tribal matrix of "primitive" objects are a subtle form of colonial exploitation. African artifacts in fiction are constructed "images of the primitive" that tell more about the novelist than his sources. Yet the interaction of the writer's imagination with "primitive" objects can be fertile, affording a critical perspective on Western culture, as in *Women in Love*.

"Primitivism" has been seen as the desire to go back to simpler, purer, or more sensual forms of life, casting off civilized repressions and accretions; the desire to live from a vital core that has not been smothered by artifice, sublimation, or deceit.[4] While such views approximate Birkin's in "Classroom" (*Women in Love*, chapter 3), Price points to traces of racism in Wingert's enthusiastic endorsement of an originary "primitive." If expressionism can be seen as "regression" or "apocalypse" (Levine), "the primitive," equally, can be associated with "degeneration" or "regeneration." Birkin first sees the wood carving of a woman in labor as the embodiment of extreme sensuality needed to regenerate European culture; later he sees another "fetish" as the icon of entropic degeneration. Torgovnick, in her challenging study *Gone Primitive*, considers Birkin's interpretation of the fetish as an "expressionist misreading" of the kind that characterized European responses to African art: "[He] sees in it the expression of violent emotions and taboo sexuality. And he believes that African and Oceanic statues provide evidence of a slide into imbalanced 'mindless sexuality' . . . " (161). She claims that Lawrence uses primitivism as a stalking horse for his own exotic or deviant forms of sexuality, but she overlooks the fact that the fetish is a symbol of "pure culture in sensation"—of sensual authenticity rather than "sexuality"—that contrasts with the self-conscious fetishism of Halliday or Loerke.

The most mentally contorted character in the novel is the overcivilized Hermione. Like the fetish, Minette, and later Gerald, Hermione wears a mask of suffering: "Her long, pale face, that she carried lifted up, somewhat in the Rossetti fashion, seemed almost drugged, as if a strange mass of thoughts coiled in the darkness within her, and she was never allowed to escape" (*Women in Love* 15). The fashionable manner of this *Kulturträger* masks a chaos of passion and intellect; she extols Gudrun's carvings as "full of primitive passion" (39), but Birkin tears her self-conscious primitivism to shreds:

> [K]nowledge means everything to you. Even your animalism, you want it in your head. . . . You've got that mirror, your own fixed will . . . your own tight conscious world, and there is nothing beyond it. . . . But now you have come to all your conclusions, you want to go back and be like a savage, without knowledge. You want a life of pure sensation and 'passion.' . . . If one cracked your skull perhaps one might get a spontaneous, passionate woman out of you, with real sensuality. (41–42)

Here Birkin directly satirizes Hermione's self-conscious civilized "primitivism." But the scene in which *she* strikes *him* with the ball of lapis lazuli repays his projected desire for release with a cathartic act that discharges *her* repressions at *his* expense. Birkin has to condone her libidinous outburst, because it fulfills, with a vengeance, the lesson of "Class-room." His words are doubly prophetic, for after she has cracked him over the head with a symbolic art object, he experiences a pantheistic return to nature, with a reflux of spontaneous, passionate being.

Birkin's spell of Rousseauesque primitivism issues from his impasse with Hermione: his primroses and fir trees are the antidote to her *willed* daffodils. He feels a "nostalgia" for nature because it lies beyond the pale of culture, but there is a trace of parody in his atavistic idyll. His "lapsing out" from the struggle with others is pleasantly pantheistic but regressive by the standards of a man "damned and doomed to the old effort at serious living" (302). His momentary retreat into isolation—the "Man Who Loved Islands" theme—comes from despair at finding a way to live with others in society. At least his nudity amid the cool vegetation is spontaneous and refreshing, unlike Halliday's self-conscious fireside cult. Despite his idyll in the pine grove, Birkin never becomes a romantic primitivist like Gauguin; neither did Lawrence, who preferred to seek "the primitive" in trees, animals, and sun rather than in actual savages, and who resisted the urge toward atavism.[5]

"Primitivism" in art is not entirely a record of expropriation, consumption, and subversion. Among its more positive aspects, Torgovnick includes "a desire to acknowledge and accept the full range of human sexual possibilities and variations in belief . . . [and] a reaching out to the natural world as our home and mother . . . " (*Gone Primitive* 246). Such motives in Birkin's—and Lawrence's—search for the primitive involve a "curve of return" that is ultimately progressive rather than regressive.

In 1905 or 1906 (if not in 1904, as often stated), Vlaminck acquired two African statuettes in a wine shop in Argenteuil and soon afterward "a large white mask and two superb statues from the Ivory Coast" (Paudrat 139). He sold the mask to Derain, who showed it to Picasso and Matisse, who were filled with enthusiasm for its strange forms. On the verge of the Cubist breakthrough that was to shatter illusionism in European art, Picasso and Braque decorated their studios with African and Oceanic objects. Like the German expressionists, "[they] first saw in African masks what they wanted to see: pure force and intensity" (Jean Decock, qtd. in Laude vi)—although they valued it for aesthetic rather than emotional reasons. Birkin, who is aware of the cumulative force of tradition behind the African fetish, is seen "admir[ing] the almost wizard, sensuous apprehension of the earth" in a Picasso reproduction that probably shows African influence (*Women in Love* 255).

The German expressionists, like the fauves, read their own conscious primitivism into African art (Grottanelli 6). Looking back, Kirchner claimed to have "discovered" the Palau roof beams in the Dresden Ethnological Museum as early as 1903, beating Vlaminck's claim by a year, although he made no actual use of his discovery until 1910. Nolde visited New Guinea and Pechstein the Palau Islands in 1914, geographic voyages contemporary with Lawrence's expressionist "voyage of discovery" in *The Rainbow*. Although they may have "shared a rather confused ideology," Nolde, Schmidt-Rottluff, Pechstein, and Kirchner "preached the necessity of rediscovering instincts, ecstasies, almost visceral reactions attributed to the original man (*Urmensch*)" (Laude 19). While African art involves a traditional, impersonal craft handed down from father to son, fauves and expressionists saw in it a magnified reflection of their own delirium. "To the Germans," writes Masheck, "and in a way that revived Romantic ideals of tapping into the lifeblood of nature, primitive art seemed to offer the possibility of emotional release from a sometimes excruciating discontent, feeding a spiritual, if sometimes quasi-pagan, longing for freely externalized feeling" (94). The cumulative influence of tribal icons in shaping group beliefs and social identities was passed over in favor of appropriating them as catalysts of an alien European aesthetic. Rubin flatly asserts: "What we call 'Primitivism' is not directly about tribal art at all; it is about the influence of tribal art on Modern art. . . . The context of primitivism is modernity!" (in Baldwin et al. 51).

The expressionists used primitivism polemically, often importing images of African objects into their canvases, as in Nolde's *Masks* (1911) or Erich Heckel's *Still Life with Negro Mask* (1912). They also used expressive distortion, exploiting angularities, concavities, and roughnesses of texture, as in Heckel's woodcuts *Sleeping Negress* (1908), *Standing Child* (1911), and *Woman Sitting* (1913); Kirchner's *Head of Schmidt-Rottluff* (1909), *Summer* (1911), *Marcella* (1909–10), and *Brücke* vignettes (1909–13); and Schmidt-Rottluff's *Woman with Her Hair Undone* (1913; see pl. 10).[6] Fauves and Cubists adapted the form language of masks and sculptures to their own needs, as in Picasso's use of elongated Fang masks and facial striations in *Les Demoiselles d'Avignon* (1907), while expressionists read their own longings for primal, authentic sensation into African sculptures. African art had become a visible commodity, whose inner meaning was unknown or neglected: European artists felt free to read their personal preoccupations into these enigmatic objects. Kirchner, Heckel, and Schmidt-Rottluff were inspired by "primitive" sculpture and Nolde by masks, their main concern (in the words of Eckart von Sydow, as qtd. in Leiris and Delange 10) being the "emotional mystic content" they saw in these forms.

Medieval and exotic forms of "primitivism" were the vital force behind German expressionism. Lawrence directly shared at least one source of inspiration with Kirchner, who expresses a primitivist sensibility in his description of the Ajanta cave paintings:

> The originals are so strong and refined that they knock the brush out of your hand. . . . We Europeans have to acquire this laboriously for ourselves . . . for it is this from which we live in the state of our dreams. These Orientals have it in their blood, perhaps because they live continually in the sun. We miserable Europeans have to sacrifice body and soul to preserve even a shadow of it. (qtd. in Donald E. Gordon, *Ernst Ludwig Kirchner* 21–22)[7]

Long before he discovered the Etruscans, Lawrence went into raptures over these same Indian wall paintings: "I *loved* them: the pure fulfilment—the pure simplicity—the complete, almost perfect relations between the men and the women. . . . They are the zenith of a very lovely civilisation, the crest of a very perfect wave of human development" (*Letters* 2: 488–89). He saw in the faint smiles of the Ajanta men and women, embracing without stress in the radiant assurance of their oneness and fulfillment, a "subtle interrelatedness" with the cosmos that was, for him, the goal of life and art.

Lawrence also has marked affinities with Emil Nolde, who sums up the vitalist appeal of tribal art: "The absolute originality, the intense, frequently grotesque expression of strength and life in the simplest possible form—that could be the factor which gives us so much joy" (qtd. in Selz 290). August Macke's devolutionist approach to "primitive art" links its simplicity, spontaneity, vividness, and force with children's art or "the form of thunder" (85). Macke and Nolde find what they seek but misconceive of "primitive" art as spontaneous, childlike, and original; such works were designed, as Lawrence knew, according to strict traditions. He compares them with classical art in order to stress their dynamism: "The African fetish-statues have no movement, visually represented. Yet one little motionless wooden figure stirs more than all the Parthenon frieze" ("Art and Morality" 168).

The term "fetish" is misleading: Lawrence uses it in the imprecise sense in which it was applied to any African artwork, while retaining a shade of its original association with magic. In the authoritative opinion of Fagg and Plass,

> The word "fetish" (from Portuguese *fetiço*) should not be applied indiscriminately to African art in general, including carvings for the divine and ancestral cults, but should be reserved for impersonal "machines" . . . "made up" (as fetish means in Portuguese) by the addition of various materials or "medicines" drawn from the animal, vegetable and mineral kingdoms, in order to draw upon the immanent life force of these substances; the witch-doctor activates the fetish by adding these medicines . . . while performing appropriate ceremonies and incantations. (35)

Pierre Meauzé adds that "the term fetish applies to a limited number of objects considered locally as dangerous, their power proceeding from that of the sorcerer-maker" (50).

Actual fetishes are often roughly or carelessly carved, for most of the carving remains hidden under a forest of nails, driven in to propitiate the power invested in the object. There is clearly a relation between the anthropological and psychological concepts of "fetish."[8] Tribally, fetishism is the investment of force in a specially made figure that can be manipulated for beneficent or destructive effects; psychologically, it is the displacement onto outward forms of vital force associated with these forms in the fetishist's mind.[9]

Jascha Kessler, while finding elements of primitivism in *The Rainbow* and *Women in Love*, considers Lawrence wholly a primitivist only in his post-European phase.[10] But Michael Bell distinguishes between the "primitive sensibility" of *The Rainbow* and the "conscious primitivism" of *Women in Love*, in which Lawrence "begins to make overtly primitive use of his anthropological reading" (*Primitivism* 60). Lawrence read Frazer's *The Golden Bough* (1890) and *Totemism and Exogamy* (1910), Tylor's *Primitive Culture* (1871, which he preferred to Frazer), and Frobenius's *Voice of Africa* (1913) and became interested in anthropological theories of the decline of "primitive" cultures. "Primitivism," in *Women in Love*, contextualizes profound reflections (beyond ethnological difference) on forces that dominate cultures and lead to their downfall.

Lawrence neither romanticized "primitives" nor shared the evolutionist theory that saw them as belonging to an earlier phase of cultural development.[11] He denied the theory of evolution because he did not feel it in his solar plexus (Huxley, *Letters* xv)—a properly primitivist attitude. Culture, to him, was not a continuum but a series of experiments along divergent lines, each with its own dynamic of development and decline:

> The savages, we may say *all* savages, are remnants of the once civilised world people, who had their splendour and their being for countless centuries in the way of sensual knowledge, that conservative way which Egypt shows us at its conclusion, mysterious and long-enduring. It is we from the North, starting new centers of life in ourselves, who have become young. The savages have grown older and older. No man can look at the African grotesque carvings, for example, or the decoration patterns of the Oceanic islanders, without seeing in them the infinitely sophisticated soul which produces distortion from its own distorted psyche, a psyche distorted through myriad generations of degeneration. ("Herman Melville's *Typee* and *Omoo*" 223)

Far from being childlike, the primitives, as Lawrence sees them, have gone further on the road to degeneration than the white race. His critique of primitivism in Melville, whom he was reading in June 1916 while working on *Women in Love*, looks beyond the formal distortion and abstraction of primitive carving to a spiritual distortion that Lawrence saw emerging in European civilization.

"Primitive" sculpture has a particular frisson for the intellectual Birkin, who feels the process of reduction imminent in himself and his society. Lawrence's use of the degeneration theory recalls Frobenius's discussion of "those laws in obedience to which forms of civilization flourished and decayed like seeds scattered on the earth . . . leaving behind them a final distribution of living seed, which, in turn, again germinated according to the soil in which it fell and blossomed into another species" (1: 42). The racist Frobenius sees colonists as seed-bearers and native populations as soil. His explanation of rise and decline in the Yoruba culture draws upon a myth of white supremacy: "The phlegmatic black had sucked up the strength and will-power of the white man's race . . . " (1: 43). Frobenius's contrast between black sensuality and white will-power may have struck Lawrence, who uses the same homology in *Women in Love*.

The German expressionist writer Gottfried Benn draws opposite conclusions from a similar dichotomy. Benn sees white civilization as succumbing to entropy: "The white peoples are on the way out. . . . Decomposition is palpable, a return to earlier conditions impossible, the substance spent; this is where the Second Law of Thermodynamics applies" (*Primal Vision* 81). Benn is writing (1937) on the eve of World War II, but his apocalyptic mood is similar to that in which Lawrence wrote *Women in Love*, once titled *Dies Irae*, in the darkest days of World War I: "We are now in a period of crisis," he wrote just after the war. "Every man who is acutely alive is acutely wrestling with his own soul. The people that can bring forth the new passion, the new idea, this people will endure. Those others, that fix themselves in the old idea, will perish with the new life strangled unborn within them" ("Foreword" 486). Expressionism was born in this climate of urgent creativity.

André Malraux offers some reflections on the compelling appeal of primitive sculpture to European artists in the first two decades of the twentieth century:

> The artist feels that he can make use of some of these forms, but is less aware that the gods lurking behind them are seeking to make use of *him*. For fetishes . . . are not just quaint museum-pieces; they are indictments. . . . The diabolical principle—from war, that major devil, to its train of minor devils, fears and complexes—which is more or less subtly present in all savage art, was coming to the fore again [in Western culture]. (538, 541)

Malraux, like Lawrence, penetrates beyond the aesthetic surface of "primitive" art to the dark gods within; he has a vision of evil welling up from

Africa into European civilization.[12] *Women in Love*, significantly, "took its final shape in the midst of the period of war" ("Foreword" 485), and Birkin's musing on parallel African and Nordic processes of degeneration in "Moony" relates closely to the sadomasochistic violence in "Rabbit."

Central themes of the novel are brought into focus by the fetish that Birkin and Gerald confront in Halliday's rooms:

> But there were several negro statues, wood-carvings from West Africa, strange and disturbing, the carved negroes looked almost like the foetus of a human being. One was of a woman sitting naked in a strange posture, and looking tortured, her abdomen stuck out. . . . [She] was sitting in childbirth, clutching the ends of the band that hung from her neck, one in each hand, so that she could bear down, and help labour. The strange, transfixed, rudimentary face of the woman again reminded Gerald of a foetus, it was also rather wonderful, conveying the suggestion of the extreme of physical sensation, beyond the limits of mental consciousness. (*Women in Love* 74)[13]

Goldwater's description of Henry Moore's work stresses primitivist qualities similar to those in Lawrence's fetish: "African inspiration can be seen in the heavy, squared-off bent legs and buttocks, the enlarged feet, and the general proportions of *Standing Woman* (1923); they are related to the 'heavy bent legs' by which African sculpture, rising upward like the tree it comes from, still is 'rooted in the earth'" (*Primitivism in Modern Art* 242).

Roger Fry, in "The Art of the Bushmen" and "Negro Sculpture" (*Vision and Design* 74–84, 85–89) discusses the distortions of African art from an aesthetic angle, and concludes: "It is for want of a conscious critical sense and the intellectual powers of comparison and classification that the Negro has failed to create one of the great cultures of the world, and not from any lack of the creative aesthetic impulse, nor from lack of the most exquisite sensibility and the finest taste" (89).[14] Much as he scorned Fry's emphasis on "plastic values," and dissatisfied as he was with "high" civilization, Lawrence was even more concerned with finding, in African art, a balance of intellect and sensuality that would empower creative being.

Birkin is no simple primitivist; Gerald, for whom as a boy "[l]ife was a condition of savage freedom," who has explored the Amazon, and who reads "books about the primitive man, books of anthropology" (*Women in Love* 221, 64, 232), is more closely identified with "primitivism," which stems from an acute, but largely unconscious, discontent with civilization.[15] At their most deathly extremes (and Gerald belongs to a "world of death") primitivism and civilization converge—the concentrated energies that go into industrial production, once exhausted, seek economic and spiritual renewal in raids on less developed cultures. The reactionary plunge into "primitivism" is marked by outbreaks of savagery, ennui, and self-destructiveness in the industrial magnate. Gerald's compulsive atavism is contrasted with Birkin's more critical interest in "the primitive."

Birkin is attracted to dark gods and African "sensuality." But he comes to see extremes of primitivism and civilization, raised to a higher level of abstraction, as equally entropic. He continues to oscillate between "primitive animism" and "conscious primitivism" (Michael Bell's terms): his ritual stoning of the moon's image leads to a meditation on the fetish as "one of his soul's intimates." African art casts a magnetic spell over his psyche and the image of an elegant, long-necked fetish surfaces as the focus of his musings.[16] The "crouched," blocklike figure of the woman in labor (78) is not the same as this "tall, slim, elegant figure," the explanation being that Birkin saw "several negro statues" in Halliday's apartment (74). His focus later shifts again, with insights derived from one figure being matched and modified by the other. Up to this point, there has been little integration of allotropic and prophetic, intuitive and intellectual responses. But in recognizing Ursula as embodying his anima—"There is a golden light in you, which I wish you would give me" (249)—Birkin begins to move toward equilibrium. His reactions to African carvings and images of dark blood-consciousness shift from empathizing to critiquing the imbalance of energy in all cultures, including the industrial.

Primitivism is generally considered to be a symptom of cultural crisis.[17] But there is a vital difference between destructive regression—the "Gadarene swine" complex that Lawrence saw in the war—and "destructive creation" such as Birkin explores in "Water-Party." Whereas Widmer regards the "primitivistic" as an amoral aesthetic force, Kessler associates it with demonic and political evil. He "[goes] so far as to claim that primitivism in its modern incarnation is the servant of Ananke, and that the extraordinary work of D. H. Lawrence shows him to have been wholly in its grip" (Kessler 471). Undoubtedly, Birkin suffers at times from the death wish that plagues his society (albeit more consciously), and would like to see civilization swept away. But knowing psychic death is not necessarily succumbing to it; it may, indeed, be the first step toward overcoming it. It is ridiculous to say that Lawrence, as a primitivist, is wholly in the grip of Ananke, when he is actively diagnosing degrees of it in Birkin and in Gerald—who *is* wholly in its grip yet hates and fears the primitive with which he is obsessed. Norman O. Brown, like Lawrence, stresses that Eros and Ananke are interdependent forces, and that there can be no fulfillment of life so long as knowledge of death is repressed (108–9). Both Birkin and Gerald have this knowledge, but while Gerald affirms it fatalistically, Birkin makes it part of a larger dialectic, in which a stubbornly held "desire for creation and productive happiness" prevents his lapsing back into "disintegration and dissolution," a recoil that Lawrence attributes to the "long African process of purely sensual understanding" (*Women in Love* 253).

Brown, following Nietzsche, says of the Dionysian artist: "Instead of negating, he affirms the dialectical unity of the great instinctual opposites: Dionysus reunites male and female, Self and Other, life and death" (175). The Dionysian strain in Lawrence's art is an overflowing of cultural barriers, an imaginative transcendence of the civilization that preached love and made war. Yet Birkin, who rejects the "Dionysic ecstatic way" along with the "African process" of mystic sensuality, advocates a reunion of Apollo and Dionysus, "the senses and the outspoken mind," rather than a simple resurrection of the "Savage God."[18] Michael Bell acutely summarizes some central issues: "Primitivism, then, is born of the interplay between the civilized self and the desire to reject or transform it. . . . [It] is the projection by the civilized sensibility of an inverted image of the self. Its characteristic focus is the gap or tension that subsists between these two selves and its most characteristic resultant is impasse" (*Primitivism* 80). This "recognition of the contradictory nature of the primitivist impulse" (80–81) provides a useful point of departure for a study of cultural dilemma in *Women in Love*.

Gerald is simultaneously attracted and repelled by "absolute" sensation in the fetish. From his Western perspective, Halliday's African carvings represent an extreme state of underdevelopment, as if African culture had been arrested at the embryonic stage. The narrative makes clear that this is Gerald's view and that he cannot see beyond "the limits of mental consciousness" that are those of his culture. Yet the carving troubles him with a dim awareness that alternative forms of living exist beyond known limits. Trapped as he is in mechanisms of the will, Gerald is fascinated by the "utter sensuality" of the fetish, its total surrender to physical consciousness. Sensation, as he knows it, is vitiated by escapism, will-to-power, or conscious demonism. Willed sensation, turning back on itself, reduces being to nothingness and his "go" to the reductive energy of the death process, which rolls on like industrial production. He is struck by the fetish and wants to wrest its secrets from it, because he senses in it the counterpart of his own monomania. The resemblance becomes almost physical when, nearing the end of his corrosive course, he "look[s] like a mask used in ghastly religions of the barbarians" (*Women in Love* 439).

To the European mind, African fetishes can suggest "great powers of violent action" (Fagg and Plass 47). But anthropologists warn against neglecting the religious or practical motives of tribal artists. The "expressionist" quality of the fetish consists in the carver's achieving an impersonal level of expression, at which the image of physical experience is embodied in extreme form. This power of abstraction can make an invisible essence visible with the aid of distortion and elimination of details. The function of tribal art is to manifest universal truth in a concrete instance. Meaning lies in "the weight of sensation beneath" and not in personal expression. African sculpture, which is innately religious, surpasses European expressionism in getting at "what the woman *is* . . . inhumanly, physiologically . . . what she *is* as a phenomenon (or as representing some greater, inhuman will). . . . " This is what Lawrence sought to express in characters who pass through "allotropic states . . . of the same single radically-unchanged element" (*Letters* 2: 183).

Birkin studies "the carved figure of the negro woman in labour": "Her nude, protuberant body crouched in a strange, clutching posture, her hands gripping the ends of the band, above her breast," while Gerald "[sees] vividly, with his spirit, the grey, forward-stretching face . . . African and tense. . . . [It was] abstracted almost into meaninglessness by the weight of sensation beneath" (*Women in Love* 78, 79). This weight is the irreducible substratum of experience reached at a certain stage of initiation. It is this "reduction of forms to what is essential and meaningful" (Robbins 14) that attracts Birkin to African sculpture. His thought, like that of an initiate, "plunges slowly into an ever-widening and infinitely profound questioning" (Laude 128). Leopold Senghor even declares that African art "is a palpable contact with the underlying reality of the universe" (Baldwin et al. 29). Gerald sees with his spirit but represses the primitivist vision with horror, as it touches on his own unconscious identity. Birkin's "visionary awareness" transcends specific knowledge, and his thinking cannot be brought to satisfactory conclusion; but the impasse inspires him to formulate a personal ideology.

Birkin, whom Hermione accuses of oscillating "between animalism and spiritual truth" (*Women in Love* 297), seems at first to advocate primitivism but later rejects both primitive and civilized extremes in order to seek wholeness and equilibrium in a "mystic conjunction" of the sexes. His attempt to enlighten Gerald about the fetish is, in a sense, fruitful; by its shocking contrast with everything that Gerald stands for, the icon stimulates in Birkin a visionary awareness of cultural dynamics. Only after a long process of gestation does he come to understand the ironic identity of civilized will-to-power and primitive barbarity, opposites that confront each other across an abyss. Ironically, Gerald lectures Birkin: "You like the wrong things . . . things against yourself" (79), not realizing that Birkin's interaction with his opposite is the only way to restore balance to a self attacked by entropy.

For the changeful Birkin, personal relations involve a search for homeostasis in a mechanically ordered world. "[White] and strangely present," he has an intuitive understanding of the black fetish as a symbol of "[pure] culture in sensation, culture in the physical consciousness" (78–79). His intuition grasps the forces that shaped the fetish but also fits Michael Bell's formula of a "projection by the civilized sensibility of an inverted image of the self." His concentration on his dream-opposite leads from empathy through initiation to abstraction and insight. Birkin's "conscious critical sense," which Fry sees as the exclusive property of civilized man, gradually overcomes his tendency to identify with "the primitive," until he achieves a standpoint of independence that contrasts with Gerald's increasing monomania.

Gerald fears and resents the abandonment to sensation he sees in the fetish:

> "Why is it art?" Gerald asked, shocked, resentful.
> "It conveys a complete truth," said Birkin. "It contains the whole truth of that state, whatever you feel about it."
> "But you can't call it *high* art," said Gerald.
> "High! There are centuries and hundreds of centuries of development in a straight line, behind that carving; it is an awful pitch of culture, of a definite sort."
> "What culture?" Gerald asked, in opposition. He hated the sheer African thing.
> "Pure culture in sensation, culture in the physical consciousness . . . mindless, utterly sensual. It is so sensual as to be final, supreme." (79)

While Gerald's attitude to "primitive" (African) as compared to "high" (European) art is typical of industrialist/colonialist culture, Birkin's insights arise from a cultural alienation that opens him to other modes of being. He corrects Gerald's ethnocentric notions—the African carving is not "primary art"[19] but classical, with a long tradition of development behind it. As Laude observes, "[African] statuary transmits 'the message of being' because . . . it refuses . . . merely to transcribe a transitory, anecdotal, or evolving reality, and . . . has the will, confirmed by myth, to represent a stable reality whose deepest nature remains untouched by time" (203). Traditional African art "'is like a silent word. Everything speaks. Everything around us imparts a mysterious enriching state of being.' . . . Form is language. Being is language" (Ba 7, 9). To Birkin, who "base[s] his standard of values on pure being" (*Women in Love* 209), the fetish is not just a fantastic object of unknown import; its power, its *aura*, is immediately apparent in its form.

The fetish fulfills the goal of African art, in which an object embodies a force,[20] rather than signifying anything outside itself. Beauty, in African sculpture, is "the identification of the object with that for which it was created (Marcel Griaule, qtd. in Laude 133). While it is difficult for Birkin to "read" the sculpture to Gerald, his sensitivity to the power of the fetish works to focus and clarify his thought. He is not a worshiper, as Moody suggests, but an empathetic critic; after prolonged reflection, he rejects another fetish as being the emblem of "knowledge in disintegration and dissolution"— simultaneously diagnosing corresponding tendencies in himself and in his culture. Pure sensuality is ultimately as entropic as pure mental consciousness. The fetish, whose otherness serves to clarify culturally repressed values, becomes the symbol of a seductive but destructive organization of energy.

All real art, Laude maintains, is "profoundly rooted in a society to whose social, religious, and semantic exigencies it responds" (132). Lawrence may be vague about the cultural context of the fetish, and the motif of a woman in labor may be largely imagined, but he understands the power of African sculpture. The face of the carved figure is "void, peaked, abstracted," as the woman gives herself completely to the experience of childbirth and the artist puts total emphasis on the life force that rends her rigid but submissive body. There is no evasion of the experience deeply incised in the woodblock.

In the "terrible face," Gerald sees Minette, masochistically yielded to him as "the passive substance of his will" (*Women in Love* 80)—a civilized perversion of the life-force, that reveals a split being. The disequilibrium of their master-slave relationship foreshadows his sadomasochistic struggle with Gudrun, which contrasts with Birkin's and Ursula's "freedom together." The connection between Minette's vulnerable sensuality and the absolute sensation of the fetish becomes clearer: "Her face was like a small, fine mask, sinister too, masked with unwilling suffering" (80). These matching primitive/civilized masks are twin faces of a single Janus-figure. Birkin's understanding of the fetish exposes the shallowness of "the whole Bohemian set"—in which, ironically, he is included by Minette. The fact that the decadent Halliday possesses an African carving allows Lawrence to satirize the inherent contradictions and presumptions of self-conscious primitivism.

The fetish, which Lawrence seems to have constructed from sculptures he had seen or heard of,[21] has the impact of a revelation in this "civilized" setting. It carries a burden of sensation "that can never be transmuted into mind content" (320), although Birkin attempts to transmute it for Gerald's benefit. As Gerald "lifted his eyes to the face of the wooden figure . . . his heart contracted" (79)—a somatic signal of the epiphany that challenges his hierarchical assumptions. The carving's truthfulness, embodied in grain of wood, stress of strokes, and cramped posture, is the exact contrary of Gerald's "life-lie." To defend himself against the realization that threatens his civilized ego, he resorts to prejudice against the "sheer African thing." Birkin is left with the task of relating "primitive" to civilized and comparing cultural counterparts.

Lawrence's understanding of West African art seems advanced for his time. But Birkin's reading of the sculptures lacks specific context and is the product of intuition. His "primitivizing" is an attempt to overcome the manifest split between blood-consciousness—"this other great half of our life active in the darkness" (*Letters* 2: 470)—and mental consciousness, or will. In his letter to Russell of December 1915, Lawrence, who had been reading Frazer, maintains that "in the transmission from the blood of the mother to the embryo in the womb, there goes the whole *blood* consciousness." He relates this process to "the origin of totem,"[22] concluding that "[this] is very important to our living, that we should realise that we have a blood-being, a blood-consciousness, a blood-soul, complete and apart from the mental and nerve consciousness" (*Letters* 2: 470–71). Lawrence's dialogue with Russell provides a clue to Birkin's with Gerald: the totem/fetish embodies blood-consciousness at the supreme moment of childbirth. The fetish, perceived as barbarous by Gerald and as expressing a complete truth by Birkin, has a profound and disturbing impact on both of them. It is the essential catalyst of several degrees of initiation, dialectically revealing the entropic tendency of all high culture.

In "Moony," the Cybele myth is secondary to the enactment of primitive animism, the moon's image rippling into life as it expands and contracts on the pool like a psychic force. Tylor observes: "First and foremost among the causes which transfigure into myths the facts of daily experience, is the belief in the animation of all nature, rising at its highest point to personification. This . . . is inextricably bound up with that primitive mental state where man recognizes in every detail of his world the operation of personal life and will" (1: 285). Lawrence strives to recover that "primitive mental state" that unites man's psyche with nature. Ritualistic, rhythmic, symbolic language re-creates a "primitive" sensibility that is precognitive, rapturous, instinctual, dynamic.

Birkin's symbolic action leads to a prophetic reflection on African and Nordic ways. He comes to see the fatal incompleteness that causes degeneration in all closed systems. Cultivation "all in one sort" leads to disequilibrium and entropy. A society animated by false ideals (or ideals it is false to) tends to relapse into the reductive process and to take unconscious delight in disintegration. This is the way of Hermione, Gudrun, Gerald, and Loerke, of sex-in-the-head, of animal movements in mirrors, of mechanical organization, of civilization rending itself in war. Birkin despairs of mass culture and looks for some "other way" through which individuals can complete their being. Recalling the fetish, he comes to realize the contradiction between his own conscious primitivism—"he was always talking about sensual fulfilment"—and the vital unconscious. He "want[s] a further sensual experience—something deeper, darker than ordinary life could give" (*Women in Love* 252). Yet, pondering the mindless sensuality of the fetishes, he sees more clearly the limits of "primitive" culture and rejects atavistic knowledge of the heart of darkness. In his long reflection on the Mendé-like fetish, he strives to grasp the inner orientation of African culture and to isolate the contrasting dynamic of Nordic civilization.

Robbins affirms that "African sculpture . . . leaps out of its cultural context and speaks to all men. If Europe and America have best communicated their vision in literature and philosophy, Africa has most perfectly embodied hers in plastic art. . . . African sculpture [is] one of the most profoundly *communicative* arts man has yet produced" (24–26). In his communings with the fetish Birkin is led, through dialectical exchanges between the sensual and intellectual, to grasp universal principles of duality and entropy. The black icon remains imprinted on his mind, as part of his psyche:

There came back to him one, a statuette about two feet high, a tall, slim, elegant figure from West Africa, in dark wood, glossy and suave. It was a woman, with hair dressed high, like a melon-shaped dome. He remembered her vividly: she was one of his soul's intimates. Her body was long and elegant, her face was crushed tiny like a beetle's, she had rows of round heavy collars, like a column of quoits, on her neck. He remembered her: her astonishing cultured elegance, her diminished, beetle face, the astounding long elegant body, on short, ugly legs, with such protuberant buttocks, so weighty and unexpected below her slim long loins. (*Women in Love* 253)[23]

Birkin's detailed description of the carving, as he remembers it, shows an eye for those distortions in African sculpture that are most striking to a European sensibility. Reacting against his own patriarchal culture, he feels a deep affinity with the probably matriarchal culture of the statuette. A striking feature is its grotesque but highly formalized emphasis on the lower body, regarded by Lawrence as the locus of unconscious libidinal energy ("Fantasia of the Unconscious" 74–75). Birkin is fascinated and repelled by the figure, which relates to fetishistic/synecdochic motifs of black and white, loins and head.

Reflections on the African fetish begin to coalesce in Birkin's mind, where they are subjected to a process of intuitive intellection[24] that enables him to discern sources of disintegration in himself and his culture. Through a two-way process of empathy and introspection—he *senses* what the fetish symbolizes and comes to *know* what is imminent in himself—Birkin rediscovers a "savage" consciousness rooted in the solar plexus and independent of the mind. But, unlike Gerald and Gudrun, he draws back from the brink of atavism, desiring to integrate bodily consciousness ("the deepest physical mind") with spiritual energy ("the desire for creation and productive happiness") (*Women in Love* 318, 253). His insights give him a degree of freedom to resist the reductive "principle of knowledge in dissolution and corruption" that he sees undermining the European psyche and rampant in African culture. As Birkin's contemplation of the fetish moves without a break from aesthetic to philosophic, his response shifts from admiration to horror:

She knew what he himself did not know. She had thousands of years of purely sensual, purely unspiritual knowledge behind her. It must have been thousands of years since her race had died, mystically: that is, since the relation between the senses and the outspoken mind had broken, leaving the experience all in one sort, mystically sensual. Thousands of years ago, that which was imminent in himself must have taken place in these Africans: the goodness, the holiness, the desire for creation and productive happiness must have lapsed, leaving the single impulse for knowledge in one sort, mindless progressive knowledge through the senses, knowledge arrested and ending in the senses, mystic knowledge in disintegration and dissolution, knowledge such as the beetles have, which live purely within the world of corruption and cold dissolution. (253)

The beetle, despite its associations with the vital/corruptive scarab in "The Ladybird," is a negative symbol that plainly shows Birkin's rejection of unmodified blood-consciousness. Compulsive channeling of energies in a single direction—a process symbolized by Yeats's gyres—leads to increasing entropy within a cultural or psychic system. "When the stream of synthetic creation lapses," Birkin tells Ursula, "we find ourselves part of the inverse process, the flood of destructive creation" (172).[25] To sustain itself, every system channels energy; certain faculties are developed at the expense of others. This tendency of one pole to draw energy away from its opposite rather than exchanging energy with it is ultimately self-negating. If those (like Gerald) who are trapped within a closed system could learn to embrace their opposite (as Birkin does) they might be saved. The irony of not liking "things against yourself" is evident; it is not a matter of yielding or merging but of salvaging something vital and repressed from the Other. Birkin, at first linking African sensuality with fulfillment of physical being, registers "the trembling instability of the balance" between his own white intellect and the black body of the fetish. Catalyzed by the fetish, his personal goals of "ultimate marriage" and integration merge with the dialectical theme of cultural synthesis. When his attempt to resolve the deadlock between African and Nordic systems breaks down intellectually, the prospect of "paradisal entry" into wholeness and harmony with a woman opens up spiritually. Thus something is salvaged from "*the passionate struggle into conscious being.*"

For Lawrence, real thought is "[a] man in his wholeness, wholly attending" (*Complete Poems* 67). Birkin's passionate attention to the fetish enables him to interact intensively with it, and also to react against it from a fuller understanding. Comprehension has its source in empathy, followed by long meditation on the object, not as a work of art in Roger Fry's sense—although Birkin can appreciate qualities of mass and form and skillful handling of material—but as a concrete symbol of vital instincts (which it *is*). Through insight into the icon's otherness he gains perspective on his own being and that of his culture. The novel's central dialectic is initiated by this encounter. Meauzé affirms that "[the] truth of African art lies in this fundamental power [whereby the form . . . stands out in all its nakedness], and if men were more curious, more clear-minded and more honest this power would explode before their very eyes" (12). In the midst of London bohemia African sculpture has the explosive impact of a challenge to "civilized" mores.

What Birkin admires in the "purely unspiritual" fetish is the completeness and integrity with which sensual experience is realized. There is absolutely no evasion or repression: with complete authenticity, the carving seems to fuse sensation with being. It emanates a life-force by which decadent characters can be judged. The inner spiritual condition of Hermione, Halliday and Minette, Gudrun and Loerke is marked by disintegration: Gudrun, like the second fetish, is left at last with "the inner, individual darkness, sensation within the ego, the obscene religious mystery of ultimate reduction . . . disintegrating the vital organic body of life" (*Women in Love* 452). This malaise of white culture shows up all the more clearly against the first icon of a black woman submitting to the life-force with passionate intensity.

The decadence of Loerke and Gudrun is explicitly associated with a cult of primitivism: "[He] liked the West African wooden figures. . . . The suggestion of primitive art was their refuge, and the inner mysteries of sensation their object of worship" (448). Only Birkin's hard-won realizations about the "awful African process" and his "star-equilibrium" with Ursula save him from falling into a similar vortex of fantasy and escapism. Amid this "flux of dissolution" the creative individual must resist inertia, struggle for awareness, make existential choices that determine his being. That is why Birkin has to go through a phase of conscious primitivizing, sharply distinguished from Halliday's self-indulgent playing at "the primitive" or Loerke's exploitation of it for mental thrills. He must resist the tide of his culture, which seems set for destruction, and draw from other cultures whatever helps to restore inner balance. While Hermione suffers the living-death of hypertrophied consciousness and Gerald dies of an atrophied will, Birkin, disillusioned and misanthropic as he is, saves himself by making a bond beyond love with the life-force in a woman. The achievement of equilibrium is more than a resolution of personal crisis; it is a faith in creation that surpasses understanding by fusing physical with spiritual.

Birkin's reflection on primitivism enables him to see the price exacted by all high culture. Instead of lapsing into mindless ecstasy, as Kessler accuses Lawrence of doing, Birkin clings to "the goodness, the holiness, the desire for creation and productive happiness"—Apollonian qualities that represent integration and the germ of culture, rather than Dionysian frenzy and disintegration. The civilization in whose toils he is caught is seen to match its opposite, insofar as both lapse from the search for equilibrium into destructive "singleness of vision." Accelerated growth of certain faculties at the expense of others causes entropy, war, and decline. The "utterly mindless" African fetish is as extreme an instance of sensual unconsciousness as Hermione is of civilized hyper-consciousness. *Her* mental contortions are caused by displacement of energy upward, *its* weight of sensation by displacement downward.

Birkin is not about to trade one monologic form of cultural conditioning for another. He has reached a level of abstraction at which cultural content is less significant than underlying drives, with their potential for fulfillment or destruction. Aware of his own psychic and sexual imbalance, Birkin finds his sickness is rooted in that of his culture. A dose of blood-consciousness might seem the proper antidote to civilized hyper-consciousness, yet willed "primitivism" is just another symptom of mental decadence, as in Halliday's bohemian games or Hermione's "false self system."[26] Culture—civilized or primitive, mental or sensual—exacts its price. To the rebel or visionary, the social contract involves more sacrifices than benefits. In 1930 Freud stressed "the extent to which civilization is built upon a renunciation of instinct, how much it presupposes precisely the non-satisfaction . . . of powerful instincts," and he attributed the rise of primitivism to "a deep and long-standing dissatisfaction with . . . civilization" (44, 34). A decade before Freud's diagnosis, Lawrence linked sexual repression and displaced drives with war and the death wish.

Birkin's interpretation of the fetish is wide-ranging; it opens up a whole metaphysic of death-in-life and life-in-death. He is a prophet of the Fall from integrity and harmony "into the long, long African process of purely sensual understanding, knowledge in the mystery of dissolution" (*Women in Love* 253).[27] For him, "primitive" and technological cultures enact parallel syndromes:

> There remained this way, this awful African process, to be fulfilled. It would be done differently by the white races. The white races, having the arctic north

behind them, the vast abstraction of ice and snow, would fulfil a mystery of ice-destructive knowledge, snow-abstract annihilation. Whereas the West Africans, controlled by the burning death-abstraction of the Sahara, had been fulfilled in sun-destruction, the putrescent mystery of sun-rays. (254)

Lawrence's climatological symbolism points forward to the apocalyptic metaphors of Gottfried Benn who, in 1937, speaks of "this white race with its compulsive pursuit of a downward path of no return, a lost, icy, heat-baked, weather-ravaged *anabasis* not held in the embrace of any *thalassa*" (*Primal Vision* 66). For Birkin as for Benn, the driving-force of civilization is Thanatos: Eros offers, at best, personal liberation from a doomed culture.[28] The history of cultures, their rise, decline, and fall, tends to repeat itself. As if by the Second Law of Thermodynamics, those components that bring about efficiency in a closed system also cause its disintegration.[29]

The theme of equilibrium versus reduction suggests that Lawrence, who was reading Gibbon and Frobenius in April 1918 (*Letters* 3: 233, 239), had entropy theory in mind. Science, as well as history, may have provided a model of cultural decline: according to the Second Law of Thermodynamics, entropy is bound to increase in isolated, noninteractive systems. This accounts for the fate of Gerald, who "cannot love," and of Gudrun, who is obsessed with the ticking of the clock. The root cause of entropy is "the single impulse for knowledge in one sort," that prevents a reciprocal flow of energy between opposing poles. Birkin and Ursula, fully in touch with each other, share "a rich new circuit, a new current of passional electric energy . . . released from the darkest poles of the body . . . " (*Women in Love* 314). Whereas *The Rainbow* ends with a vision of blood and spirit fused in radiant new being, *Women in Love* offers no such visionary transcendence of the historical and psychological. Interaction between civilized and "primitive" leads to no ideal synthesis but rather points to imminent disaster. Birkin and Ursula do find a way out that involves an equilibrium of upper and lower, mental and sensual centers. But it remains a way for them alone—not a solution for the dying culture from which they must extricate themselves.

Lawrence's view of history is vitalist and mystical[30]—the creative and destructive forces that well up from the unconscious group-soul are unknowable in their genesis. Man can only respond to or resist these forces by becoming aware of what is taking place in himself. Birkin's empathy with "primitive" blood-consciousness stimulates his understanding of cultural growth and decline. His response to African fetishes integrates "the deepest physical mind" with an otherwise alienated intellect and points to a mode of being beyond the pervasive entropy of his culture. The African/Nordic reflections in "Moony" are followed by the Greek/Egyptian, mind/senses allotropism of "Excurse," symbolizing the construction of a whole being from potentially entropic cultural opposites. That, however, remains an allotropic fantasy. Neither Birkin nor Lawrence is a "primitivist" in any simple sense; yet in *Women in Love*, "primitive art," seen empathetically and critically, plays a crucial role in an ongoing quest for vitalized being.

6

FUTURISM AND MECHANISM IN *WOMEN IN LOVE*

Futurism was the catalyst that enabled Lawrence to break through to a new style;[1] but, as the ferment of ideas in his letters shows, his response was an ambivalent mixture of attraction and repulsion. Delavenay points out that "the stress has been laid so far on the divergences," and he argues that "a closer study of the points of convergence [is now] possible" ("Lawrence and the Futurists" 140). In this chapter, I shall be concerned with Lawrence's divergence from, and denunciation of, the futurist ideology of the machine and his convergence with futurist form-language in expressing extreme states of being.

Futurism made an impact on Lawrence when he was living in Italy and exploring new means of expression in "The Sisters." On 2 June 1914, he wrote to Arthur McLeod:

> I have been interested in the futurists. . . . I read Marinetti's and Paolo Buzzi's manifestations and essays—and Sofficis essays on cubism and futurism. . . .
> The one thing about their art is that it *isn't* art, but ultra scientific attempts to make diagrams of certain physic or mental states. . . . [E]verything is appraised according to its mechanic value. . . . (*Letters* 2: 180–81)

Lawrence repudiates futurist "mechanism"—for him the future of art lies in cocreative relations between men and women—but he is interested in Marinetti's focus on the physical basis of phenomena.

Although specific references to futurism in *Women in Love* are negative, futurist art had a positive impact on Lawrence's style. Three days after announcing his interest in the futurists, he wrote a letter to Edward Garnett that is a key to understanding the changes in his art:

> I think the book is a bit futuristic—quite unconsciously so. But when I read Marinetti . . . I see something of what I am after. . . . [T]hat which is physic—

117

non-human, in humanity, is more interesting to me than the old-fashioned human element—which causes one to conceive a character in a certain moral scheme and make him consistent. (2: 182)

There follows a striking case of creative convergence. Lawrence, who translates the neologism *fisicologia* as "physiology," missing the hybrid sense of physiology/psychology (2: 182n3),[2] comes to see his own expressive means more clearly through Marinetti's "obfuscated" Italian. Out of the critique of Marinetti's supposed "physiology of matter" he forges his own theory of "allotropic states."

In the *Technical Manifesto of Futurist Literature*, Marinetti proclaims, "Destroy the 'I' in literature," and in a passage preceding the one that Lawrence translates, he proposes:

> To capture unawares, by means of freely moving objects and capricious motors, the respiration, the sensitivity and the instincts of metals, rocks, wood, etc. Substitute the psychology of man, now depleted, with the LYRICAL OBSESSION OF MATTER.
>
> Be careful not to lend human sentiments to matter, but deduce, instead, the different directive impulses, their power of compression, dilation, cohesion and dissolution, motion of the electrons. (Marinetti 18, qtd. in Carrieri 80)

Lawrence accuses the futurists of "only look[ing] for the phenomena of the science of physics to be found in human being" (*Letters* 2: 183). His own aim is to discover the Lost Atlantis of the unconscious. Thus he changes the focus from matter to life, while applying chemical and metallurgical metaphors to human phenomena of consciousness and sensation.

As part of his "struggle into conscious being," Lawrence wanted to articulate a fuller response to futurism. He ends the letter to McLeod by saying: "I want to write an essay about Futurism, when I have the inspiration and wit thereunto," and he adds a postscript to Garnett: "Please keep this letter, because I want to write on futurism and it will help me" (2: 182, 184). Instead of writing an essay, Lawrence worked out his creative response to futurism in *The Rainbow* and *Women in Love*.

On the strength of the letters, Lawrence seems to have been influenced mainly by futurist ideas and rhetoric rather than painting and sculpture. In "Study of Thomas Hardy," however, he shows a thorough knowledge of Umberto Boccioni's sculptural aesthetic, recasting it within the framework of his own sexual philosophy. Whereas for Lawrence man and woman must come closer together in the search for equilibrium, he sees the Italian as going over to

> the northern conception of himself and the woman as two separate identities. . . . So that the Futurist Boccioni now makes his sculpture "Development of a Bottle through Space", try to express the withdrawal, and at the same time he must adhere to the conception of this same interlocked state of marriage between centripetal and centrifugal forces, the geometric abstraction of the bottle. ("Study" 75)[3]

Lawrence sees the Latin race's clinging to Woman as centripetal, as opposed to the centrifugal movement of passionate male desire and action. Centering life on the man-woman relationship, he sees the futurist movement as an aggressive reaction against dependence on Woman that bogs down in a failed dialectic:

> So that when I look at Boccioni's sculpture, and see him trying to state the timeless, abstract being of a bottle, the pure geometric abstraction of the bottle, I am fascinated. But then, when I see him driven by his desire for the male complement into portraying motion, simple motion, trying to give expression to the bottle in terms of mechanics, I am confused. (75)

Lawrence here zeroes in on the conflict between cubist abstraction (stasis) and futurist dynamism (kinesis) in Boccioni's art. For Lawrence, futurism, with its scientific materialism and purely "masculine" or abstract values, confuses art with science. He admired the organic structure of Cézanne's art that had inspired the geometric trend in cubism; he was also attracted to dynamism as a form of vitalism, but he rejected the cult of mechanism through which it was expressed. His insights into Boccioni's *Bottle* show that he had studied futurist form-language closely and curiously, even though he imposed his own symbolic interpretation on what he saw there.

Boccioni's "plastic dynamism," as in the drawing *Muscular Dynamism* (1913; see pl. 11), and his sculpting of muscular movement in *Unique Forms of Continuity in Space* (1913; Taylor 94, 95) are close to the verbal/plastic form-language of "Gladiatorial." The form-language of the wrestling scene has affinities with Boccioni's futurist aesthetic, which emphasizes "interpenetration of planes" and the role of individual limbs or bodies as "element[s] in the plastic rhythm of the whole" (Boccioni, qtd. in Apollonio 52, 63).

> [Birkin] seemed to *penetrate* into Gerald's more solid, more diffuse bulk, to *interfuse* his body through the body of the other. . . . It was as if Birkin's whole physical intelligence *interpenetrated* into Gerald's body. . . . Often, in the white, *interlaced knot* of violent living being that swayed silently, there was no head to be seen, only the swift, tight limbs, the solid white backs, the physical junction of two bodies clinched into oneness. (*Women in Love* 270 [my italics])

While Lawrence's symbolism includes homoerotic and metaphysical over-tones (the struggle into oneness or conjunction of opposites), the plastic values of movement in "Gladiatorial" are strikingly similar to those of futurist sculpture. The chapter title has sculptural connotations, and the "interlaced knot" of living, depersonalized being might be described as Lawrence's Laocoön. But the alternating "inter-" compounds, emphasizing impulses of fusion, penetration, linking, match the futurist device of interpenetrating planes. The physical imagery dramatizes submerging of identities and interpenetration of two beings within a moving mass; although the two are "clinched into oneness," affinities are neither with classical stasis nor "geometric abstraction" but with Boccioni's attempt to capture the fluidity of muscular dynamism in sculpture, and particularly with his goal of "physical transcendentalism," whereby "[the] physical seems to lift itself by its own strength into the realm of the spirit" (Taylor 93).

"Electricity for the futurists," says Carrieri, "was always an excellent and stimulating source of metaphors" (41), and so it became for Lawrence. The vorticists also drew heavily on electromagnetic imagery. Ezra Pound wrote in 1913: "We might come to believe that the thing that matters in art is a sort of energy, something more or less like electricity or radioactivity, a force transfusing, welding, and unifying" (qtd. in Perloff 173). The embrace of Gerald and Gudrun in "Death and Love" is a process of galvanization described in dehumanizing futurist imagery: "[She melts] into his limbs and bones, as if he were soft iron becoming surcharged with her electric life" (*Women in Love* 331). Here Lawrence focuses on the allotropic forces that invest characters with an impersonal dynamism as they relinquish themselves to sensation.

Electrical imagery combines with radioactivity in the negative tropisms of "Death and Love": "her soul was destroyed with the exquisite shock of his invisible fluid lightning. . . . How much more of him was there to know? Ah much, much, many days harvesting for her large, yet perfectly subtle and intelligent hands, upon the field of his living, radio-active body" (332). Although the harvesting metaphor is organic, the "inorganic principle" reas-

serts itself in the image of radioactivity and the process of transmuting living impulses into commodities of knowledge to be exploited for power. Like
Marinetti stressing "the phenomena of physics" in human being, Lawrence
gives full weight to the chemical analogy, with "radio-active" meaning "un-
dergoing spontaneous nuclear decay, involving the emission of radiation."[4]

It is ironic that Gerald, who has imported "iron men" and electrified the
machinery of the mines, should have his own body reduced to the functions
of a battery. Gudrun's manipulation of the range of sensations it affords is not
far removed from Marinetti's futurist vision of harnessing the sea for electrical power and of engineers, "[seated] at control panels . . . [with] the rich
gleam of polished levers . . . [feeling at] a brief pass of the hand . . . the fullness and solidity of their own will" (qtd. in Banham 125). With Gerald, as
with the futurists, it is all a question of transmission of energy ("where does
his *go* go to . . . ?") and, as Ursula rightly says, "It goes in applying the latest
appliances" (*Women in Love* 48). Just as Marinetti applauds "workmen who
have already undergone the education of the machine, and in some way are
affiliated to machinery" (qtd. in Banham 123), so Gerald promotes mechanization. But, as he devotes his energies to modernizing the mines, his own
impulses become mechanized and he is left feeling drained and hollow.

In the "Foreword to *Women in Love*," Lawrence observes that "the bitterness of the war may be taken for granted in the characters" (485). The futurists, on the contrary, glorified war and regarded it as "hygienic," even
aesthetic. Marinetti proclaimed: "War is beautiful because it initiates the
dreamt-of metalization of the human body." Carlo Carrà added: "The war is
creating in man a really new love for machinism and metallism, which inspire an entire new art in formation . . . " (qtd. in Carrieri 165). Mechanolatry and idolatry of industry tend in the same direction. Walter Benjamin,
quoting a lyrical celebration of military mayhem by Marinetti, observes: "All
efforts to render politics aesthetic culminate in one thing: war" (241). The
cult of the machine continued after the war, when Fernand Léger exclaimed:
"I love the forms imposed by modern industry. . . . Steel has a thousand col-
ourful reflections which are both more subtle and more solid than any of the
so-called classical subjects" (qtd. in Carrieri 156). And the American artist Joseph Stella wrote: "Two elements—steel and electricity—are capable of
transforming the physiognomy of the world. . . . [Painting] will use as its key
a language which will have the precise ductility of steel and the radiance of
electricity" (147).

In describing the tense battle of wills between Gudrun and Gerald, Lawrence uses metallic imagery with a dehumanizing futurist intensity:

> The passion came up in him, stroke after stroke, like the ringing of a bronze bell. . . . His knees tightened to bronze. . . . He felt strong as winter, his hands were living metal, invincible and not to be turned aside. . . . She moved convulsively, recoiling away from him. His heart went up like a flame of ice, he closed over her like steel. He would destroy her rather than be denied. (*Women in Love* 401–2)

Kinesthetic sensations are expressed in metallurgical images and reciprocal movements of sexually aroused bodies as a play of forces involving inertia and propulsion, attraction and recoil. Electromagnetic imagery emphasizes the destructive effect of two wills locked in combat, leaving no room for spontaneous impulse: "A fierce, electric energy seemed to flow over all his limbs, his muscles were surcharged. . . . He and she were separate, like opposite poles of one fierce energy" (399). This frictional separation recapitulates the concept of "separate identities" that Lawrence projected into Boccioni's sculpture.

Futurist dynamism—the cult of speed (*la velocità*) and momentum—is a feature of Loerke's art as it is of Gerald's alpine sports. On the toboggan,

> [Gudrun] felt as if her senses were being whetted on some fine grindstone, that was keen as flame. The snow sprinted on either side, like sparks from a blade that is being sharpened, the whiteness round about ran swifter, swifter, in pure flame the white slope flew against her, and she fused like one molten, dancing globule, rushed through a white intensity. Then there was a great swerve at the bottom, when they swung as it were in a fall to earth, in the diminishing motion. (420)

The frenetic motion, where sensation reaches a pitch of mindless abstraction, points forward to the correlative "frenzy of chaotic motion" in Loerke's frieze. Marinetti had proclaimed the ecstatic sense of flight in a poem that Lawrence must have read:

> Between my hands, the steel, with blazing crash
> lacerates the light, and the cerebral
> fever of my propellor
> makes its roar blossom in the air.

>   (qtd. in Carrieri 34; my trans.)

It was Marinetti, of course, who exclaimed in his manifesto that "[a] racing car whose hood is adorned with great pipes, like serpents of explosive breath—a roaring car that seems to ride on grapeshot—is more beautiful than the *Victory of Samothrace*." He wanted "[to] sing of the vibrant nightly fervour of arsenals and shipyards blazing with violent electric moons . . . bridges that stride the rivers like giant gymnasts, flashing in the sun with a glitter of knives . . . deep-chested locomotives whose wheels paw the tracks like the hooves of enormous steel horses bridled by tubing . . . " (qtd. in Apollonio 22).

The "flying sledge" becomes a weaponlike extension of Gerald's body, "his strength spread out," as it responds to his own perfect instrumentality. Mindless momentum materializes the spirit, rather than etherealizing the senses. Earlier, the "demon-like" rabbit, "spread on the air as if it were flying," became the symbolic embodiment of Gerald's own mechanized impulses, "lunging wildly . . . like a spring coiled and released . . . " (*Women in Love* 240). For the expressionist/futurist Franz Marc, animal impulses had a spontaneous grace lacking in human movements. But for Boccioni, "[the] opening and closing of a valve creates a rhythm which is equally beautiful but infinitely newer than that of an animalistic palpitation" (qtd. in Carrieri 74). Lawrence fuses animal and mechanical in "Rabbit," to highlight the mechanization of impulses that occurs when the delicate balance between will and senses breaks down. Sledge and rabbit, like the Arab mare, respond to Gerald's machinelike willpower in controlled or convulsive motions. Gerald finds an illusory satisfaction in the vibrational contraction and expansion of his own will. The image may be that of a steel spring coiled and released or of an electrical discharge. With the bohemian slave girl, Minette, he finds "[the] electricity [is] turgid and voluptuously rich, in his limbs. He would be able to destroy her utterly in the strength of the discharge" (*Women in Love* 65). This sense of destructive power shows a dangerous confusion of eros with mecha-thanatos. Gerald is easily assimilated with Boccioni's "great mechanised individuals" as with the electrical drilling machines he imports from America.

Boccioni rejects primitive art as the premechanical stutterings of savages; but Renato Poggioli analyzes a paradoxical dialectics of progression and retrogression within the European avant-garde that simultaneously comprises primitivism and futurism. Gerald encounters both primitive sculptures and futurist paintings in Halliday's bohemian flat—the fetishization of sensuality in the African icon has its counterpart in the mechanization of impulses in futurist art. Ambivalent impulses to leap forward and fall back appear in Gudrun's doublethink notion of *reculer pour mieux sauter* and are metaphysically articulated in Birkin's dual concepts of "the stream of synthetic creation" and its "inverse process, the flood of destructive creation" (172).

Gerald's alpine sports exemplify futurist cults of danger, speed, and physical exertion that ultimately obliterate identity. Such mindless cults can be linked both with primitivism and with the agonism and nihilism of the avant-garde (Poggioli 61–68), suggesting parallels between Gerald's athletic exertions and Loerke's art of mechanical motion:

> The first days passed in *an ecstasy of physical motion*, sleighing, ski-ing, skating, *moving in an intensity of speed and white light that surpassed life itself*, and carried the souls of the human beings beyond into *an inhuman abstraction of velocity and weight* and eternal, frozen snow.
>
> Gerald's eyes became hard and strange, and as he went by on his skis he was more like some powerful, fateful sigh than a man, *his muscles elastic in a perfect, soaring trajectory, his body projected in pure flight*, mindless, soulless, *whirling along one perfect line of force*. (*Women in Love* 421 [my italics])

The abstraction, rigidity, muscularity, and linearity of the alpinist are essentially futurist. In a culmination of the Nordic motif, Gerald's being "materializes"; his impulses, ruled by an iron will, become mechanical. His physical propulsion—more that of a projectile than a human being—approaches "the sheer movement of substance in its own paths, free from all human postulation or control," that Lawrence finds in Melville and the futurists (*Symbolic Meaning* 237). The concept of *lines of force* (*linee forze*) is central to the futurist aesthetic. As Boccioni declared in his *Technical Manifesto of Futurist Sculpture*, "Our straight line will be alive and palpitating; it will lend itself to all the necessities of the infinite expressions of the material, and its fundamental, naked severity will be the iron-severe symbol of the lines of modern machinery" (qtd. in Carrieri 74). Gerald's alpine sports relate to his role as Industrial Magnate; the aggressive vigor of the Nietzschean Superman, exalted by the futurists, is the outward expression of a destructive will-to-power.

Futurist/vorticist mechanism becomes an explicit theme in the discussion of Loerke's factory frieze. The design of the frieze, representing mechanical swings and roundabouts, offers "a frenzy of chaotic motion"—unlike the frozen motion of its vorticist source, Mark Gertler's *The Merry-Go-*

Round.[5] Gertler's painting, of which Lawrence had seen only a photograph, is now in the Tate Gallery. It presents a blend of naive or folk art with the geometrical forms of vorticism. As Quentin Bell observes: "Everything is held, as though within some whirling, metallic labyrinth, by a system of ellipses and verticals"; Frances Spalding comments on the painting's "extreme fixity; one part is locked into the next . . . " (qtd. in *Mark Gertler* 11, 5). Against the disruptive frenzy of the futurists, "the Vorticists set up the neoclassical ideal of a rigorously selective [order]" (Cianci 48). The streamlined stasis of Gertler's *Merry-Go-Round* reflects the vorticist aesthetic of Wyndham Lewis and Pound, for, as Lewis wrote in *Blast* (20 June 1914), "[T]he Vorticist is at his maximum point of energy when stillest" (qtd. in Cianci 50). While Gertler's painting reduces mechanical motion to ritualized automatism, Loerke's frieze intensifies the image of chaotic activity.[6]

The frieze follows futurist aesthetic principles in that centrifugal motion accompanies interpenetration of planes. Ardengo Soffici explains that "futurist plastic dynamism consists in movement . . . of volumes and planes intersecting each other in vital synthetic concurrence" (66; my trans.). Less abstractly, Boccioni claims "a mechanical wheel can emerge from the armpit of a mechanic. . . . [The] sidewalk can climb up onto our table and your head can cross the street . . . " (qtd. in Carrieri 73). Futurists dramatize the constant motion and agitation of big city life by obliterating the integrity of objects whose force-forms are made to intermingle in an undefined spatial field. This promiscuous confusion of objects and planes is antithetical to the "austere 'nordic' severity" of the vorticists (*Cianci* 48), with their imposition of mechanical order.

It was the forward-thrusting energy of futurism that attracted Lawrence. Boccioni, for instance, in his painting *The City Rises* (1910–11), was stimulated by the energies of a construction site and " '[tried] for a great synthesis of labor, light, and movement' " (Taylor, *Futurism* 35, illustration 37). Loerke, like the futurists, glorifies "machinery and the acts of labour" as "extremely, maddeningly beautiful" (*Women in Love* 424). He revels in "the opportunity to make beautiful factories, beautiful machine-houses" to replace the temples of religion, now considered *passatista* by the futurists. Marinetti, in his *Manifesto of Geometrical and Mechanical Splendour* (1914), proclaims: "Nothing is more beautiful than a great humming central electric station . . . " (qtd. in Apollonio 155). Loerke's statement, "Art should *interpret* industry, as art once interpreted religion," echoes futurist doctrine. In *Manifesto of the Futurist Painters* (1910), Boccioni declares:

> As our ancestors drew the material of their art from the religious atmosphere
> that was incumbent on their souls, so we must be inspired by the tangible
> miracles of contemporary life, by the iron net of velocity which envelops the
> earth . . . by the marvelous flights which furrow the sky, by the dark daring of
> underwater navigators and by the anguished struggle for the conquest of the
> unknown. And can we remain insensitive to the frenzied activity of the great
> capital cities . . . ? (qtd. in Carrieri 28)

Mechanized amusements and crowd scenes attracted the futurists, as
they do Loerke, because they could abstract from them depersonalized
rhythms of city life. The worker subjected to "the stern rhythm of the work-
shop" (Boccioni, *Futurist Painting and Sculpture*, 1914) does not want the
sense of isolated individuality in his off hours. He can escape from the onus
of alienation only by mingling with crowds at mind-numbing spectacles
such as circuses or fairs. As Marinetti noted, "[the] Variety Theater is absolutely practical, because it proposes to distract and amuse the public with
comic effects, erotic stimulation, or imaginative astonishment" (qtd. in Perloff
96). Loerke is equally pragmatic on the use of mass entertainment to distract
factory workers, while reinforcing and internalizing the mechanical rhythms
that bind them to their work. If he cannot escape from the machine, the
worker must escape from himself by submitting to it and eroticizing its
rhythms: "What is man doing, when he is at a fair like this? He is fulfilling
the counterpart of labour—the machine works him, instead of he the machine. He enjoys the mechanical motion, in his own body" (*Women in Love*
424). The mechanization of impulses leaves no gap between human and mechanical, no space for spontaneity.[7] This is the consummation of alienation—
the machine is no longer an external entity but becomes a pervasive, internalized principle. Ursula reflects: "No flowers grow upon busy machinery,
there is no sky to a routine, there is no space to a rotary motion. And all life
was a rotary motion, mechanised, cut off from reality" (193).

Loerke propounds the futurist ideology of the machine and its supremacy
over human life:

> "But is there nothing but work—mechanical work?" said Gudrun.
> "Nothing but work!" he repeated. . . . "No, it is nothing but this, serving a
> machine, or enjoying the motion of a machine—motion, that is all." (424–25)

The avant-garde artist and the Industrial Magnate are in odd complicity here.
Gerald's father, a nineteenth-century capitalist/philanthropist, had tried un-
successfully to link religion and "the Godhead of the great productive ma-

chine" (225). Gerald's futurist hubris is to identify with the mechanical principle and *become* "the God of the Machine":

> It was this inhuman principle in the mechanism . . . that inspired Gerald with
> an almost religious exaltation. . . . And this is the God-motion, this produc-
> tive repetition ad infinitum. . . . He had to begin with the mines. . . . It would
> need a marvellous adjustment of myriad instruments, human, animal, metal-
> lic, kinetic, dynamic, a marvellous casting of myriad tiny wholes in to one
> great perfect entirety. (228)[8]

Exaltation of the machine, along with the will to impose unity on multiplicity, are life-denying: the inorganic principle replaces harmony in industry or
art. The Industrial Magnate resembles the futurist artist in mechanolatry—
although the industrialist's organizing principle is coercively centripetal, like
that of the Vortex, whereas the futurist's "form/force" is "centrifugal," according to Boccioni.[9] The difference is only partial, however; Marinetti's
metaphor of "crystalliz[ing] . . . a new concept of the infinite" in "plastic
form" (Clough 136) is just as centripetal as Gerald's "casting of myriad tiny
wholes in to one great perfect entirety"—a rational, reductive ordering of a
complex material network that resembles the streamlined vorticist aesthetic.
For the futurists, mechanolatry supersedes human culture. Marinetti
claims that "[modern man] should be in love with the machine," which
embodies "the concepts of strength, velocity, light, will, discipline, method,
and synthesis"—a group of Apollonian/Nordic qualities contrasted with
Dionysian/African values in Lawrence's dialectic. Marinetti goes so far as
to proclaim that "[the] esthetic interpretation of the machine is [the futurist's] only salvation." For him, "[the] machine is the symbol of the 'mysterious force' of the infinite—it is the symbol of life" (Clough 164, 136). One
can imagine how such an apotheosis of the machine would grate upon
Lawrence's "passionately religious" sensibility.
In his *Manifesto dell'Estetica della Macchina*, Enrico Prampolini later compounds the confusion of mechanical with vital:

> Our age, he wrote, differs from previous ages in that it is inspired by a new
> beauty: that of the machine. Fast trucks, glittering steel rods and pistons, bil-
> lowing smoke-stacks, noisy automobile horns, panting locomotives, express
> the new spiritual necessities and form the basis of a new art. The machine no
> longer has a merely functional value; it rises to the spiritual realm of art and
> becomes the 'illustrious and prolific inspirer.' . . . Man is so bound up with the
> engine . . . that he, too, has become mechanized. (Clough 136)

Loerke consciously celebrates this inverted tendency toward "mechanical pantheism in which the machine acquires a soul and the mind becomes a motor" (Clough 136).

The inorganic metaphor of crystallization relates to the splintering, angular lines of force in futurist painting—what Boccioni describes as "the poetry of the straight line and the mathematical calculation—[in which] everything becomes rectangular, square, pentagonal, etc." (qtd. in Carrieri 25). Crystallization also appears in Gudrun's aesthetic visions: she "settle[s] down like a crystal in the navel of snow, and [is] gone" and later becomes "a pure, thoughtless crystal" (*Women in Love* 401, 420). Gerald, in the intensity of his sexual obsession, experiences a similar crystallization: "His brain seemed hard and invincible now like a jewel . . . " (444). But the apex of the motif is Gudrun's vision of the mountains, "glistening like transcendent, radiant spikes of blossom" (403)—a crystalline image that highlights the triumph of the inorganic principle in aesthetic and visionary spheres.

Dynamism, velocity, propulsion are the demiurgic forces of futurism. As machine rhythms come to pervade modern life, so the image of muscular movement tends to become mechanical, especially when fixed in the sculptural block, while mechanical rhythms invite muscular metaphors, as in Marinetti's "deep-chested locomotives." Animating energies are displaced from the human soul or unconscious, with its spontaneous impulses, to "the Godhead of the machine," that icon of dehumanized power. The vorticist notion of dissolution through production that Birkin articulates in "Water-Party" is implicit in the willingness of alienated factory workers or miners to become cogs in an endlessly spinning mechanism. Loerke's frieze, like Gertler's *Merry-Go-Round*, reveals the insidious power of the machine to dominate life and leisure.

Gudrun, after teaming up with Loerke, finds herself enslaved to the machine of her own consciousness, her fate analogous to Gerald's in "The Industrial Magnate." Despite her illusions about the pleasures and freedoms of bohemian life in Dresden, she is crushed by a horrific vision of mechanized humanity that reflects not only her knowledge of Gerald but also the gradual mechanization of her own consciousness: "the wheels within wheels of people—it makes one's head tick like a clock, with a very madness of dead mechanical monotony and meaninglessness" (464). She has come a long way from "Sketch-Book," where she had a "sensuous vision" (119) of organic forms (including Gerald's physique) to this dead reckoning of being and time as a "mechanical succession of day[s]" (464). The insistent repetitions and forced rhythms of her consciousness reflect the negative side of futurist mechanolatry that superimposes machines on life. Gudrun no longer *generates* (or regenerates) her consciousness by spontaneous acts. She is cut off from the source that Birkin and Ursula are in touch with, relegated to the position of a spectator (like the schizophrenic Hermione who watches her own acts): "She was watching the fingers twitch across the eternal, mechanical, monotonous clock-face of time. She never really lived, she only watched" (465). The chaotic state of her mechanically driven consciousness is prophetically foreshadowed by that of the miners who have sacrificed their freedom to the machine: "It was . . . the first great phase of chaos, the substitution of the mechanical principle for the organic, the destruction of the organic purpose, the organic unity. . . . It was pure organic disintegration and pure mechanical organisation" (231). Trying to know spontaneous life and overcome it by a mechanical use of the will (in art and love), Gudrun has placed herself outside of organic life, as the futurists did. She has instrumentalized her own being, which makes her all the more critical of Gerald's cruder instrumentation/instrumentalism. She who had a sensuous, and at least partly intuitive, vision has become an intricate automaton. Her fate, in Lawrence's view, is that of a vital, organic art, reduced to futurist abstraction, mechanization, and alienation.

Loerke's fairground frieze, with its "frenzy of chaotic motion," is the very image of Gudrun's machine-driven consciousness, where inorganic order is streamlined chaos. Loerke himself seems to share many of the futurists' propensities, although "[he is] not satisfied with the Futurists" (448).[10] Max Kozloff observes that the futurists' "protean theatrical behavior and shifting masquerades concealed great inner alienation" (125). Loerke's attitudes are symbolic of his own disintegrated, unbalanced nature. His struttings, gesticulations, and bombastic proclamations remind one of the "manic, burlesque character" of early futurism (219), with its theatricality and rites of provocation.[11] Brought up in a slum as Gertler was in a ghetto, Loerke has rejected all ideals, especially those of love: "L'amour, l'amore, die Liebe—I detest it in every language. Women and love, there is no greater tedium . . . " (*Women in Love* 458). There is a subtle link here between Loerke and Birkin, who repudiates love in "An Island" and, at the beginning of a chapter entitled "Man to Man," curses the need for sexual union with Woman. A similar downgrading of love and women was a feature of futurist polemics. "'I wish to conquer the tyranny of love,'" declares Marinetti's hero in *Mafarka il futurista* (qtd. in Martin 84).

Ortega y Gasset asks: "Why is it that the round and soft forms of living bodies are repulsive to the present-day artist? . . . Why this desire to dehumanize?" (38–39). And Poggioli comments: "[W]hat we have to see is whether the 'recoiling from the forms of life and living beings' [Ortega] is related only to geometric abstraction, to the mathematical figures of cubism and its derivatives, or to the plastic dynamism and machine aesthetic of the futurists as well" (176). Like the futurists, who despised the rounded contours of the female nude, the homosexual or bisexual Loerke prefers the immature, "bud"-like form of the girl on the massive stallion. As Poggioli points out, in relating futurism to agonism, "[d]egeneration and immaturity equally aspire to transcend the self . . . " (76). Loerke is an almost caricatural embodiment of such hybridity; "the wizard rat that swims ahead," guiding those who "want to explore the sewers" (*Women in Love* 428), is also the puny "little brat" or "mud child." This inner conjunction of discordant qualities goes along with a modernist disjunction of art from life and a concomitant nihilism. Loerke exclaims: "[T]hat is a Kunstwerk, a work of art. . . . [It] is a picture of nothing, of absolutely nothing. It has nothing to do with anything but itself, it has no relation with the everyday world. . . . I and my art, they have *nothing* to do with each other. My art stands in another world . . . " (430–31).

While the mythic Loki is the negative principle that seeks to undermine the gods, Loerke is the avant-garde demolitionist of humanist aesthetic values. His art grows from a "rock-bottom" of nihilism and is therefore a profound statement of the inorganic principle in modernism. Lawrence wrote to Gertler regarding *The Merry-Go-Round*: "But I *do* think that in this combination of blaze, and violent mechanical rotation and complex involution, and ghastly, utterly mindless human intensity of sensational extremity, you have made a real and ultimate revelation" (*Letters* 2: 660). The complicity of life and art with industry, and the consequent mechanization of impulses, signify for Lawrence a perversion of the life-force and ultimate annihilation of human values. His encounter with futurism and its celebration of mechanical energies led him to focus on this theme explicitly and prophetically in *Women in Love*.

7

VITALISM IN LAWRENCE AND VAN GOGH

While many of Lawrence's readers and several of his friends have sensed his affinity with Van Gogh, the present study is the first to consider, at more length, how that affinity is manifested in his work. Lawrence's writing and Van Gogh's painting share a preternatural intensity of vision and expression.[1] In this chapter, I want first to explore more fully the "imaginative context" in which Lawrence and Van Gogh invite comparison,[2] and then specific connections between their writing and painting. While techniques differ from one artistic medium to another, verbal and visual arts share aspects of perception and vision rooted in the unconscious ground of Being. Focusing on Lawrence's affinity with Van Gogh, therefore, highlights distinctions and resemblances of expression *and* of ontological vision.

Lady Ottoline Morrell noted a personal resemblance that went beyond physical appearance:

> [Lawrence's] mind [was] so vivid and flame-like, his whole being so active and alive. . . . His small, pale face was rather overshadowed by a mass of red hair and a short beard. I have sometimes thought that he had a strong resemblance to the portraits of Van Gogh, and, indeed, in many ways he resembled him in character, especially in the intensity of his imaginative insight into people and his power of seeing and even exaggerating the essence of what he saw. . . . (qtd. in Nehls 1: 271)

This power of seeing and articulating a vision with hallucinating clarity links Lawrence with Van Gogh. Lady Ottoline writes convincingly of Lawrence's vitalism, comparing his mind to a "red flame": the intensity of Lawrence's awareness and aliveness comes through in her portrait, interfaceted with the self-portraits of Van Gogh.[3] Catherine Carswell, like so many others, was struck by this vital quality in Lawrence: "[W]hen I first set eyes on him," she writes, "the immediately distinguishing thing was his swift and flamelike quality . . . " (qtd. in Nehls 1: 227).

Lawrence must have recognized his own affinity with Van Gogh. He tells Lady Ottoline, who had loaned him Van Gogh's *Letters*: "I am also doing a Van Gogh—one of those sketches in a letter, with colour directions—of a dock and raising bridge" (*Letters* 2: 303).[4] The sketch is of the Langlois bridge at Arles (see pl. 12), with the words "jaune," "lilas," "emeraude," "rose," "vert" written in as on a coloring model. Van Gogh describes the motif as "a little scratch of a study that engrosses me . . . sailors returning with their sweethearts to the town which profiles the strange silhouette of its drawbridge against an enormous yellow sun" (*Complete Letters* 3: 477). Switching to Lawrence's fictional counterpart, we find Birkin telling Hermione that "One gets more of China, copying this [drawing of geese], than reading all the books" (*Women in Love* 89). When she presses him, he explains: "I know what centres they [the artists] live from—what they perceive and feel. . . . " The homology is clear: copying Van Gogh's drawing is no idle exercise for Lawrence; in empathizing with the hand and eye that drew the bridge, he aims to penetrate Van Gogh's creative being, testing his affinities with the painter.[5]

In Van Gogh's vital vision, eye, mind, and hand are instinctively one: "In the immemorial depth of the visible, something moved, caught fire, and engulfed his body; everything he paints is in answer to this incitement. . . . Vision encounters, as at a cross-roads, all the aspects of Being" (Merleau-Ponty, "Eye and Mind" 188). For Lawrence, however, optical vision is incomplete, because the eye too readily turns perception into "mental consciousness," passing over the deeper, instinctual flow of "blood-consciousness" (*Letters* 2: 470). "Real thought," writes Lawrence, "is an experience. It begins as a change in the blood, a slow convulsion and revolution in the body itself. It ends as a new piece of awareness, a new reality in mental consciousness" ("Making Pictures" 616). According to him, Cézanne "wished to displace our present mode of mental-visual consciousness . . . and substitute a mode of consciousness that was predominantly intuitive, the awareness of touch" ("Introduction to These Paintings" 578). Merleau-Ponty sees the approach to Cézanne's art through "touch" as a reductive solecism; yet his phenomenology of perception, applied to painting, bears close resemblance to Lawrence's creative thinking.

The extraordinary vitality of their art led to a mysterious conjunction of

Van Gogh and Lawrence in the mind of the poet H.D. She combines, transposes, imbricates images of "old shoes, a rush-bottomed chair and a Devonshire pottery jug filled with sunflowers" with "that cypress-tree twisted in a whirlwind, the field at the second turning before Zennor, and the self-portrait" (166–67)—in Van Gogh's painting or in Lawrence's writing. For the poet H.D., the world springs into being through a dual vision simultaneously refracted through images of the painter and the writer. Seeing the interior of a room, a branch against the sky, a green wheat field, she says: "I can see it through your eyes, through Vincent's" (181), as if the creative energy of Lawrence and Van Gogh formed a single "tremulation" uniting their vision with hers. H.D. adds: "And you [Lawrence] see things as Vincent saw them, that upturned pot or basket of pansies and those old shoes. He would draw that magnetism up out of the earth, he did draw it. His wheat stalks are quivering with more than the wind that bends them" (183). Both artists had a genius for empathy, an urge to express "the life-thrust," as Lawrence puts it. H.D., feeling "the flame and the fire, the burning, the believing," was inspired to identify Lawrence's genius with Van Gogh's: "I would goad you on to writing, writing as Vincent painted" (52, 182). Vital vision calls on depths of being where separate identities dissolve. Such visionary expression embraces things of the world, so that "[s]ome particular entity"—be it sunflowers or gnarled peasant hands—"comes . . . to stand in the light of its being" (Heidegger, "Origin" 36)—and in the light of the artist's being.

For Van Gogh, "the great thing after all is to express oneself strongly." He saw "*colour* seeking *life*"[6] (*Complete Letters* 3: 508; 2: 513) and the objects in his still lifes "as mystic symbols of obscure vital instincts" (Nordenfalk 84). In Arles he aimed at "intensity, a firm, clear, advancing image exalted by daring colour . . . a kind of vitalism, an art of unbounded joy in life" (Schapiro, *Van Gogh* 13). Matching this vitalism, Lawrence proclaims: "We ought to dance with rapture that we should be alive and in the flesh, and part of the living, incarnate cosmos" (*Apocalypse* 149). In *The Escaped Cock*, "the natural world, thronging with greenness," has a vital sensory impact by contrast with the twilight zone of death-in-life: "Leaping out of greenness, came the black-and-orange cock with the red comb, his tail-feathers streaming lustrous. . . . So the green jets of leaves unspread on the fig-tree, with the bright, translucent green blood of the tree" (17, 30). The reclaimed phenomenal world has a color, glamour, and force lacking in the world of shadowy ideals:

> The man who had died looked nakedly on life, and saw a vast resoluteness ev-
> erywhere flinging itself up in stormy or subtle wave-crests, foam-tips emerging
> out of the blue invisible, a black and orange cock or the green flame-tongues
> out of the extremes of the fig-tree. . . . They came like crests of foam, out of the
> blue flood of the invisible desire, out of the vast invisible sea of strength, and
> they came coloured and tangible. . . . (21)

Van Gogh's senses, too, awaken to the "circumambient universe"; he paints
the surging sea of life and embodies his imagination in solid forms, "har-
monis[ing] brutal extremes" with "intense colour" (*Complete Letters* 2: 513).
This substantiality, made vibrant by thickened texture and contrasting tones,
is the quality Lawrence admired in Cézanne and Van Gogh, in contrast with
the floating light of the impressionists.

The vital art of Van Gogh and Lawrence does not aspire to "luminous
silent stasis" (with Joyce) nor "continual extinction of the personality" (with
Eliot). For Van Gogh and Lawrence, "the man who suffers and the mind
which creates" are *not* "completely separate"; on the contrary, there is an expressive, disturbing, challenging unity between life and art that springs from
ontological grounds. As Heidegger writes, "[p]rojection always pertains to
the full disclosedness of Being-in-the-world. . . . Understanding is either
authentic, arising out of one's own Self as such, or inauthentic. . . . The
world belongs to Being-one's-Self as Being-in-the-world" (*Being and Time*
186). If the art of Joyce and Eliot stills and cools sensation in contemplation,
the art of Van Gogh and Lawrence stirs the "pulsing frictional to-and-fro" of
a heightened sensory response. "Kinetic emotions" are not "refined out of
existence," as with Joyce's Stephen Dedalus, but "remain *within*" the work,
distorting it with the "flow" and "recoil" of "sympathetic consciousness."[7]
Lawrence, while writing *Lady Chatterley's Lover*, realized that erotic, creative, and vitalist responses are closely related. Van Gogh, with shocking di-
rectness, links aesthetic apprehension ("the enjoyment of a beautiful thing")
with coitus—both present "a moment of infinity" (*Complete Letters* 3: 503)
or what Lawrence calls "[the] source, the issue, the creative quick" ("Poetry
of the Present" 183). For Van Gogh, Christ's parables of the sower, the harvest, the fig tree "make us see the art of creating life, the art of being immor-
tal and alive at the same time. They are connected with painting" (*Complete
Letters* 3: 496). A painting by Van Gogh or a novel by Lawrence is not a
modernist heterocosm but the animated record of a passionate encounter of
self with world.

The insights of a handful of critics suggest an affinity between the visual expression of Van Gogh and the "art speech" of Lawrence. Some of these insights take negative form. In a formalist attack, R. P. Blackmur declares: "Lawrence the poet was no more hysterical in his expressive mode than the painter Van Gogh. But where Van Gogh developed enough art to control his expression objectively, and so left us great paintings, Lawrence developed as little art as possible, and left us the ruins of great intentions . . . " (267). Blackmur's strictures ironically match Lawrence's on Van Gogh, for each bases his case on the "fallacy" of self-expression. Emile Delavenay, discussing Lawrence's revision of "Christs in the Tirol" (1912) for *Twilight in Italy* (1916), deplores "the determination to achieve expressionism at all costs, the swamping of reality by interpretation, the distortion of the object of observation in an attempt to wring out meaning," and adds: "Lawrence was not altogether immune from the influence of Van Gogh, from a tendency to paranoiac distortion of objects. . . . But *creation* added to *statement* is more revealing of the sufferings and torments of the poet than of the innate nature of the object . . . " (*D. H. Lawrence* 343). While Delavenay's bias in favor of representational realism is clear, he recognizes expressionist qualities that link Lawrence with Van Gogh. In praising the teachable humanism of *Sons and Lovers*, Delavenay finds that novel "almost exempt from the distortions and exaggerations . . . in some of the later novels, from those Van Gogh-like effects one comes across, in *Women in Love* for example" ("Lawrence's Major Work" 142). Harry T. Moore finds a lyrical expressionism in Lawrence's treatment of void space toward the end of *Sons and Lovers*, comparing that scene with Van Gogh's *The Starry Night* ("The Prose" 249). R. E. Pritchard, however, states the affinity most clearly: "Van Gogh, in particular," he writes, "seems very like [Lawrence], in the early sympathetic portrayals of the industrial proletariat, the passionate identification with Christ, and the visionary intensity of the gaze directed upon the symbols of fierce (phallic) energy, the flame-like cypresses and blinding sun" (15).[8]

Lawrence and Van Gogh were exposed to mining at formative stages—Lawrence in childhood, Van Gogh on the verge of turning from religion to art—and for both the mines occupied a deep substratum in their imagination, subject to endless transformations.[9] A series of stylistic oscillations in Lawrence's use of the motif may be compared with similar effects in Van Gogh's writing and drawing. Images of collieries—pit-bank, headstocks, railway lines, trucks—are scattered throughout Lawrence's work. The mining countryside becomes a psychological and aesthetic phenomenon, as well as a social reality.

The realistic mode of perception in *Sons and Lovers* grasps contingent facts of the socioindustrial environment and provides a mimetic basis for later stylistic variations. In combination with realism, Lawrence employs geometric abstraction. The dehumanizing rigidity of industrialization appears at the start in a graphic, or cartographic, abstraction—"six mines like black studs on the countryside, linked by a loop of fine chain, the railway"— extended to a mathematical image of houses in "two rows of three, like the dots on a blank-six domino" (10). Such abstraction, which goes beyond the minimalist precision of Van Gogh's drawing, is the formal image of dehumanization, substituting number and line for the random detail of life. This thematic equation becomes explicit in *The Rainbow*, where "activity [is] mechanical yet inchoate," the great colliery "mathematical," and the mining town a "hideous abstraction" (321).

Whereas abstraction is reductive in its elimination of details, impressionism transforms reality by blurring outlines, as in darkness or snow. Lawrence at times transforms the image of the ugly mining countryside through atmospheric effects or post-impressionist contrasts of light and dark with strong spatial values. As Durant, in "Daughters of the Vicar," emerges from the darkness of the mine,

> [the] upper world came almost with a flash, because of the glimmer of snow. . . . The hills on either hand were pale blue in the dusk, and the hedges looked savage and dark. The snow was trampled between the railway lines, but far ahead, beyond the black figures of miners moving home, it became smooth again. . . . Below, the lights of the pit came out crisp and yellow among the darkness of the buildings, and the lights of Old Aldecross twinkled in rows down the bluish twilight. (69)

The hollowing out of space and play of complementaries recall Van Gogh's sketches or Cézanne's early snowscapes, such as *L'Estaque, Melting Snow* (1870–71).[10] After studying drawings by Dürer, Vincent wrote to Theo: "[It] was an intriguing sight to see the miners going home in the white snow in the evening at twilight. . . . [T]he light shines kindly through the small-paned [cottage] windows" (*Complete Letters* 1: 183). Lawrence describes nightfall over the coalfields in similar impressionist terms, with "the miners troop[ing] home, small, black figures trailing slowly in gangs across the white field. Then the night [coming] up in dark blue vapor from the snow" (*Sons and Lovers* 92). Distant mines are signaled by "a few yellow lamps . . . and the red smear of the burning pit-bank on the night" ("Odour of Chrysanthemums" 188).

"Japanese" stylization involves a radical restructuring that is the counterpart of abstraction. Heightening of formal outlines signals a search for structure amid amorphousness; raw shapes, purged of detail, become signs. An urgent desire for order and meaning, that paradoxically foregrounds their absence, is inscribed on the industrial landscape. Van Gogh defines art as "'*l'homme ajouté à la nature*' . . . nature, reality, truth, but with a significance, a conception, a character, which the artist brings out in it, and to which he gives expression . . . " (*Complete Letters* 1: 189 [my italics]). In grasping the subjective significance of a scene, his eye and pen eliminate some details and heighten others as in a Japanese print. He sees hedges in the snow "like black characters on white paper" (*Complete Letters* 1: 183) and, if he piously compares fields to "pages of the Gospel," the aesthetic impression retains a vitality of its own. "Japanese" stylization throws outlines into relief, making shapes stand out like stark ideograms on a black background.

In Lawrence's fiction, the mode of vision can create a gap between subject and object so that a scene seems cut off and curiously externalized. There is a "Japanese" precision of design in such scenes that increases the sense of alienation. A few examples will illustrate: "At Bretty pit the white steam melted slowly in the sunshine of a soft blue sky, the wheels of the headstocks twinkled high up, the screen, shuffling its coal into the trucks, made a busy noise" (*Sons and Lovers* 166). The spellbound detachment comes from Paul's realization of his brother's death, and the visual symmetry and bright animation are all the more clear-cut by contrast. "Japanese" artifice combined with automatic movement creates some oddly heraldic effects: "In the valley that was black with trees, the colliery breathed in stertorous pants, sending out high conical columns of steam that remained upright, whiter than the snow on the hills, yet shadowy, in the dead air" ("Daughters" 63). The emblematic flatness points to a mechanized mystery imposed on nature.

Most peculiar is an aesthetic of ugliness that inverts plain realism. Although Lawrence carries on Carlyle's and Ruskin's crusade against industrial squalor, he also glamorizes it on occasion, giving the blackened underworld a sinister seductiveness. Nowhere is this curious aesthetic more potent than in the "Coal-Dust" chapter of *Women in Love*, where "[the] heavy gold glamour of approaching sunset lay over all the colliery district, and the ugliness overlaid with beauty was like a narcotic to the senses" (115). The strangeness, distortion, "unnatural stillness," and "abstraction" Gudrun senses in the miners are the formal qualities she substitutes for life-values in her art. Lawrence also applies his negative aesthetic to the urban sprawl that "plasters" the landscape. In one panoramic view, "smoke waved against steam, and patch after patch of raw reddish brick showed the newer mining settlements, sometimes in the hollows, sometimes gruesomely ugly along the skyline of the slopes" (*Lady Chatterley's Lover* 156). Lawrence reveals this layer of blight all the more starkly by manipulating perspective and thus strives to wring from "amorphous squalor" the essence of industrialism that threatens to engulf Old England.

Finally, Van Gogh and Lawrence, having explored a panoply of perceptual possibilities, transform reality into mythic vision. In one of his panoramic verbal canvases, Van Gogh describes a thunderstorm over the coal mines, modulating from realism through impressionism to an apocalyptic symbolism close to that of *The Rainbow*:

> Quite near our house there is a spot from which one can see, far below, a large part of the Borinage, with the chimneys, the mounds of coal, the little miners' cottages, the scurrying little black figures by day, like ants in a nest. . . . Generally there is a kind of haze hanging over it all, or a fantastic chiaroscuro effect formed by the shadows of the clouds. . . . But during that thunderstorm in the pitch-dark night the flashes of lightning made a curious effect: now and then everything became visible for a moment. Near by the large, gloomy buildings of the Marcasse mine stood alone, isolated in the open field, that night conjuring up the huge bulk of Noah's Ark as it must have looked in the terrible pouring rain and the darkness of the Flood, illuminated by a flash of lightning. (*Complete Letters* 1: 188–89)

The mythic image reminds one that Van Gogh's religious impulses came to him through the senses, manifested in emotional responses to human or natural phenomena. His apocalyptic image of the Flood is matched by Lawrence's prophetic vision of Fire in the industrial Midlands (*Letters* 3: 302).

In Van Gogh's letters, writing and sketching flow together in a "stream that consists of two undulations." In his letters from Arles, says Hammacher, "an amazing lucidity and intensity of living" momentarily coheres into "a primitive vital force" animating the "auditory, oral and visual" expression ("Van Gogh and the Words" 36, 37). This fusion of visual and verbal is also a feature of Lawrence's vital imagination, seen at its freshest in letters, travel books,[11] essays, and poems. Van Gogh and Lawrence use rhythm, color, and contrast in words or paint to express their vision of the physical world.

Reacting against the repressive darkness of the industrial north, writer and painter felt "the need for completion and deliverance through the completely other, the south, the brightness, clarity and lightness, the gift of the beautiful" (Thomas Mann, qtd. in Meyers, *D. H. Lawrence* 6). Their senses awoke to the south like those of a man suddenly let out of a dark room. Van Gogh's path led from blackened coal fields and gloomy moors to the golden wheat fields of Provence. The mythic paradigm is that of a Dionysian journey. The artist-to-be descends into the depths to share the burden of human suffering and strengthen his own imaginative grasp of reality; after his self-inflicted ordeal, he is ready to rise into "the greater day" of sun-filled art. Along the way, Van Gogh abandoned the earth-tones of his Northern palette for the dazzling rays of Parisian light and the violent colors of the Midi. When he moved from wintry Paris to Arles in February 1888, the clear sunshine struck him with the force of a revelation. His response to the south was all the more dynamic because of the Nordic substratum in his soul. By a logic of polarities, the countryside "[aroused] the old power of the unforgettable North . . . and he recalled his first great motifs, landscapes and peasant figures" (Hammacher, *Genius* 109). Julius Meier-Graefe romantically stresses the conflict of "the old world and the new" in Van Gogh's art, saying "he was conscious of the demon in him, whom he served, and whose northern extraction forbade him to surrender to the ecstasy of the south" (122). Yet Van Gogh did surrender to the southern sun. He wanted "to see this stronger sun . . . because one feels that the colors of the prism are veiled in the mist of the North" (*Complete Letters* 3: 208). Under Japanese influence, he attempted to fuse polar extremes into a unified art.[12] The shock of confrontation may have led to his eventual collapse, as Tralbaut suggests: "Vincent's northern temperament was inspired and intoxicated by the brilliant southern sun. In the end the violent confrontation of Apollo and Dionysus was more than his sanity could stand, as it had been for Nietzsche and Hölderlin and so many others" (261).

For Lawrence, too, "life depends on duality and polarity" ("The Two Principles" 186): the north-south dialectic mobilizes his imagination. While Delavenay calls his philosophy "the passionate quest for unity of a divided man" (*D. H. Lawrence* 458), Janik sheds light on the philosophical relation of duality to wholeness in Lawrence's cosmology (*Curve of Return* 87–88). Zoll traces Lawrence's tendency to think in opposites to Schopenhauer, to whom "polarity (*Polarität*) is the 'sundering of a force into two qualitatively different and opposed activities striving after reunion'" (6). Lawrence sees cultural wholeness as the fruit of an interracial marriage that would reunite the "blonde, blue-eyed, northern [races] . . . born along with the ice-crystals and blue, cold deeps" with the southerners, "[born of] the sun and hav[ing] the fiery principle predominant . . . " ("The Two Principles" 185). Only such a fusion of opposites, whose basic elements are fire and water, can produce cultural vitality and creative growth.[13]

Van Gogh and Lawrence sought the sun as a regenerative force. On coming to Arles, Van Gogh exclaimed: "Oh! those who don't believe in this sun here are real infidels" (*Complete Letters* 3: 7). He was stimulated to a new boldness of color and exulted in work like a cicada in a heat wave. Charged with the sun's apocalyptic energy, he projected his creative tension and suffering into the portrait of the *Old Peasant (Patience Escalier)* (August 1888):[14] "I imagine the man I have to paint," he wrote, "terrible in the furnace of the height of harvesttime, as surrounded by the whole Midi. Hence the orange colors flashing like lightning, vivid as red-hot iron, and hence the luminous tones of old gold in the shadows" (*Complete Letters* 3: 6). Concentric, sunlike circles surround the old man's red-rimmed eyes: he seems to live scorched and shriveled in the glare and blood-heat of the sun, his stare a blind persistence. The figure is less an individual than an archetypal emanation of sun and earth.

The sun itself looms large and solid in several studies of an even less personalized son of the soil, the Sower. Here the golden orb symbolizes creative energy and the cycle of human life and seasons. The version of *The Sower* painted in June 1888 shows a huge sun, radiating gold flecked with green, flooding the fields with orange and violet-blue as it sinks below the horizon.[15] Across this arena strides the expressionless Sower, scattering seed with an imperious gesture, at once a force of nature and the embodiment of purposeful human activity.[16]

In August 1888, Van Gogh wrote to Bernard:

I am thinking of decorating my studio with half a dozen pictures of "Sunflowers," a decoration in which the raw or broken chrome yellows will blaze forth on various backgrounds—blue, from the palest malachite green to *royal blue*, framed in thin strips of wood painted with orange lead. Effects like those of stained-glass windows in a Gothic church. (*Complete Letters* 3: 511)[17]

He was ecstatic about the "Japanese" motif of large bright canvases in small rooms, with sunflowers symbolizing vitality, joy, and companionship. He planned a burst of color, "a symphony in blue and yellow," to celebrate Gauguin's arrival. The sunflower motif was transformed from an emphasis on destruction and decay in the Paris version of 1887, with its broken stalks and ragged red-tinged petals, to an exultant celebration of life. The sunflowers are at once an expression of his being and a Dionysian hymn to the sun; in possessing and painting them once and for all time, he achieved self-realization.

Through the motif of the sunflowers and his passion for yellow, Van Gogh became the painter of the sun, while Lawrence, more than any other modern writer, celebrated the sun as a living force. To him "the sun, like the rest of the cosmos, is alive" (*Letters* 5: 262). This sun-worship was a significant part of Lawrence's attempt to recover a state of primitive animism. Sun-rituals, sun-sacrifices, and solar religion abound in his work. "[The] great fiery, vivifying pole of the inanimate universe" ("Fantasia" 184) becomes fully mythicized as "this vast dark protoplasmic sun from which issues all that feeds our life" ("The Hopi Snake Dance" 172). Linking solar energy with blood-consciousness (*Apocalypse* 76–77), Lawrence draws on Aztec, Mayan, and Egyptian sources for sun-sacrifices or rituals in "The Woman Who Rode Away," *The Plumed Serpent*, and *The Escaped Cock*. In that final fable, the natural or macrocosmic "great sun" has its counterpart in the regenerative "inner suns" of Isis and Osiris.

But even the natural sun, in Lawrence, is a potent source of regeneration, as in the poems "Sun-Men" and "Sun-Women" (*Complete Poems* 525–26) or "in works like *Sun* [in which] the battering effect of light is as violent and explosive as the most demoniac Van Gogh . . . " (Lindsay 53). Here Lawrence's art of excess, like Van Gogh's, is directly inspired by the sun, which streams forth its male potency. The reader, like the woman in the story, confronts the sun as a molten source of energy and divine fire: "She looked up through her fingers at the central sun, his blue pulsing roundness, whose outer edges streamed brilliance. Pulsing with marvellous blue, and alive, and streaming white fire from his edges, the sun!" (*Complete Short Stories* 2: 530). Color, as

Van Gogh and Lawrence are aware, is a relative phenomenon created by the sun. Here the sun's orange/yellow fire is transposed into complementary blue as masculine object symbolically enters feminine subject to create the sensation of vision. (Optically, a blue afterimage is caused by shutting one's eyes against the sun.) This is no mythical dark sun at the center of the earth but the actual sun of the Mediterranean that struck Van Gogh and "stood above the horizon" as Lawrence sailed for Sardinia, "like the great burning stigma of the sacred flower of day" (*Sea and Sardinia* 52).

Lawrence cultivated an animistic response to trees as living presences, and his poem "Trees in the Garden" (*Complete Poems* 646–47) is the verbal analogue of a Van Gogh painting. Van Gogh expressed his animistic vision directly in colors laid thickly on the canvas and rhythmic brush strokes that gravitate toward symbolic gestures. He projected his psychic states into paintings of trees—"He would get into the cypress tree, through his genius, through his daemon," says H.D. (181).[18] Lawrence, who hated the tendency to subsume otherness in anthropomorphism, attacks a tendency to projection in Van Gogh that he feared in himself: "myself plucking my own flowering" ("New Heaven and Earth," *Complete Poems* 257). But the earth Van Gogh serves up with such intensity is not just "subjective earth"; it is otherness entered, absorbed, and permeated with vital perception—Van Gogh in touch with the vitalizing earth. As Lawrence recognized in the *Sunflowers*, it is the life flow between artist and object that gives the work life. Vital art is not just an interrelation of lines and colors in virtual space, as in Fry's formalist aesthetic; it is the expression of a dynamic interaction between self and world at a given moment. It is this *act* of art, opening the self to otherness in ever-varying interpenetrations, that constitutes significant or vital form for Lawrence. Empathy penetrates the attractive/resistant surface of the object and renders it luminous. The creative process neither subsumes the sunflower nor leaves it unchanged: the object, restructured by perception and expression, becomes an image that bears its creator's signature in every line. The artwork is a new thing in another dimension that can be entered only imaginatively.

Baudelaire observed that "one of the characteristic symptoms of the spiritual condition of our age [is] that all the arts aspire, if not to take one another's place, at least reciprocally to lend one another new powers" (qtd. in Meyers, *D. H. Lawrence* 139). This is particularly true of literary works and paintings that focus on visual motifs: Van Gogh's writing reinforces his drawing and painting, while Lawrence's painting relieves and supports his writing. Close resemblances between words and paint can be observed in the two artists' expressive rendering of trees. In "Flowery Tuscany," Lawrence offers a post-impressionist vision of layered greenness:

> The pear and the peach were out together. But now the pear-tree is a lovely thick softness of new and glossy green, vivid with a tender fulness of apple-green leaves, gleaming among all the other greens of the landscape, the half-high wheat, emerald, and the grey olive, half-invisible, the browning green of the dark cypress, the black of the evergreen oak, the rolling, heavy green puffs of the stone pines, the flimsy green of small peach and almond trees, the sturdy young green of horse-chestnut. So many greens, all in flakes and shelves and tilted tables and round shoulders and plumes and shaggles and uprisen bushes, of greens and greens, sometimes blindingly brilliant, at evening, when the landscape looks as if it were on fire from inside, with greenness and with gold. (234)

With its strong sense of paint and brush strokes, color and texture, plane and relief, this passage is the verbal equivalent of a post-impressionist painting. While the cumulative composition by tonal gradations of a single color suggests the art of Cézanne or Gauguin, the dramatic contrast of green with incandescent gold has the impact of Van Gogh. Sap circulates like a bloodstream through "the translucent membranes of blood-veined leaves" (234), and Lawrence's vitalism appears most clearly in the final image of sunset suffusing greenery with fire.

Lawrence's Sicilian poem "Almond Blossom" is about new life springing from suffering; this theme, so relevant to Van Gogh's life or Lawrence's, emerges from the concrete phenomenon of blossoming:

> Knots of pink, fish-silvery
> In heaven, in blue, blue heaven,
> Soundless, bliss-full, wide-rayed, honey-bodied,
> Red at the core,
> Red at the core,
> Knotted in heaven upon the fine light.

(Complete Poems 307)

The conjoint adjectives are semantic equivalents of painterly brush strokes, "fish-silvery" fusing with the pink tone and adding a quick glint of variation, "wide-rayed, honey-bodied" making light seem to emanate from or condense within thickly clustered blossoms that radiate against a blue sky. Van Gogh's *Branches of an Almond Tree in Blossom* (February 1890; see pl. 13), which he painted in a lucid interval during his stay at the asylum in Saint-Rémy, is a paean of joy bursting out of suffering. The dance of blossoms on an arabesque of gnarled branches set against a cerulean sky celebrates the birth of Vincent's nephew and namesake. Blossoming, for Van Gogh and Lawrence, symbolizes the perennial triumph of the life-spirit over the crucified body. When he visited Sardinia in January 1921, Lawrence found the almond trees already in blossom, "their pure, silvery pink gleaming so nobly, like a transfiguration . . . " (*Sea and Sardinia* 165). This glimpse of spring at Orosei has the ecstatic lightness of Van Gogh's Provencal orchards: almond blossom brings out the Apollonian side of each artist's nature. The artist's vision and expression transfigure the object, as does the life-force that they celebrate.

Lawrence vies directly with the painter and shows a "Japanese" sensitivity to thinning or condensing light and the isolation or grouping of objects. His description of trees in Sardinia shows knowledge of Japanese prints as well as of Van Gogh but is stamped with Lawrence's own casual mastery of verbal rhythms and preternatural intensity of vision. In this luminous vignette, he seems ready to drop the pen and pick up the brush: "If I were a painter I would paint [the naked poplars]: for they seem to have living, sentient flesh" (96–97). He is attracted to the trees, not as a play of forms that the eye abstracts, but for the vital, protoplasmic life that suffuses and gives them outline: "If not phosphorescent, then incandescent: a grey, goldish-pale incandescence of naked limbs and myriad cold-glowing twigs, gleaming strangely" (96). The trees impress their existence on the mind by reflecting light in shadowy space, and the composition achieves completeness through a "living relatedness" of animate and inanimate that subsumes formal relations in a "quick" intuitive response. "The knowing eye watches sharp as a needle; but the picture comes clean out of instinct, intuition and sheer physical action" ("Making Pictures" 603). With words, an imaginative, metaphoric dimension is added, but words only go so far. To express the poplars' living otherness one would need "tree-speech," a kind of plasmic communication.

Van Gogh was attracted by the violent gestural configurations and subtle color of olive-trees at various seasons and in various weathers. Like Lawrence, he found the phenomenal world far more wonderful in its irreducible energy than any abstract spiritual image imposed upon it, as in Emile

Bernard's *Christ Among the Olive Trees* (1889). A letter from Auvers, written the month before he died, is an act of attention and verbal re-creation of the visual:

> The effect of daylight, of the sky, makes it possible to extract an infinity of subjects from the olive tree. Now, I on my part sought contrasting effects in the foliage, changing with the hues of the sky. At times the whole is a pure all-pervading blue, namely when the tree bears its pale flowers, and big blue flies, emerald rose beetles and cicadas in great numbers are hovering around it. Then, as the bronzed leaves are getting riper in tone, the sky is brilliant and radiant with green and orange, or, more often even, in autumn, when the leaves acquire something of the violet tinges of the ripe fig, the violet effect will manifest itself vividly through the contrasts, with the large sun taking on a white tint within a halo of clear and pale citron yellow. At times, after a shower, I have also seen the whole sky colored pink and bright orange, which gave an exquisite value and coloring to the silvery gray-green. (*Complete Letters* 3: 232)

Now here is Lawrence writing to the painter Ernest Collings from Garganano, twenty-three years later: "[It] is a perfect place for you, would rejoice you: the cypresses, the olives, the great high rocks and gorgeous contours. And who has ever done the lovely glimmer of olive trees in black, and white—or in colour" (*Letters* 1: 518). If Lawrence in February 1913 had little knowledge of Van Gogh's *Olive Orchards*, he was clearly drawn to the same motifs and imagined painting them.

Van Gogh painted olive groves with a dynamism that brings all the senses into play; through "the seethe of phenomena" (Lawrence, *The Escaped Cock* 31) he attuned himself to cosmic energies. He was painting "the flame of life," the "shimmeriness" in the twisted trees, not the dead husk but the sap that sends the branches spiraling in a mad dance toward the sun. In *Olive Orchard* (September–October 1889), Van Gogh fuses sky, trees, and earth in a single dancing rhythm of blue, green, and ocher. Flickering green brush strokes interweave with blue of sky, gyrating blue trunks with green of leaves, green-blue flecks with surging flamelike ochers of earth. All the separate forms and colors unite in a wavelike/flamelike motion to form a kind of Heraclitean vision. A view of the Alpilles, *Landscape with Olive Trees* (October 1889; see pl. 14) has the tremendous plasticity of Van Gogh's animistic vision. The earth is alive and everything is in motion: the blue mountain mass billows in waves like the sea, the foreground heaves in great undulations, and the upspringing olive trees gesticulate in a spiral dance.[19]

Lawrence, who understood such "pantheistic sensuality," wrote of his

New Mexican pine tree: "It vibrates its presence into my soul, and I am with Pan. . . . Something fierce and bristling is communicated. The piny sweetness is rousing and defiant, like turpentine. . . . I am even conscious that shivers of energy cross my living plasm, from the tree . . . " ("Pan in America" 25). He shared with Van Gogh an openness to nature that surcharges their painting and writing with vitalizing energy. Lawrence's animistic vision makes landscapes dynamic in *The Rainbow* and in *Lady Chatterley's Lover*, where it reflects the awakened life of the body: "As she ran home in the twilight . . . the trees in the park seemed bulging and surging at anchor on a tide, and the heave of the slope to the house was alive" (178). Connie's subjective response sets the landscape in undulating motion, emphasized by heavy dactylic measures that express a surging rhythm in the language, recalling the intensity of Van Gogh's vision.

Pritchard finds an affinity between Van Gogh and Lawrence in "the visionary intensity of the gaze directed upon the symbols of fierce (phallic) energy, the flame-like cypresses and blinding sun." But to both artists, cypresses and pine trees are *more* than human and sexual symbols: in their otherness, they incarnate a cosmic energy deeper and more ancient than the "ithyphallic" force that derives from it. For Van Gogh and Lawrence, dark cypresses standing rigid in the southern sun express a polarity, a Heraclitean tension of opposites. "It is so still and transcendent," Lawrence writes; "the cypress trees poise like flames of forgotten darkness. . . . For as we have candles to light the darkness of night, so the cypresses are candles to keep the darkness aflame in the full sunshine" (*Twilight in Italy* 154). The cypresses embody a solar-telluric polarity. In "Sun," Juliet offers her body to the sun at the foot of a cypress tree that is the phallic connector between opposing principles of light and darkness: "Out of this blue-grey knoll of cactus rose one cypress tree, with a pallid, thick trunk, and a tip that leaned over, flexible, up in the blue. It stood like a guardian looking to sea; or a low, silvery candle whose huge flame was darkness against light: earth sending up her proud tongue of gloom" (*Complete Short Stories* 2: 530). The visual image becomes visionary as Van Gogh and Lawrence reach out toward the palpable otherness of trees in acts of attention that extend their own being.

The dark luminosity of Van Gogh's cypresses complements the brilliant yellow of his wheat fields. He saw the cypress as "a splash of black in a sunny landscape," a black that was almost impossible to transfer to canvas because it was really the darkest green. It became an obsessive image, a reminder of his northern origins, and possibly a memento mori looming up under the sun or between the night fires of moon and stars. Van Gogh was driven to paint the cypresses that he felt no one had ever fully *seen* before, absorbing and transforming them as with the sunflowers that represent the complementary side of his nature. In *Cypresses with Two Figures* (1889)[20] and *Road with Cypress and Star* (1890; see pl. 15), the upright form of the trees, exaggerated and contorted into dense spiral movements, becomes the expressive gesture of Van Gogh's being.

The fact that Van Gogh and Lawrence respond so positively, in different phases of their careers, to opposing poles of light and darkness, sun and moon seems to signify an Apollonian-Dionysian duality in their creative activity.[21] Van Gogh was torn between Apollo and Dionysus. As he gave himself to the blazing sun of Provence, he was also strongly attracted by "primeval, nocturnal life forces" (qtd. in Hammacher, *Genius* 83) and spoke of "tak[ing] death to reach a star (*Complete Letters* 2: 605). After long gestation, he painted two distinct versions of *The Starry Night*, one in Arles in September 1888 and the other in Saint-Rémy in June 1889.[22] He describes the first as "a study of the Rhône—of the town lighted with gas reflected in the blue river. Over it the starry sky with the Great Bear—a sparkling of pink and green on the cobalt blue field of the night sky, whereas the lights of the town and its ruthless reflections are red gold and bronzed green" (*Complete Letters* 3: 84). It is a dance of above and below, a fusion of fire and water in the glowing and flowing of southern night. Before he painted the first *Starry Night*, Vincent wrote to Theo about the colors he experienced during a night stroll along the shore at Les Saintes-Maries:

> The deep blue sky was flecked with clouds of a blue deeper than the fundamental blue of intense cobalt, and others of a clearer blue, like the blue whiteness of the Milky Way. In the blue depth the stars were sparkling, greenish, yellow, white, pink, more brilliant, more sparklingly gemlike than at home— even in Paris: opals you might call them, emeralds, lapis lazuli, rubies, sapphires. The sea was very deep ultramarine—the shore a sort of violet and faint russet . . . and on the dunes (they are about seventeen feet high) some bushes Prussian blue. (*Complete Letters* 2: 589)

Lawrence may or may not have seen reproductions of Van Gogh's *Starry Night* paintings, but he certainly felt the splendor of starry skies and tried to express his vision in words:

The stars were marvellous in the soundless sky, so big, that one could see them hanging orb-like and alone in their own space, yet all the myriads. Particularly bright the evening star. And he hung flashing in the lower night with a power that made me hold my breath. Grand and powerful he sent out his flashes, so sparkling that he seemed more intense than any sun or moon. And from the dark, uprising land he sent his way of light to us across the water, a marvellous star-road. So all above us the stars soared and pulsed, over that silent, night-dark, land-locked harbour. (*Sea and Sardinia* 183)

Van Gogh's *Starry Night* of June 1889 is an apocalyptic vision of the cosmos; the dream overtakes reality and submerges it in a tidal expansion of the painter's being. The very fact that Van Gogh saw the world through bars and between bouts of hallucination intensified his reaching out for freedom in the otherness of space. A precarious balance of genius and madness, self-surrender and will-to-form sustains his ecstatic vision. Stability is represented by tiny buildings that cling to earth, but the ground-level of existence is subjected to the turbulent night sky and dynamism of space. White and blue clouds contort themselves in spiral undulations,[23] like living mating forms, while enlarged stars like pale suns and a burning crescent moon pulse in wild gyration. The soaring vertical of the cypress intersects the surging waves of clouds, that may be seen as cosmic/spiritual forms of energy, and points toward infinity, grazing the stars. Vertical, spiral, rotary movements create plastic tension and keep the canvas alive with restless motion. It is a vision of clustering, nucleolating forces, that Van Gogh, for once, did not attempt to describe in words.

Van Gogh projects the whole drama of his being into this image of the night sky. The sense of unlimited space and power, with electromagnetic waves of energy creating and dissolving worlds, surpasses the expressionist and futurist modes of vision that it foretells. But the forces unleashed in Van Gogh's canvas are also found in the imagery of Lawrence's novels. The apocalyptic imagination that produced *The Starry Night* vibrates with the same frequency as that which produced *The Rainbow* and *Women in Love*. In "First Love," "The Bitterness of Ecstasy," and "Moony," Lawrence, who had himself been smitten with "moon-madness" on the Lincolnshire coast, creates a language of the unconscious to express energies radiating from the moon and stirring up blood-consciousness in his characters. In Van Gogh's *Starry Night*, as in those moonlight scenes, cosmic energy is transfigured by human vision and passion. Lawrence conveys cosmic reverberations within allotropic states of consciousness, and there is a reflective dimension in his writing that painting lacks. But a deep affinity links the nocturnal visions of painter and novelist.

In *The Rainbow*, Will Brangwen feels the shadowy presence of angels as he goes to meet Anna—a presence that symbolizes a vitalizing of his being. The deep resonance of space is expressed in a Van Gogh-like intensification of colors:[24] "[The] evening glowed in its last deep colours, the sky was dark blue, the stars glittered from afar, very remote and approaching above the darkening cluster of the farm, above the puther of crystal along the edge of the heavens" (113). As a prelude to the corn harvest ritual, Lawrence heightens spatial values by contrasting round with vertical, as Van Gogh does with his moons, stars, and cypresses, and by choosing animistic verb forms: "A large gold moon hung heavily to the grey horizon, trees hovered tall, standing back in the dusk, waiting" (113). As Van Gogh repeatedly sketched the gestures of men and women stooping, carrying sheaves, harvesting, so Lawrence, who had experienced these rhythms, assimilates them to the ritual of courtship. Successive movement and repetition in phrasal structures reproduce wavelike rhythms of attraction. In addition to this kinetic element, Lawrence emphasizes the interplay of moonlight and shadow in visual images like the "flaring" focus on Anna's bosom, that recall the eerie illumination of Munch's *Summer Night's Dream (The Voice)* (1893),[25] with its "dark column" and "dazzle of moonlight" (*Rainbow* 115), and its sense of ghostly erotic presence.

In Lawrence's harvest dance scene of Anton and Ursula (*Rainbow* 294–99), in the following generation, surging rhythms and waves of energy correspond to the dynamism of Van Gogh's forms, in which brush strokes cross, reverse directions, or interweave in spiral paths—"There was a wonderful rocking of the darkness, slowly, a great, slow swinging of the whole night, with the music playing lightly on the surface, making the strange, ecstatic rippling on the surface of the dance . . . " (chapter 11, "First Love" 295). The "turgid, teeming night, heavy with fecundity" (413) and the swinging motion of the tides and surge of moonlight on the shoreline, in "The Bitterness of Ecstasy" (chapter 15, 443–45), are part of a universal undulation that animates all matter, sense, and spirit.

Van Gogh's *Starry Night* and Lawrence's "Moony" are mythic expressions of nonvisual, nonverbal struggle, shadowed forth in paint or print. The dynamism of plastic or verbal rhythms and the extreme boldness of imagery are outward expressions of convulsive inner movement. While illuminating the darkness within, Van Gogh and Lawrence seem to penetrate the veil of matter around them to reveal those principles of cosmic energy that "roll through all things." Being and space, consciousness and matter meet and mingle in a sundering-merging dance of forms. Individual being is the merest particle in this dance of light and darkness. As religious artists, Van Gogh and Lawrence dare to "leap from the known into the unknown" (*Rainbow* 295) and to affirm the endless flux of being that lies beyond the self.

Just as Van Gogh projected the turbulence of his psyche into images of sun, moon, and stars, so Lawrence expressed his vitalism in images of flame.

> There is a swan-like flame that curls round the centre
> of space
> and flutters at the core of the atom,
> there is a spiral flame-tip that can lick our little atoms
> into fusion
> so we roar up like bonfires of vitality
> and fuse in a broad hard flame of many men in a oneness.
>
> ("Spiral Flame," *Collected Poems* 440)

Apart from the Whitmanesque image of male solidarity—so far removed from Van Gogh's or Lawrence's actual isolation—the motif of the vivifying flame makes this stanza extraordinarily close in spirit and form to *The Starry Night* and *Road with Cypress and Star* (see pls. 5, 15). Heraclitus proclaimed fire to be the vital principle of the cosmos, and Lawrence, whose philosophy in "The Crown" is Heraclitean, was a flame-loving vitalist. In the novel, which he felt to be the most vital form of expression, the real hero "[is not] any of the characters, but some unnamed and nameless flame behind them all. . . . [Character] is the flame of a man . . . rising or sinking or flaring. . . . God is the flame-life in all the universe" ("The Novel" 182, 186, 189).

Lawrence's vitalism is expressed through the Spirit of Place in novellas like "St. Mawr," "The Woman Who Rode Away," and *The Escaped Cock*, and in travel writings like "Pan in America," "New Mexico," and *Sketches of Etruscan Places*. The "latent fire of the vast landscape" in "St. Mawr" (140) has the passionate animism of Van Gogh's olive orchards, while the cosmic dynamism that creates forms and impinges on human life is figured forth in the huge pine tree that towers above the cabin, "a bristling, almost demonish guardian. . . . Its great pillar of pale, flakey-ribbed copper rose there in strange callous indifference. . . . A cold, blossomless, resinous sap surging and oozing gum, from that pallid brownish bark" (144). Lawrence's para-sexual imagery emphasizes substance and texture, the tree's rebarbative otherness, but "the flame-life in all the universe" is also concentrated in this "non-phallic column." For Lawrence, as for Van Gogh, the painter's vision of light and color transforming objects signifies the mysterious urgency of life:

> Strange, those pine-trees! In some lights all their needles glistened like polished steel, all subtly glittering with a whitish glitter. . . . Then again, at evening, the trunks would flare up orange red, and the tufts would be dark, alert tufts like a wolf's tail touching the air. (144)

Lawrence's metaphors and similes link the visual and external hard shiny surface reflecting sunlight with the instinctual and internal alertness behind animal motion.

In "The Woman Who Rode Away," pine trees in the sunset—as in Van Gogh's *Pine Trees with Setting Sun* (1889)[26]—are more than material forms. They become the focus of a savage, animistic vision of the earth: "The sun was setting, a great yellow light flooded the last of the aspens, flared on the trunks of the pine trees, the pine trees bristled and stood out with dark lustre, the rocks glowed with unearthly glamour" (556). In "Pan in America," the pine tree comes alive and stimulates the observer's intuitive being, as "shivers of energy cross [his] living plasm, from the tree" (25). Lawrence's "pantheistic sensuality" makes him aware "that the tree has its own life, its own assertive existence, its own living relatedness to me" and that magnified life "consist[s] in [such] a vivid relatedness" (26–27). This sense of being in touch with a living cosmos vitalizes the vision and expression of Lawrence and Van Gogh.[27]

The intense light of "St. Mawr"—"that vast, white, back-beating light which rushed up at one and made one almost unconscious, amid the snow" (146)—has the physically aggressive quality of Van Gogh's Provencal sunlight—a light he virtually worshiped and for which he was willing to sacrifice his sanity (this being the negative-sublime aspect of his vision). So Lawrence's vision took a quantum leap forward in New Mexico,[28] as he embraced new dimensions of light-filled space in that "vast and living landscape" (146). The battle for life in the arid New Mexican desert is projected into images of flowers that are botanically precise yet heavy with apocalyptic overtones, like Van Gogh's blazing or burnt-out sunflowers. The wild honey-suckle is

> a tangle of long drops of pure fire-red, hanging from slim invisible stalks of smoke colour. The purest, most perfect vermilion scarlet, cleanest fire-colour, hanging in long drops like a shower of fire-rain. . . . [Then] there came another sheer fire-red flower, sparking, fierce red stars running up a bristly grey ladder, as if the earth's fire-centre had blown out some red sparks. . . . (148)

The writer, like the painter, first grasps the natural form and then reveals its vital significance, as in "a vision."[29] Just how much Lawrence's apocalyptic imagination has projected into the forms of the red honeysuckle can be seen by comparing the second half of the description, with its cluster of metaphors, with the first. The tension between the act of attention, that reproduces concrete forms in line and color, and the act of imagination, that penetrates and transforms them, characterizes Lawrence's vision. While Van Gogh's vision is latent in the sensuous forms and colors of his painting—so that loneliness, for instance, can be strongly felt in the deep blue backgrounds of *Wheat Field Under Clouded Sky* or *Crows Over the Wheat Field* (both July 1890)[30]—Lawrence's writing has the extra dimension of thoughts that emanate like sparks from the object. His vital image of life highlights difference, variety, and coruscating interaction of colors, as in Van Gogh's *Irises* (May 1889), with their "wavy, flaming, twisted, and curling lines, broken and pointed" (Schapiro, *Van Gogh* 96), or in the glints of red poppies among yellow-green grass in *The Enclosed Field* (May–June 1889).[31] In "St. Mawr,"

> [the] alfalfa field was one raging, seething conflict of plants trying to get hold. . . . the spiky, blue-leaved thistle-poppy with its moon-white flowers, the low clumps of blue nettle-flower . . . the rush of red sparks and michaelmas daisies, and the tough wild sunflowers, strangling and choking the dark, tender green of the clover-like alfalfa! (148)

No one can deny that this landscape, with its violence and conflict, is a very subjective way of seeing a field of flowers.[32] Only Van Gogh saturates nature with a vision of such explosive force while sustaining the outline of objective forms, however contorted.[33] Accurate perception of the real and objective mediates and empowers the expressive vision of Lawrence and Van Gogh.

The more Van Gogh wrestled with colors and forms, the more ruthlessly religious his dedication to art became. Early in his career (April 1884), he wrote of his "positive consciousness of the fact that art is something greater and higher than our own adroitness or accomplishments or knowledge; that art is something which, although produced by human hands, is not created by these hands alone, but something which wells up from a deeper source in our souls . . . " (*Complete Letters* 3: 399–400). He added: "My sympathies in the literary as well as in the artistic fields are most strongly attracted to those artists in whom I see the working of the soul predominating." These words might well have been written by Lawrence, who believed religiously in the power of the unconscious. After his struggle "[to come] at the real naked essence of our vision" in *Sons and Lovers*, he wrote:

> I often think one ought to be able to pray, before one works—and then leave it to the Lord. Isn't it hard, hard work to come to real grips with one's imagination—throw everything overboard. I always feel as if I stood naked for the fire of Almighty God to go through me—and it's rather an awful feeling. One has to be so terribly religious, to be an artist. (*Letters* 1: 519)

Defending "The Sisters," Lawrence declared: "But primarily I am a passionately religious man, and my novels must be written from the depth of my religious experience" (*Letters* 2: 165). This daimonic capacity to articulate the depth of one's being is what makes the art of Van Gogh and Lawrence so stirring. In both, there is a sense of man's ontological relation with the cosmos. In August 1927, Lawrence wrote to Dr. Trigant Burrow: "There is a *principle* in the universe, towards which man turns religiously—a *life* of the universe itself. And the hero is he who touches and transmits the life of the universe" (*Letters* 6: 114). The painter of *The Starry Night* and the author of *The Rainbow*, reaching through seen to unseen, create a vital art in touch with being. In their creative work, they offer a "splendour of living" that overcomes alienation, and a force of expression that fuses the spiritual with the natural.

8

LAWRENCE, VAN GOGH, AND CÉZANNE

Expression seems such a natural, God-given
thing—and yet it's not either. It's a lifelong
struggle to find yourself. Think of Cézanne, Van
Gogh, Gauguin, Lawrence.
>   —Henry Miller to Lawrence Durrell, *A Private Correspondence*

The interaction of visual imagination with verbal expression is an intuitive process. Influence is a thorny issue, for "the strong imagination comes to its painful birth through savagery and misrepresentation," and Lawrence is one of "the great deniers of influence" (Bloom 86, 56). As Henry Miller observes: "The men to whom he owed everything, the great spirits on whom he fed and nourished himself, whom he had to reject in order to assert his own power, his own vision, were they not like himself men who went to the source?" (136). Miller proposes Christ, Nietzsche, Whitman, and Dostoevsky as "forerunners" and links Lawrence with Cézanne and Van Gogh as pioneers of expression. Lawrence must have encountered Van Gogh in 1912, when the Cologne Sonderbund established the painter's reputation. Such expressive power leaves strong impressions. "Van Gogh's paintings," writes Merleau-Ponty, "[once seen] have their place in me for all time, a step is taken from which I cannot retreat, and, even though I retain no clear recollection of the pictures . . . my whole subsequent aesthetic experience will be that of someone who has become acquainted with the painting of Van Gogh . . . " (*Phenomenology* 393). Despite the anxiety that may have led Lawrence to distort his response to Van Gogh and distance himself from the painter's subjectivity, they share a vitalist aesthetic.

Lawrence's deep interest in Van Gogh appears in three major statements: a long letter to Lady Ottoline Morrell (1 March 1915; *Letters* 2: 296–99) and the essays "Morality and the Novel" (1925) and "Introduction to These Paintings" (1929).[1] In his letter, sympathy outweighs criticism. Lawrence is spiritually drawn to Van Gogh and implicitly uses the painter's career to define his own position. He was reading Van Gogh while completing *The Rainbow*, for the day after this letter was dispatched he wrote to Viola Meynell: "I have finished my *Rainbow*, bended it and set it firm. Now off and away to find the pots of gold at its feet" (299). His spatial metaphors corroborate the wholeness and solidity that were part of Lawrence's architectonic vision. In this euphoric mood, he saw the tragedy and triumph of Van Gogh's life from the perspective of his own creative achievement. He empathized strongly with Van Gogh's lonely struggle and yearning for community. Both Van Gogh and Lawrence were fired by the idea of medieval art guilds and by the religious art of Renaissance "primitives."

Although Lawrence intuitively grasps Van Gogh's existential and social aims, he compounds them with his own obsessions:

> He couldn't get out of the trap, poor man, so he went mad. . . . He wanted that there should be a united impulse of all men in the fulfilment of one idea—as in Giotto's and Cimabue's time. But in this world there is as yet only chaos. So he struggled to add one more term to the disorderly accumulation of knowledge. But it was not living. It was submitting himself to a process of reduction. (296–97)

In Lawrence's metaphysic of revitalization, life must either break the shell of the old or turn back on itself in a series of known reactions that become mechanical and ultimately destroy growth and feeling. He may have seen Van Gogh as caught in a "process of destructive creation" such as Birkin defines in "Water-Party" (*Women in Love* 172).

He may also have seen the extremity of Van Gogh's vision, his helpless plunge into the unconscious, as allied with madness. In the "nightmare" years of 1915–16, Lawrence himself suffered from personal conflicts, paranoia, and apocalyptic visions leading to megalomaniacal pronouncements and uncontrollable outbursts, so that some of his friends believed he had stepped over the border into madness. His spirit was much darkened by the war, which he saw as "the spear through the side of all sorrows and hopes" (*Letters* 2: 268). In April 1915 (less than two months after his Van Gogh letter), he wrote to Lady Ottoline: "How dark my soul is! . . . All the beauty and light of the days seems like [an] iridescence on a very black flood" (330).

The mood is that of Van Gogh's darkest days in the mental hospital at Saint-Rémy. In May 1915, he admits: "Everything has a touch of delirium—the blackbird on the wall . . . even the apple-blossom. And when I see a snake winding rapidly in the marshy places, I think I am mad" (339). Middleton Murry describes Lawrence as "overwhelmed by the horror of the war" and "radiating desolation," or as "passionately angry" at Frieda (Nehls 1: 255–56). The consumptive Katherine Mansfield, who also suffered from black rages, found herself and Lawrence "*unthinkably* alike" (Nehls 1: 476). With his cult of "equilibrium," reservations about "ecstasy," and determination to play down his "genius," Lawrence himself may have feared that he was too much like Van Gogh and that he shared his creative/destructive instability.

If Lawrence mixes his own problems and prophecies with the Van Gogh legend, it is at least a sign of deep interest in Van Gogh's life. The author of *Sons and Lovers* and *The Rainbow* would certainly see something of himself in a genius split between spiritual and physical drives. Although Van Gogh's "very sad" history differs from the reductive process in *Women in Love*, Lawrence saw in it a tendency to sacrifice life to art. He himself always stood for the integral wholeness of an artist's life and work. The extreme opposite of such integrity is the heterocosmic notion of art put forward by Loerke and Gudrun; their denial of all vital links between life and art makes art a mechanical game. But art that manipulates techniques and feeds on its own substance is an obscenity to Lawrence.

Van Gogh's frustration with life led him to pour all his energy into art and left him a burnt-out case with an almost savage disregard for ordinary living. It was a question of life for art's sake rather than art for life's sake or "art for my sake" (Lawrence's vitalist slogan). His view of Van Gogh is tinged with sadness rather than censure. He was enough of an apocalyptist to know, with Bakunin, that "the passion for destruction is also a creative passion." He saw Van Gogh as a victim trapped between quasi-religious yearnings for community and the disintegrative effects of all his actual relationships—with women, with fellow artists, and with God. Lawrence, who was trapped in England for the duration of the war, projected some of his own creative and existential conflicts onto Van Gogh, foreshortening complexities with an abrupt tone of omniscience. Yet the degree of aptness in the abruptness confirms Lawrence's empathy with his subject.

In this same letter, Lawrence's prophetic vision of a "new life," whose source is "the dark fire, the hidden, invisible passion, that has neither flame nor heat" (*Letters* 2: 298), is flanked by two extended reflections on Van Gogh. The concluding paragraph focuses on a disequilibrium of angel and animal, art and life, in which Lawrence explicitly sets life above art—or, rather, unites them in a mutual incarnation. He sees art as "the final expression" of life, a supplement, an overflow, an articulated vision rather than an epiphenomenon or substitute. There is a conceptual continuity, in his view, between the life-changing power of art and "that piece of supreme art, a man's life." Lawrence's attitude toward art was vitalist: he believed it should serve the artist's quest for fulfillment. What he could never accept was that life should be sacrificed to art. Ironically and heroically, Van Gogh, in the very depths of disaster, *did*, in a sense, "achieve that piece of supreme art, a man's life." In *The Starry Night* (June 1889; see pl. 5) and *Road with Cypress and Star* (May 1890; see pl. 15),[2] he expressed a cosmic vision that is the expression of man's soul driven to extremes of passion, yet creating order out of chaos and form from the void. *The Starry Night* has rightly been considered one of the most authentic religious masterpieces of the twentieth century (Paul Tillich and Theodore M. Green, cited in Graetz 212).

Van Gogh comes to play a central role in Lawrence's thinking on art and literature. In his essay "Morality and the Novel," in which he defines the quick of every vital art as "subtle interrelatedness," Lawrence builds his ideas from a concentrated meditation on Van Gogh's *Sunflowers* (August 1888)[3]—those flowers that exist as a whole world, sun and earth, growth and decay, as well as becoming a profound expression of Van Gogh's subjective existence. In Lawrence's meditation on art, Van Gogh, the subjective artist, is first factor; the sunflower, object of perception, is second; and "the vision on the canvas" is "a third thing," existing "in the fourth dimension." That is to say, the artwork is seen as a separate entity, existing apart from spatial and temporal, personal and phenomenal circumstances. It springs from a "momentaneous" interaction yet has "the quality of eternity." What comes across from the canvas is "a revelation of the perfected relation, at a certain moment, between a man and a sunflower" ("Morality and the Novel" 171). According to Remy C. Kwant, "man himself, in interaction with reality, makes the world appear as a visual field. Seeing is an existential, intentional activity . . . " (23). There is no consciousness that is not consciousness of something, no life that does not involve contact. Painting—like that "tremulation on the ether," the novel—is not only virtual space but also virtual life. The object in painting may be even more vivid than objects in ordinary life because it is seen through the burning glass of the artist's perception and transformed by his imagination. In upholding a paradoxical fusion of subject and object, moment and eternity, Lawrence's view of art anticipates the phenomenology of Merleau-Ponty.

Both Lawrence and Van Gogh were able to focus with complete empathy on things outside themselves. This self-effacement in the act of attention to flower or chair, bedroom or wheat field, can lead to deeper self-expression. The object stimulates the poet or painter, who in turn saturates and animates the image with his own creative energy, making it an extension of his seeing and being. There is no room for self-consciousness, with its reflexive limitations, in this fuller response to otherness. The mirror in Van Gogh's *Bedroom at Arles* (1888) remains empty. Only through vital contact of self with other does a third thing—the visionary artwork—come into being. Lawrence's meditation on Van Gogh leads to a vitalist definition of art:

> The business of art is to reveal the relation between man and his circumambient universe, at the living moment. . . .
>
> When Van Gogh paints sunflowers, he reveals, or achieves, the vivid relation between himself, as man, and the sunflower, as sunflower, at that quick moment of time. His painting does not represent the sunflower itself . . . .
>
> The vision on the canvas is a third thing, utterly intangible and inexplicable, the offspring of the sunflower itself and Van Gogh himself. The vision on the canvas is forever incommensurable with the canvas, or the paint, or Van Gogh as a human organism, or the sunflower as a botanical organism. You cannot weigh nor measure nor even describe the vision on the canvas. It exists, to tell the truth, only in the much-debated fourth dimension. In dimensional space it has no existence. ("Morality and the Novel" 171)

Lawrence's location of the art image in the Einsteinian/Ouspenskyan fourth dimension anticipates Susanne Langer's more formalist concept of "virtual space" in painting.[4] As for expression of being, all Van Gogh's frustrated love and spiritual hunger were poured into his celebration of the sunflowers, conceived as heraldic decorations of the Yellow House in Arles, which was to be the nucleus of an artistic community. The sunflowers in oil on canvas became an incarnation of his pent-up creative energy.

Lawrence's aesthetic of "perfected relation" is an extension of the Heraclitean philosophy of "The Crown" (1915) and "Reflections on the Death of a Porcupine" (1925), in which all life is seen to be based on constant interaction of opposites: "The Holy Ghost is that which holds the light and the dark, the day and the night, the wet and the sunny, united in one little clue. There it sits, in the seed of the dandelion" ("Reflections" 359). If one pole— earth or sun, lion or unicorn, sense or soul, body or mind, darkness or light, male or female, blood-consciousness or mental consciousness—dominates completely, the result will be entropy and collapse. A successful artwork is the "fourth dimensional" image of a momentary equilibrium between self and other, perceiver and perceived, lover and beloved.

In his discourse on Van Gogh, Lawrence presents a paradox. Art appears to be transcendent, aspiring to a stillness that lies beyond the flux of space and time yet it arises from immanence, being the fullest possible expression of "the quick," "*the incarnate moment*"[5]—a fleeting perception or vision that articulates the artist's being at a certain moment of existence. Neo-Platonic Kantianism is replaced by Heraclitean vitalism. "Man and the sunflower both pass away from the moment, in the process of forming a new relationship. The relation between all things changes from day to day, in a subtle stealth of change. Hence art, which reveals or attains to another perfect relationship, will be forever new" ("Morality and the Novel" 171). The painter or novelist embraces his material and achieves a moment's empathy with it; "[he] wants to produce himself as self in that which he is not, but in which he then can recognize himself" (Kockelmans 39). The viewer of the painting or reader of the novel rediscovers the product of this relationship, unchanged by time. This theory of art, epitomized by Van Gogh, who struggled to penetrate nature, culminates in Lawrence's claims for that "one bright book of life," the novel ("The Novel" 195), as "the highest complex of subtle interrelatedness that man has discovered" ("Morality and the Novel" 172)—a concept that relates his vital aesthetic dynamically to Van Gogh and formally to Cézanne. But Lawrence stresses the novel's affinity with the flux of existence, which it expresses in dialogic form, rather than any transcendence of phenomena in a Flaubertian heaven of art. He is fully aware of the novel's close relation to the reader's life and its powers of revitalization.

By "morality in the novel," Lawrence refers to a fusion of ethics and aesthetics that stimulates vital awareness, and to an interactive process that shapes the artist's perception and expression. A vitalist writer preserves "the trembling instability of the balance" and resists the tendency "to pull down the balance to his own predilection" ("Morality and the Novel" 172). Lawrence's notion of aesthetic integrity incorporates Keats's empathy and "negative capability." Van Gogh achieved maximum intensity in *The Starry*

Night by letting the vision well up from his unconscious "without any irrita-
ble reaching after fact and reason" (Keats 72). In all his work, he is one
of "the pure in spirit," as Lawrence defines that term in "Making Pictures"
(604). The artist's dedication to his art involves being able to "see the divine
in natural objects," the infinite in the concrete and particular. Van Gogh developed this ability to a marked degree. Yet Lawrence did not always stick to
the concrete sensuousness he advocated in painting—indeed, it is harder for
the novelist to refrain from preaching than it is for the painter with his silent
language. Lawrence could not resist, at times, giving vision a conscious direction; like Sartre, he believed that a writer's art should be approached
through his metaphysics. Yet in a complex novel like *Women in Love*, there
are many checks and balances; dialogic exchanges are matched by allotropic
changes within a single character. The "subtle interrelatedness" of everything, as Lawrence sees it, appears on a vaster and more complex scale in the
novel than in painting or poetry.

Although Lawrence mentions canvas and paint in his remarks on Van
Gogh, his theory of one-to-one interaction between artist and object does not
really account for the artist's response to his medium. The physical involvement of a writer with writing is, of course, much less evident than that of a
painter with paint. Yet, in "Why the Novel Matters," Lawrence describes the
spontaneous movements of his own hand, which is just as integral a part of
him as brain, mind, or soul (193). The hand, a synecdoche of physical consciousness, is an extension of the mind: "My hand is alive, it flickers with a
life of its own. It meets all the strange universe, in touch, and learns a vast
number of things, and knows a vast number of things. My hand, as it writes
these words, slips gaily along, jumps like a grasshopper to dot an i . . . "
(193). Lawrence is describing a rhythmic quickness and manual dexterity
that embody intuitive knowledge and expression.[6] Similarly, he considers the
movement of the painter's hand part of a kinetic/spiritual totality: "The
knowing eye watches sharp as a needle; but the picture comes clean out of
instinct, intuition and sheer physical action. Once the instinct and intuition
gets into the brush-tip, the picture *happens* . . . " ("Making Pictures" 603).
Here Lawrence emphasizes the painter's active involvement with his medium, as Merleau-Ponty does in "Eye and Mind."

Instead of simply mirroring the world, Van Gogh projects his being into
objects, animating their surfaces with rhythmic brush strokes that move this
way and that across the canvas, in convoluted masses or spiraling centripe-

tal paths. Antonin Artaud claims that "van Gogh is a painter, because he recollected nature, because he reperspired it and made it sweat, because he squeezed onto his canvases in clusters, in monumental sheaves of color, the grinding of elements that occurs once in a hundred years . . . " (499). The flickering movement of his brush was like another form of thought, rooted in the senses yet mediating between consciousness and the object. Perhaps any artist who lives in his medium loves it above all others and sees it as more living. In *Road with Cypress and Star*, the dark green flame of the trees, flanked by a huge rotating star and crescent moon, could never be mistaken for a landscape seen through the conventional window of illusion. The frenzied brush strokes, vibrating with contrasts of color and direction, record the painter's impulsive movements in shaping his vision. Such impulses, "felt in the blood" (Wordsworth, "Tintern Abbey"), arouse the viewer's response, drawing him into the life of the work.

Roughened surfaces manifest the author's or sculptor's or painter's active involvement with his medium; physical existence is integrated into the vision. In his "Foreword to *Women in Love*," Lawrence defends "the continual, slightly modified repetition" of his style on the grounds that "it is natural to the author"—part of his total kinesthetic/perceptual/instinctual being. In this sense, language is being, and the novel "a record of the writer's own desire, aspirations, struggles: in a word, a record of the profoundest experiences in the self" (485). Few artists have grasped the motif so intensely or left so much of themselves in the texture of their work as Van Gogh and Lawrence.

Lawrence's major statement on painting is "Introduction to These Paintings," written for his exhibition at the Warren Gallery, London, in 1929. In the first ten pages, he attempts to account, by pathology, for the English fear and hatred of the body. This phobia, he says, accounts for the English preference for landscape. He is mistaken, I think, when he says that landscape in general "doesn't call up the more powerful responses of the human imagination" (561). Having copied the English water-colorists as a young man, he takes them as his norm; he does not consider vital changes in landscape painting made by European expressionists such as Nolde, whose seas and clouds surge with power and who (like Van Gogh) seems spiritually akin to Lawrence (see chapter 3). When Lawrence says "there is no deep conflict" in landscape, he seems to be thinking in literary rather than plastic terms. Nighttime in Provence released a surge of Dionysian energy in Van Gogh; out of his passion, he created an expressionist order in which road, tree, sky, and faceless figures share. Lawrence's argument is really a double-bind; first, he says there is no deep conflict in landscape painting; then, when conflict forces itself on his attention, he dismisses it as not belonging rightly to the genre:

> Some of Turner's landscape compositions are, to my feelings, among the finest that exist. They still satisfy me more even than Van Gogh's or Cézanne's landscapes, which make a more violent assault on the emotions, and repel a little for that reason. Somehow I don't want landscape to make a violent assault on my feelings. Landscape is background with the figures left out or reduced to minimum, so let it stay back. Van Gogh's surging earth and Cézanne's explosive or rattling planes worry me. Not being profoundly interested in landscape, I prefer it to be rather quiet and unexplosive. ("Introduction to These Paintings" 561)

This dismissal is not without a trace of uncertainty, as if Lawrence were writing from one side only and unconsciously imposing a novelist's ideology on painting. He admits that Van Gogh's landscapes do have emotional impact; however he does not relish disturbance in landscape, being accustomed to the tranquillity of Constable and the English watercolorists. Whereas Cézanne's still-lifes and portraits, and all but his late landscapes, move toward equilibrium, Van Gogh's landscapes of Saint-Rémy and Auvers (1889–90) display an alarming tendency to disequilibrium as inner forces struggle for domination. Lawrence, very much aware of this dialectic of motion and rest, shares Cézanne's desire for a dynamic equilibrium in art.[7]

The disturbing quality of Van Gogh's landscapes appealed strongly to Antonin Artaud, who had spent nine years in mental institutions. "Carded by Van Gogh's nail," he writes, "the landscapes show their hostile flesh, the anvil of their eviscerated folds." In one, "[an] enormous mass of earth . . . like a musical introduction, seeks to form itself into a frozen wave"; in another, one sees "the pure enigma . . . of the countryside slashed, plowed, and harried on all sides by his intoxicated brush." In *Crows Over the Wheat Field* (July 1890),[8] "the earth become[s] equivalent to the sea" (Artaud 488, 497, 505, 508). At the same time, Cézanne's versions of *Mont Sainte-Victoire* (1885–87, 1904–06) wrestle with the structure of the land, locking lyrical and compositional impulses into a tight harmony.[9]

Lawrence's lack of interest in landscape must be taken in the context of an "introduction" to his own paintings, which emphasize the naked human figure. Turner's landscapes and seascapes, which Lawrence admires, often have a nonhuman protagonist such as a ship (*The Fighting Téméraire* [1839]) or a train (*Rain, Steam, and Speed* [1844]) that gives the work a dramatic or "literary" focus. Even when they approach abstraction, as in *Shade and Darkness: The Evening of the Deluge* or *Light and Color: The Morning after the Deluge* (both 1843),[10] they are apt to have an operatic or theatrical aura. Lawrence's largely negative response to post-impressionist landscape seems partly the consequence of youthful copying of milder English paintings and partly of a literary/artistic philosophy that stresses the body. Even so, he does acknowledge the *power* of Van Gogh's "surging earth,"[11] its impact on the feelings, and he admits that "the English delight in landscape is a delight in escape" ("Introduction to These Paintings" 561). While Cézanne's and Van Gogh's landscapes vibrate with emotional or plastic intensity, Lawrence reserves the fullness of his response for human figures. In terms of painterly values of color, line, mass, and shape, his preference for fully rounded forms may be seen as the limitation of a literary man. Yet Lawrence consistently puts life ahead of purely aesthetic values, in painting as in the novel.

Lawrence regards the impressionists' excursion into light and color as a glorious escapade ending in illusion, after which the post-impressionists (and later the cubists) come back to substance in a frustrated rage, splitting matter and the body into every variety of geometrical form. "As for landscape," he adds, "it comes in for some of the same rage. It has also suddenly gone lumpy. Instead of being nice and ethereal and non-sensual, it was discovered by van Gogh to be heavily, overwhelmingly substantial and sensual. Van Gogh took up landscape in heavy spadefuls" (565). Artaud strikingly echoes Lawrence's image when he says that "Van Gogh flings his earth as with a hoe" (508); Schapiro more technically explains that "[the] loading of the pigment is in part . . . a drastic effort to preserve in the image of things their tangible matter and to create something equally solid and concrete on the canvas" (*Van Gogh* 32).

Lawrence's metaphor of "spadefuls" recalls Van Gogh's many drawings of peasants and miners digging, in which the painter identifies with the toilers of the earth. After years of drawing the earth and its workers, culminating in his masterpiece *The Potato Eaters* (1885), and after studying Rembrandt, Hals, Rubens, and the human figure in Amsterdam and Antwerp, Van Gogh went to Paris, where his palette lightened and brightened in response to the impressionists and neo-impressionists. When he discovered his imaginary Japan in Provence, he no longer served up landscape in heavy spadefuls; he laid it down in sun-drenched vistas and subtly asymmetrical planes, patterns, and formal rhythms. Lawrence, ignoring these changes, discusses the broad outlines of Van Gogh's art rather than its specific historical phases.

In "Introduction to These Paintings," Lawrence sheds his expressionist affinity with Van Gogh in order to link his own art implicitly with that of Cézanne.[12] He finds Cézanne "[the] most interesting figure in modern art . . . not so much because of his achievement as because of his struggle" (571), which he identifies with his own. Despite doubts and defects, Cézanne stuck by "the little flame of life where he *felt* things to be true" and thus produced a vital art. Lawrence admires Cézanne's organic, tactile solidity rather than the "crystallization" of forms that appealed to Roger Fry.[13] In "The Artist's Vision," Fry gives an extremely formalist, antinatural definition of *creative vision*; for him, "impassioned vision" depends on detachment (48). This nonnatural vision involves *crystallization* and *distortion* to fit an evolving pattern, with a radical heightening or exclusion of forms. The identity of objects is submerged in the "mosaic of vision"; every percept submits to the hegemony of form.

With Clive Bell's *Art* (1913) and Fry's *Cézanne* (1927) in his sights, Lawrence gleefully ridicules "significant form" and "plastic values." Having disposed of the formalist mystique with an ironic "Cézannah!" he goes on to praise Cézanne for contrary, but subtly related, reasons:

> The actual fact is that in Cézanne modern French art made its first tiny step back to real substance, to objective substance, if we may call it so. Van Gogh's earth was still subjective earth, himself projected into the earth. But Cézanne's apples are a real attempt to let the apple exist in its own separate entity, without transfusing it with personal emotion. ("Introduction to These Paintings" 567)

Schapiro points to "the extraordinary search for compactness and solidity" in Cézanne's *Still Life with Apples* (1890–94), and adds: "It is hard to remember another painting of fruit so densely colored and so appealing to the touch" (*Cézanne* 100).[14] Merleau-Ponty, similarly, contrasts Cézanne's solidity with the impressionists' diffuseness: "The object is no longer covered by reflections," he writes, and lost in its relationships to the atmosphere and to other objects: it seems subtly illuminated from within, light emanates from it, and the result is an impression of solidity and material substance" ("Cézanne's Doubt" 12).

Lawrence's emphasis on substance contradicts Fry's on form. Pondering Cézanne's epistemology, Fry suggests that "reality," for the artist, "lay always behind this veil of colour, but it was different, more solid, more dense, in closer relation to the needs of the spirit" (*Cézanne* 37). In mystical fashion, he goes on to claim that "[Cézanne] gave himself up entirely to this desperate search for the reality hidden beneath the veil of appearance . . . " (38). The reality that Cézanne tried to see and express is, for Lawrence, neither behind nor "beneath the veil," but inherent *in* physical objects perceived by the senses.[15] In "the incarnate cosmos" there is no disjunction of spirit and matter, perception and reality.

When Fry says of Cézanne's *Still Life with Fruit Dish* (see pl. 16) that "[e]ach form seems to have a surprising amplitude. . . . [T]he spherical volumes . . . enforce, far more than real apples could, the sense of their density and mass" (*Cézanne* 47), he is expounding the composition of a higher, formal reality in art. But Cézanne himself had reminded Bernard that "[the] writer expresses himself through abstractions whereas the painter is concrete through line and color, his feelings, his perceptions" (*Letters* 297). To counter Fry's tendency to mystical formalism, Lawrence coined the notably concrete and nonconceptual metaphor "appleyness." Yet he does derive key ideas from Fry,[16] such as the suppression of emotion in an attempt to see the object-in-itself, unclouded by preconceptions or clichés. According to Fry, Cézanne painting a self-portrait "looks at his own head with precisely the same regard that he turned on an apple on the kitchen table" (*Cézanne* 56). Lawrence adopts Fry's phenomenology of "external vision" (35) but articulates it quite differently—as an element of sensuous vision rather than formal aesthetic.[17] Art, for Lawrence, is a matter of knowing the object all round, in the senses and not just in the mind:

> It is the appleyness of the portrait of Cézanne's wife that makes it so permanently interesting: the appleyness, which carries with it also the feeling of knowing the other side as well, the side you don't see. . . . For the intuitive apperception of the apple is so *tangibly* aware of the apple that it is aware of it *all round*, not only just of the front. The eye sees only fronts. . . . But intuition needs all-aroundness, and instinct needs insideness. The true imagination is for ever curving round to the other side, to the back of presented appearance. ("Introduction to These Paintings" 579)

Cézanne undercuts or "forgets" the concept, in order to paint the phenomenal perception of objects in space. "In the concentric waves of this visual space," writes Edwin Jones, "objects are seen in their roundness as well as their 'aroundness'" (97). Despite his "striving to realize that part of nature that, falling under our eyes, yields up the picture to us" and his dictum that "[c]onsulting nature provides us with the means for achieving our goal" (Cézanne, *Letters* 311, 313), Fry's formalist doctrine highlights "[the] transposition of all the data of nature into values of plastic colour" (*Cézanne* 69). The aesthetic effect exceeds apprehension of reality: "Though all comes by the interpretation of actual visual sensations," Fry insists that "[it] belongs to a world of spiritual values incommensurate but parallel with the actual world" (69). This Kantian disjunction of aesthetic and spiritual values from their perceptual and sensual coordinates characterizes Fry's formalism, which he himself relates to "creative illusions." Fry's privileging of abstract, formal values over the living or material body must have annoyed Lawrence. Of Cézanne's attraction to the female nude, Fry says: "His plastic feeling would alone have urged him to the contemplation of forms so eminently suited to embody his ideas, his love of ample, simply defined volumes" (83). Although Fry goes on to discuss Cézanne's attitudes to women and how they affected his art, one can imagine Lawrence spitting at the critic's prioritization of *abstract* volumes. Lawrence maintains that Cézanne, in his art, desired to realize more fully the sensuous life of objects, in their "thingness" or "thereness," rather than the "plastic volumes" that could be abstracted from them.

Yet Lawrence and Fry have something in common, for Fry is an aesthetic vitalist. Of one of Cézanne's landscapes, he writes that "it is by the accumulation of innumerable slight variations that he is able to construct for the imagination this immensity of space filled with light and vibrating with life" (62–63). But Fry's vitalist vision finds life in formal structures rather than in objects. Of the rigidly posed *Portrait of Mme. Cézanne*, he writes: "Every particle vibrates, the palpitation of life is revealed in the delicacy and sensitiveness of all these innumerable touches so freely and lightly inscribed on the canvas, to kindle what a smouldering glow of colour!" (68–69). Treatment is everything and it would be heresy to ask about the artist's relation with his sitter. When Fry declares that "the impression of living reality" in Cézanne's *Portrait of Gustave Geffroy* is "overwhelming,"[18] it becomes clear that his epistemology depends more upon articulation of formal relations within a static pattern that reduces the maximum amount of complexity to order than on any rhythmic process of "creative vision," let alone "the trembling instability of the balance." Form *is* reality for Fry—but a virtual reality, as Langer would have it, that exists alongside the substantial reality of objects without participating in it. In Fry's epistemology, the mind can know only a version of reality through abstract structures or spiritualized constructs of art. But Lawrence boldly asserts the tangible, palpable reality of material substance, embodied in Cézanne's apple and apprehended directly through the senses.

Lawrence admires Cézanne for qualities that are not necessarily, or naturally, his own. His earth, like Van Gogh's, is still very much "subjective earth," for what else is Spirit of Place but an ambiguous fusion of subject and landscape? As Georg Brandes says of Zola, *"He who paints the landscape is of it"* (qtd. in Nordenfalk 176). Yet L. D. Clark justly maintains "that [Lawrence] has brought back from the hinterland of self conspiring with place a great deal of the actual 'spirit' of the place itself" (letter to the author, 8 February, 1994). The artist's vision gives the landscape life. "In the best landscapes [writes Lawrence] we are fascinated by the mysterious *shiftiness* of the scene under our eyes; it shifts about as we watch it" ("Introduction to These Paintings" 580). The alternative to subjective responses would seem to be severely formal plastic values, but the dichotomy is false and Lawrence has no patience with Fry's aesthetic principles. Unlike all previous critics, he takes his stand on phenomenological grounds: if the apple can be painted in the round, so can the body in its sensuous and physical fullness. "Appleyness" becomes the vital ontological quality of Cézanne's art.

A central problem in aesthetics, as in epistemology, is the relation of subject to object. "Probably the chief gain from phenomenology," writes Merleau-Ponty, "is to have united extreme subjectivism and extreme objectivism in its notion of the world or of rationality" (*Phenomenology* xix). He describes something very like Lawrence's "fourth dimension" when he says: "The miracle of consciousness consists in its bringing to light, through attention, phenomena which re-establish the unity of the object in a new dimension at the very moment when they destroy it" (30).[19] The painter's analysis of his motif leads to a new synthesis. "Thus attention is . . . the active constitution of a new object . . . " (30). By this reckoning, the relation between art and perception is close; art discloses phenomena, thrown into relief by "acts of attention" and reshaped by plastic or verbal expression. When Merleau-Ponty declares that perception not only discovers but also *constitutes* meaning,[20] he comes close to describing the empathetic relation of an artist like Van Gogh to an object like the sunflower. Lawrence likewise identifies the "trembling and changing *balance*" between subject and object as the measure of integrity in art and life.

In "Introduction to These Paintings," Lawrence, having observed that Van Gogh "projected [himself] into the earth," projects his own philosophy into Cézanne's painting. As usual, even in Lawrence's most brilliant critical pronouncements, subjective and objective intermingle so that the figure that emerges is an interesting hybrid—Lawrence's Cézanne. Yet so striking is this figure that critics have been impressed with his insights.[21] Cézanne, says Lawrence, wanted to escape "the sky-blue prison" of mental consciousness by expressing the real "existence of matter." In a very direct way, Lawrence identifies Cézanne's struggle to realize his "petite sensation" in paint with his struggle to *be*, in the "procreative body." And here, of course, Cézanne's struggle becomes Lawrence's own: everything positive he says of Cézanne's painting applies equally well or better to his own writing. The "fight with the cliché" is a distinctly literary, as well as philosophical, concept that puts Lawrence close to Merleau-Ponty in his view of Cézanne's struggle.[22]

Instead of discussing his own paintings, Lawrence projects an inner dialectic onto Cézanne and Van Gogh. Pritchard comments: "Cézanne's attempt at objectivity was also Lawrence's, *who feared that he was too much like Van Gogh*, that is, subjective, a solipsist, a solitary being in an unreal world that reflected and manifested only himself" (19 [my italics]).[23] Van Gogh, fearing the vortex of the unconscious, clung all the more desperately to solid objects: "He needs objectivity, the most humble and obvious kind, as others need angels and God or pure forms . . . " (Schapiro, *Van Gogh* 32). It could be said that Van Gogh's shoes or chair or bed are *more* objective, more clearly seen and rendered as things with a function in space, than Cézanne's freely distorted fruits or jars or tables. Of course, no art is simply objective or subjective. As John Walker observes, "the painter fixes and heightens perceptual signs via the medium of oil painting simultaneously reproducing and transforming those perceptual signs" (68). In Van Gogh, objects are transformed by emotional energy, in Cézanne by structural vision, so that Van Gogh's art seems more personal, Cézanne's more classical. But it should not be forgotten that Van Gogh, objectively, places more importance on "the feeling for the things themselves, for reality . . . than [on] the feeling for pictures" (qtd. in Schapiro, *Van Gogh* 32), while Cézanne, subjectively, strives to give plastic form to his sensations. The strength of their painting lies in a "subtle interrelatedness" of subject and object.

In Lawrence's ethically charged aesthetic, vitality and wholeness are prime values. A work of art, he affirms, should give "a whole conception of the existence of Man—creation, good, evil, life, death, resurrection, the separating of the stream of good and evil, and its return to the eternal source" (*Letters* 2: 263). Very few artists would attempt such an epic synthesis amid the chaos of a world at war; but in 1915, Lawrence, about to complete his "one bright book of life," *The Rainbow*, was filled with enthusiasm for a religious conception of art stemming from the Renaissance. The complete iconic work, from his point of view, was Fra Angelico's triptych *The Last Judgment*, and he was in no mood for tolerating meaningless concatenations of geometrical figures. Such formal experimentation in contemporary art seems frivolous because it allows no vital interpenetration of subject and object. What Lawrence looks for is life-sustaining vision and the form that expresses it. "*Do* rub this into Duncan Grant," he urged Lady Ottoline, "and save him his foolish waste. Rembrandt, Corot, Goya, Monet have been preparing us our instances—now for the great hand which can collect all the instances into an absolute statement of the whole" (263). It was hardly fair to expect Grant to be the new Renaissance artist. But if eternity can be reflected in a grain of sand, man's relation to the cosmos can be reflected in a work of art, and Lawrence aspired to such unifying vision.

For Lawrence's comments on his own painting one has to go to the short autobiographical piece "Making Pictures," which is fresher and freer from polemics than "Introduction to These Paintings." There he describes the interplay of attention and intuition in his painting. In November 1926, Maria Huxley had brought four canvases to the Villa Mirenda, near Florence, and Lawrence had attacked them with house paints and brushes: "I disappeared into that canvas. It is to me the most exciting moment—when you have a blank canvas and a big brush full of wet colour, and you plunge" ("Making Pictures" 603). Writing is inevitably a "struggle into conscious being," but painting was liberation for Lawrence because he could tackle it more or less spontaneously. "[W]hen you start to paint," he says, "shut your theoretic eyes and go for it with instinct and intuition" (603). Although grateful for practical hints from Earl Brewster, he was not concerned with accepted techniques but solely with the art of "making pictures"—of expressing a whole conception in paint. "A picture lives with the life you put into it" (604), he says, and no amount of technical perfection can, in itself, make a picture live.

Lawrence describes some long-stemmed camellias he had seen on a stall in Barcelona as a "vision" that he would like to paint. But he could not have painted them from nature, he says, because "by staring at them I should have lost them" (605). In this he resembles Gauguin, who believed the artist should dream in front of nature,[24] rather than Cézanne or Van Gogh, who studied their motifs and tried to grasp them, even while they transformed them. Van Gogh craved direct contact through his art with sitters or sunflowers; modestly but stubbornly he resisted Gauguin's gospel, maintaining that he himself had "no imagination." He had learned all he needed to know about formal techniques by putting himself through an intensive two-year apprenticeship in drawing before he started to paint. At the end of this training, his hand was an extension of his eye and he could paint instinctively from nature. The act of feeling his way into a motif created rhythms that give his compositions unity. He would study the object profoundly, then immerse himself in the act of painting. Few artists, if any, have painted faster or with more prodigious energy. Van Gogh slowly and painstakingly prepared himself for the creative explosion of his last two years. When the upsurge of his being threatened to engulf the universe in waves of force, he had the technical mastery to hold the vision—and the picture—firmly together.

Through copying masterpieces by Fra Angelico, Lorenzetti, and Carpaccio, Lawrence "*really* learned what life, what powerful life has been put into every curve, every motion of a great picture. Purity of spirit, sensitive awareness, intense eagerness to portray an inward vision . . . " (606). He shared Van Gogh's hero worship of "the great Rembrandt" and his modified admiration for the lavish, fleshly, Rubens;[25] he copied several Dutch masters, such as Peter de Hooch and Vandyck. However, it was not until Maria Huxley presented him with those canvases that he took the plunge and discovered he could do original work: "Then it became an orgy, making pictures" (606). He tried not to copy objects but to paint untrammeled visions: "The picture must all come out of the artist's inside, awareness of forms and figures. We can call it memory, but it is more than memory. It is the image as it lives in the consciousness, alive like a vision, but unknown" (606). Lawrence's "nostalgic" image of Cagliari as the Jerusalem of his childhood imagination (*Sea and Sardinia* 58–59) exemplifies such a vision.

Lawrence painted to relieve the pressure of his writing and for the sheer joy of seeing his visions appear on canvas. He was more concerned with getting these visions out wholesale than with transmuting feeling into form. Some of his images, like *Fire Dance* (1926), *Yawning* (1927–28), or *Dance Sketch* (1928),[26] have an immediate, almost expressionist impact, but most are representations of sensual *ideas* and, to that extent, "literary." Lawrence wrote to Brewster: "I . . . put a phallus, a lingam you call it, in each one of my pictures somewhere. And I paint no picture that wont shock people's castrated social spirituality. I do this out of positive belief . . . " (*Letters* 5: 648). In the verbal medium he was wiser, subtler, harder to pin down. But in his paintings, he tries to hammer home a central theme, the supremacy of the phallic and procreative body, as in *A Holy Family* (1926), *Boccaccio Story* (1926), *The Mango Tree* (1927–28), *Family on a Verandah* (1928), *Rape of the Sabine Women* (1928), and *Contadini* [*Peasants*] (1928).[27] The results are often grotesque, due to unplanned anatomical distortions, yet Lawrence's desire to make pictures that will be complete expressions is a healthy one. After a visit to Alberto Magnelli's studio in Rome, he wrote to Brewster: "I'm not so conceited as to think that my marvellous ego and unparalleled technique will make a picture. I like a picture to be a picture to the whole sensual self, and as such it must have a meaning of its own, and concerted action" (637).

Lawrence realized that the living novel depends on "quick relatedness" of characters with everything else, "snow, bed-bugs, sunshine, the phallus, trains, silk-hats, cats, sorrow, people, food, diphtheria, fuchsias, stars, ideas, God, tooth-paste, lightning, and toilet-paper" ("The Novel" 183). The list is a surreal conjunction of things that apparently have nothing to do with each other. Painting is less eclectic than fiction in this regard, and Lawrence stressed the visionary wholeness of a picture rather than the interrelation of its parts. He had no intention of sharing a platform with Roger Fry, who insisted that a proper response to painting is always a response to formal relations. But there is a parallel: Lawrence insisted that art comes out of vital *human* relations—of man with woman, man with man, and man with God or cosmos. Fry, with his repudiation of the anecdotal, and Lawrence, with his repudiation of pure form, represent two extremes.[28] Lawrence's painting illustrates his values and vision, rather than creating "plastic equivalents" (Fry). Here and there he does make the medium come alive, as in the flamy color of *Red Willow Trees* (1927), the expressive gestures of *Dance Sketch* (1928), or the physical solidity of *Contadini*.[29] But Lawrence, who paradoxically found that "the joy in words goes deeper and is for that reason more unconscious. The *conscious* delight is certainly stronger in paint" ("Making Pictures" 606) was too intent on transferring his vision direct from mind to canvas to lavish much care on plastic expression. His paintings are known today only because of his writing.

All artists turn to earlier artists in whose works they see the image of their own creative struggle upheld, illuminated, or foreshadowed. "If no painting comes to be *the* painting, if no work is ever absolutely completed and done with, still each creation changes, alters, enlightens, deepens, confirms, exalts, re-creates, or creates in advance all the others" (Merleau-Ponty, "Eye and Mind" 190). Or as Birkin puts it, "only artists produce for each other the world that is fit to live in" (*Women in Love* 208). Van Gogh, despite his tragic life, was such an artist for Lawrence, although Cézanne is his model for formulating how physical, sensual reality can be expressed in art. He wished with Cézanne to lay hold on life in its palpable forms and, above all, on "the procreative body." Sensing that his affinity with Van Gogh lay all too deep, Lawrence struggled away from the vortex of self-expression toward Cézanne's impersonal classicism.[30] If he consciously identifies with Cézanne's painstaking attempt to express otherness, his own language of the unconscious seems closer to Van Gogh's projective self-expression. Actually, both poles are integral to Lawrence's verbal art, where their tension is a source of strength. Cézanne's art, like Van Gogh's, helped Lawrence to expound his vitalist æsthetic. But his primordial and expressionist affinities with Van Gogh, based on a plunge into immanence that fuses subject and object, mark his style more deeply than his elective affinities with Cézanne, based on classical objectivity and solidity of form.

9

LAWRENCE, GAUGUIN, AND JAPANESE ART IN *KANGAROO* AND *THE PLUMED SERPENT*

Lawrence's "savage pilgrimage" (*Letters* 4:375; cf. Carswell) began in November 1919, when he left England for Florence; his self-imposed exile lasted the rest of his life, broken only by brief visits to England in 1923–24 and 1926. Lawrence's impressions were changing—accumulating, shifting, recombining, diverging—as he responded alertly to Spirit of Place,[1] and developments in his writing reflect this changing external vision. The voyage outward exposed Lawrence to new sensations—the dazzling sun, the surge and sweep of space, the interrelation of planes and colors—that greatly expanded his powers of perception and led him to experiment with new forms of expression. Lawrence's vision and expression alter subtly as new sensations of space and color in landscape converge with renewed aesthetic responses to heightening and clarification, blurring and harmonizing of forms in painting. While he readjusted his focus to geographical Spirit of Place, new ways of seeing—sparser, more long-range, oriented to a background of deep space in Australia; exotic, colorful, dreamlike, decorative in Mexico— also reflect his knowledge of Gauguin, whose Tahitian journal Lawrence read in Sicily, of Puvis de Chavannes, whose painting he studied in Melbourne, and of Japanese Ukiyo-e prints, which had left an indelible imprint on his imagination. The challenge for Lawrence was to rearticulate these sensory and plastic sources in ways that express his own seeing and being.[2]

Kangaroo (1923) can be read as a travel book describing the Lawrences' experiences in Australia, its rather ramshackle plot superimposed on a vital background. The freshest and most vivid writing in the novel describes the new/old land. "[When] the landscape painter in [Lawrence] feels the setting of a story," wrote T. E. Lawrence, "miracles happen" (qtd. in Alcorn 90).

While he was contemptuous of Australian society and boasted of having isolated himself from human contact, Lawrence was drawn to the primordial quality of the land, where "earth and air are new, and the spirit of place untouched" (*Letters* 4: 260).

Lawrence found "a great fascination in the country itself: a sort of lure in the bush" (280). While critics have faulted *Kangaroo* for its loosely structured, fragmented quality, John B. Humma finds that the novel "[has] a unity, a dark god of its own, the bush" (32). This magical nonhuman presence appears when the newly arrived Somers takes a walk at night: "[He] had just come to a clump of tall, nude dead trees, shining almost phosphorescent with the moon, when the terror of the bush overcame him. . . . There was a presence" (*Kangaroo* 14). Somers, who is sensitive to what Lawrence Durrell calls "hidden magnetic fields which the landscape is trying to communicate" (161), attributes his terror to "the roused spirit of the bush."[3] From the safety of a township on the hill, he looks back on the panorama, with "somebody burning off the bush in a ring of sultry red fire under the moon in the distance, a slow ring of creeping red fire, like some ring of fireflies, upon the far-off darkness of the land's body, under the white blaze of the moon above" (*Kangaroo* 15). The land, even as perceived by an alienated white consciousness, is alive and has a spirit in it, as the New Mexican mountains have in "St. Mawr."

The primordial silence, stillness, and strength of the land, its indifference to human life, impress themselves on Somers:

> That curious sombreness of Australia, the sense of oldness, with the forms all worn down low and blunt, squat. The squat-seeming earth. And then . . . dark old rocks, and sombre bush with its different pale-stemmed, dull-leaved gum-trees standing graceful, and various heathy looking undergrowth, and great spikey things like yuccas. As they turned south they saw tree-ferns standing on one knobbly leg, among the gums. . . . It was virgin bush . . . The strange, as it were *invisible* beauty of Australia, which is undeniably there, but which seems to lurk just beyond the range of our white vision. You feel you can't *see*—as if your eyes hadn't the vision in them to correspond with the outside landscape. (76–77)

The question is how to envision the invisible. The landscape overpowers any effort to conceptualize it: it is "aboriginal," "out of our ken," "virginal," "aloof." Its haunting yet evasive presence invites animistic responses. The antiquity of the land manifests an unbridgeable time gap between the aboriginal past and the white settlers' present. The land has become invisible because "perceptual habits," bred by interaction with it,[4] have been lost or never acquired.

In Lawrence's metaphoric style, human consciousness is subtly related to visualization of the environment. Somers's reaction to the veiled quality of the land recalls Birkin's desire to get beyond Ursula's visual appeal, his desire for "a woman I don't see" (*Women in Love* 147). Ursula "[has] fallen strange and dim, out of the sheath of the material life, like a berry falls from the only world it has ever known, down out of the sheath on to the real unknown," and Birkin tells her (as he might be telling himself): "I want to find you, where you don't know your own existence, the you that your common self denies utterly" (144, 147). Somers, more radically, "[has] fallen apart out of the human association" (*Kangaroo* 345). The animism he feels in the Australian bush has a similar appeal: the land seems unfathomably old and mysterious, and at the same time, pristine, new. It has the lure of Conrad's African coast, "with [its] air of whispering—'Come and find out'" (*Heart of Darkness* 16).

The bush seems to contain some ancient knowledge that Lawrence associates with the aboriginal race: "Somers always felt he looked at it through a cleft in the atmosphere; as one looks at one of the ugly faced, distorted aborigines with his wonderful dark eyes that have such an incomprehensible ancient shine in them, across gulfs of unbridged centuries" (*Kangaroo* 77). The primordial Australian landscape is associated with a beauty and power that are "formless" because unshaped by human will and consciousness. The bush is the antithesis of the cultivated landscapes of Italy that had given Lawrence back so much of himself (*Sea and Sardinia* 131) or the romantic landscapes of the English Lake District as divined by Wordsworth.[5] In Humma's formulation, "The bush is the aboriginal, mysterious symbol of our 'unconscious,' 'blood' self" (39). But the bush is not a "symbol" of anything human; it exists as an extrahuman presence, *correlative* with the unconscious. To Somers it is sublime, expanding his being while overwhelming his individual identity.[6]

Australia presents bare views of earth and sky, space and distance; the bush is vaster and more daunting than the rugged hills and moors of

Sardinia. Part of its appeal is its vagueness, its dull tints and half-submerged tones. The dreamlike vision of the landscape finds a correlative in paintings of Puvis de Chavannes, a replica of whose mural *Winter* (1891–92) Lawrence saw in the Melbourne Art Gallery. To the artist Earl Brewster he writes:

> It is extraordinarily subtle, *unknown* country. The gum trees are greyish, with pale trunks—and so often the pale, pure silver dead trees with vivid limbs: then the extraordinary *delicacy* of the air and the blue sky, the weird bits of creek and marsh, dead trees, sand, and very blue hills—it reminds me of Puvis de Chavannes more than any country I have seen: so apparently monotonous, yet when you look into it, such subtly different distances, in layers, and such exquisite forms—trees, flat hills—strange, standing as it were at the *back* of the vision. It needs Japanese treatment—or Puvis. . . . I still hated his self-conscious sentiment. . . . But love that detaily pattery subtle layering of distances. (*Letters* 4: 265)

Lawrence does not approach Australia with a blank mind but tries to seize its essence by filtering his vision through aesthetic models. He shares the love of Japanese design with Zola, who spoke of "these transparent horizons, this beautiful, transparent colouring of the Japanese" (qtd. in Wichmann 24), and with Van Gogh and Gauguin, who collected Japanese prints and saw the shimmering landscape of the Midi as "colored Puvis mixed with Japan" (Gauguin, *Writings of a Savage* 27). Lawrence, similarly, found a happy conjunction of "Provence, Japan, and Italy" under an almond tree in London (*Complete Poems* 58). For the writer, as for the painters of the Yellow House, a way of seeing derived from Japanese woodcuts (see pl. 17)—"Look closely at the Japanese," Gauguin tells Bernard; "they draw admirably and yet in them you will see life outdoors and in the sun without shadows" (27)—came to subtly interfuse the act of looking and sharpen his perception.[7]

Van Gogh imaginatively transposed Provence to Japan—"[We] like Japanese painting, we have felt its influence, all the impressionists have that in common; then why not go to Japan, that is to say the equivalent of Japan, the South?"—and identified his own vision with Japanese perception and expression: "[O]ne's sight changes: you see things with an eye more Japanese, you feel color differently. The Japanese draw quickly . . . like a lightning flash, because their nerves are finer, their feeling simpler" (*Complete Letters*

2: 589, 590). In mid-July 1888 Van Gogh wrote to Bernard about his pen-and-ink drawings of the wheat fields. In the vast panorama of that landscape, in which details contrast with empty space, he had tried to suggest infinity:

> [An] immense stretch of flat country, a bird's-eye view of it seen from the top of a hill—vineyards and fields of newly reaped wheat. All this multiplied in endless repetitions, stretching away toward the horizon like the surface of a sea, bordered by the little hills of the Crau.
>
> It does not have a Japanese look, and yet it is really the most Japanese thing I have done; a microscopic figure of a laborer, a little train running across the wheat field—this is all the animation there is in it. (*Complete Letters* 3: 501)

Van Gogh admired the economy and precision of Japanese art, its ability to suggest so much with so little. The paradox of not looking "Japanese" yet being intrinsically so implies an internal modification of Van Gogh's vision rather than formal imitation. Lawrence also derived acuity of aesthetic vision from the Japanese, plus a rhythm of the eye that selects, frames, isolates, and connects figures and objects in a landscape.

Lawrence sometimes creates Japanese effects in the more decorative passages of his letters, but his concept of "Japonaiserie" seems to differ from Van Gogh's in the treatment of space. Thus he writes from Lerici on the Gulf of Spezia: "The pines on the little peninsula were very dark and snowy, above a lead grey sea. It was queer and Japanesy: no distance, no perspective, everything near and sharp on a dull grey ground. The water cut out a very perfect, sweeping curve from the snow on the beach" (*Letters* 2: 141). Lawrence is probably thinking of Japanese snow scenes, such as Hiroshige's *Mountain Stream in Snow* (see pl. 18), in which shapes of trees, riverbanks, and bridge are sharply cut out against a muted white background, or of *Evening Snow* scenes with their leaden skies and melancholy poetry.[8] He knew Japanese woodcuts well enough to speak of a print reproduced on the cover of the American edition of *Tortoises* as "surely Hiroshige's" (*Letters* 5: 175).[9]

Just as Van Gogh and Gauguin found Japan in Provence, Lawrence found it in Italy, Australia, and Mexico. Many of his landscape sketches have a Japanese stamp, as does this Italian scene overlaid with transcendent tones of Puvis de Chavannes:

> [H]igh up on the lovely swinging road, in the strong evening sunshine, I saw a bullock wagon moving like a vision. . . .
>
> Everything was clear and sun-coloured up there, clear-grey rocks partak-

ing of the sky, tawny grass and scrub, browny-green spires of cypresses, and then the mist of grey-green olives fuming down to the lake-side. There was no shadow, only clear sun-substance built up to the sky, a bullock wagon moving slowly in the high sunlight, along the uppermost terrace of the military road. I sat in the warm stillness of the transcendent afternoon. (*Twilight in Italy* 110)

The theme of timeless human activities played out against a luminous backdrop is typical of Oriental art, as is the motif of the bullock wagon, whose "clanking . . . resound[s] close in [the watcher's] ears" (110); while the daring viewpoint, looking up from a deep chasm at a road winding up the mountainside with "beautiful curves" and "clear leaping bridges," transposes the Italian scene into a Japanese key[10]—as in Hiroshige's *Tsumagome*,[11] or *Sakanoshita: The Throwing-Away-the-Brush Peak* (see pl. 19). The visual effect is enhanced by planar gradations of light and color and the contrast of misty olive trees with sun-drenched slopes. The arrangement of the scene in piled-up planes exemplifies "that detaily patterny subtle layering of distances" that Lawrence admired so much in Puvis.

Van Gogh described the layering of colors and animated action in a quayside scene on the Rhône as "pure Hokusai" (*Complete Letters* 2: 624). Hokusai's art, as described by Muneshige Narazaki, has clear affinities with the vital art of Van Gogh and Lawrence:

Hokusai . . . sought to apprehend nature in its more universal aspects—that is, in its physical reality and as a source of unending energy and continuous creation. He felt his own creativity as part of the process of creation that he saw going on all about him. His art was subjective insofar as he refashioned and reorganized nature to suit his own will; he also seems to identify the energy of nature with his own inner energy. . . . (*Hokusai* 24)

What Van Gogh and Lawrence apparently learned from Japanese art is a preexpressionist heightening of forms that makes one aware of the ceaseless rhythms of life. Seen through the lens of Japanese art, a landscape can become a palimpsest or a vision in which the accidental has been eliminated or reconstructed as a timeless harmony.

The bush alone does not unify *Kangaroo*, as Humma suggests, for there is total alienation between its brooding presence and the fragmentary foreground activities of the characters. The human plot, involving ups and downs in the marriage of Harriet and Somers and his flirtation with fascist and socialist movements, is dwarfed by the looming, nonhuman forces of bush and sea. Landscapes are not artfully woven into the plot as in *The Plumed Serpent* (1926) but overshadow the action, which is founded on antinomies of human and nonhuman, political and primordial.

Empty space makes the viewer aware of the prehuman architecture of the earth. The pristine, unspoiled landscape contrasts with the tawdriness of social and political intrigue. The light seems new and the air alive.

> There was an unspeakable beauty about the mornings, the great sun from the sea, such a big, untamed, proud sun, rising up into a sky of such tender delicacy, blue, so blue, and yet so frail that even blue seems too coarse a colour to describe it, more virgin than humanity can conceive; the land inward lit up . . . and then rising like a wall, facing the light and still lightless, the tor face, with its high-up rim so grey, having tiny trees feathery against the most beautiful frail sky in the world. Morning! (*Kangaroo* 82–83)

Rejecting the dead world of wartime, Lawrence in Cornwall was already affirming "[a] rarer reality: a world with thin, clean air and untouched skies, that have not been looked at nor covered with smoke" (*Letters* 2: 498). In Australia, these tropes of ecological purity and refinement find objective correlatives in a vaster landscape. It is the precivilized, "virgin" element and the living sun that attract Lawrence; his paeans to the nonhuman mark stages in a savage pilgrimage that leads to deification and politicization of natural forces in *The Plumed Serpent*.

Somers responds to "the voice of Australia" in spring, and the animism of "the great gum-trees [running] up their white limbs into the air like quicksilver" (*Kangaroo* 342) recalls the painterly images of poplars and fig tree in *Sea and Sardinia* (96–97). The arabesque motif of "white, naked nerves" or "stark grey limbs" (*Kangaroo* 344) configures organic forms in an intricate network of living and dead. The animistic imagery is carried over to a view of flame trees in the sunset that implies a vision of life and death:

> So the land swooped in grassy swoops, past the railway, steep up to the bush: here and there thick-headed palm trees left behind by the flood of time and the flood of civilisation both: bungalows with flame-trees. . . . And so the great tree-covered swoop upwards of the tor, to the red fume of clouds, red like the flame-flowers, of sunset. . . . And the thick aboriginal dusk settling down. (344)

Like the bush, the ocean is a forceful presence. There are many descriptions of its surging rhythms and color:

The waves rolled in pale and bluey, glass-green, wonderfully heavy and liquid. They curved with a long arch, then fell in a great hollow thud and a spurt of white foam and a long, soft, snow-pure rush of forward flat foam. Somers watched the crest of fine, bristling spume fly back from the head of the waves as they turned and broke. The sea was all yellow-green light. (81)

This painter's vision of changing forms and colors catches the nonhuman power and beauty of the ocean, as Nolde does in *The Sea* (1913).[12] Even on a rainy day, sea-light and colors have a hypnotic fascination: "Under the dark-grey sky the sea looked bright, but coldly bright, with its yellow-green waves and its ramparts of white foam" (146). The plasticity and color of Lawrence's images are similar to those of Nolde, who, after surviving a storm in a small boat, "painted seas with wildly rolling green waves, and only a tiny bit of yellow sky at the upper corners" (Nolde, *Years of Struggles* [1934], qtd. in Haftmann, facing pl. 13).

Metonymic scanning appears in vivid vignettes of action, a couple of which involve steamers toiling in heavy seas: "And through the light came a low, black tramp steamer, lurching up and down on the waves, disappearing altogether in the lustrous water, save for her bit of yellow-banded funnel and her mast-tips: then emerging like some long, out-of-shape dolphin on a wave-top" (*Kangaroo* 81). Synecdochic glimpses of the wallowing steamer have the visual luster and roughness of Nolde's *Tug-boat on the Elbe* (1910).[13] Beaming the viewpoint back from the storm-tossed boat makes a clump of trees on the shore look "like ragged Noah's Ark trees" (82). Metonymic spatial representation is reflected in verbless phrases set off by semicolons, and in shifting directional signals: "the jetty"—"the foreshore"—"northwards"—"inland."

Lawrence's metaphorical ramparts form part of a fortress whose other wall is the bush. In Australia, he communed more willingly with land and ocean than with people, and his images of waves, "turning like mill-wheels white all down the shore" (329), show verbal invention and variety. Figurative images intensify perceptions of shape and color; through an accumulation of momentary glimpses, Lawrence builds a composite image of the sea in its otherness. As Somers strolls the beach alone, glistening seabirds perch "like opalescent whitish bubbles on the dark, flat, ragged wet rock, in the sun," and a strange octopod unfurls its tentacles in a rock pool (331, 332–33).

If the sea in *Sea and Sardinia* stimulates a sense of freedom, in *Kangaroo* it symbolizes "surging passional forces" (Clark, *Minoan Distance* 263). The flux and reflux of moonlit waves has an animistic force, a terrible vitalism, that recalls moon-drenched scenes in *The Rainbow*: "A huge, but a cold passion swinging back and forth. Great waves of radium swooping with a down-curve and rushing up the shore. Then calling themselves back again, retreating to the mass. Then rushing with venomous radium-burning speed into the body of the land. Then recoiling with a low swish, leaving the flushed sand naked" (*Kangaroo* 340). Here Lawrence reaches beyond ordinary perception to radiochemical allotropy and futurist imagery to convey the ruthless rhythm of natural forces.

Bush and ocean converge under a sunset sky as Lawrence seeks to express the elusive spirit of the land:

> The west, over the land, was a clear gush of light up from the departed sun. The east, over the Pacific, was a tall concave of rose-coloured clouds, a marvellous high apse. Now the bush had gone dark and spectral again, on the right hand. You might still imagine inhuman presences moving among the gumtrees. And from time to time, on the left hand, they caught sight of the long green rollers of the Pacific, with the star-white foam, and back of that, the dusk green sea glimmered over with smoky rose, reflected from the eastern horizon where the bank of flesh-rose colour and pure smoke-blue lingered a long time, like magic, as if the sky's rim were cooling down. It seemed to Somers characteristic of Australia, this far-off flesh-rose bank of colour on the sky's horizon, so tender and unvisited, topped with the smoky, beautiful blueness. (32)

Distance and blueness create a reflective atmosphere, while the primordial ethos is felt in "subtle layering of distances", through repetition and symmetrically matched directional signals, that combines metonymy with subliminal metaphors of the earth's birth. The layering of space is matched by a play of complementary colors and half-tones, overlapping and transmuting, as in the mornings Harriet "watch[es] the lovely, broken colours of the Australian dawn"—primrose yellow, "bluey primrose," "smoky red-purple," "rose and mist-blue," "the sea all reddish, smoky flesh-colour, moving under a film of gold . . . with the foam breaking blue as forgetmenots or frost" (101). It is a vision that seems to herald the breakup of white mental consciousness, leaving the senses open, "dawn-kaleidoscopic within the crack" (Lawrence, "Pomegranate," *Complete Poems* 279).

In July 1920 Lawrence wrote to Compton Mackenzie: "I've got a *very good* book from America about the Marquesas Islands . . . also Gauguin's

Noa-Noa which is Marquesas too" (*Letters* 3: 563). Although he makes derisory comments about Gauguin, Lawrence read Somerset Maugham's *The Moon and Sixpence* (1919) and must have been interested in the painter's attempt to live like a "savage" in the tropics. His readings and musings on voyages to the South Seas are reflected in visual images that have the dimly glowing tones, lit by brighter touches, of Gauguin's palette. In depicting the Australian dawn, he uses "strange, mixed colours" and hazy, misty, smoky, glazed tints rather than clear tones; the result is both sensuous and atmospheric, conveying the spirit of the vast continent as "a kind of virgin sensual aloofness" (32).

As Somers turns to sky, sea, and land for silence and relief, his mood subtly alters. The other side of his misanthropy is a religious celebration of that pristine world that lies beyond the scattered fringe of civilization. Feeling absolved from human ties, he turns to "[the] soft, blue, humanless sky of Australia, the pale, white unwritten atmosphere of Australia. Tabula rasa. The world a new leaf. And on the new leaf, nothing. The white clarity of the Australian, fragile atmosphere. Without a mark, without a record" (*Kangaroo* 332). Lawrence's protagonist seeks empathy with nonhuman qualities in land and sky. The atmosphere is "unwritten" because no one has yet captured it in words; the land is "virgin" territory, uncontaminated by literary, historical, or human associations. Australia is seen as the radical Other of European civilization; projecting himself against this background, the narrator is revealed as someone who has cared too much, who is all too human despite his cult of the "humanless," who wants to transcend writing, and who needs a new start. Somers reads his destiny in the landscape; his own existence merges with his sense of Australia, and the Spirit of Place with a deepening awareness of his own being. His "act of pure attention" employs all the senses in "divination" (*Sketches of Etruscan Places* 62), and the doubling of subject and object, spirit and place, produces the following homologies: conscious ego is to Being as Europe is to Australia and human settlements to the Land.

A casually referred to "Japanese" aesthetic[14] again separates distance into clearly marked planes and emphasizes design by leaving empty space between objects. Lawrence exploits "those elements in Japanese art that create form by simplification rather than elaboration" (Wichmann 24). After a regressive dream of an Italian palazzo and a Gothic cathedral, Somers awakens to haphazard Australian reality: "Since then he had loved the Australian landscape, with the remote gum-trees running their white nerves into the air, the random streets of flimsy bungalows, all loose from one another, and temporary seeming, the bungalows perched precariously on the knolls, like Japanese paper-houses, below the ridge of wire-and-tuft trees" (*Kangaroo* 346). The structures of Lawrence's vision and style are modified by the genius loci as he withdraws from European symbolism into a looser and more carefree Oriental/antipodal mode of perception. Disrupting the closed forms and metaphoric emphases of Northern Gothic, Lawrence develops a metonymy of the formless, "amorphous," "foundationless," random, unplanned, remote, temporary, and precarious among which one can breathe freely.

> No no, the flimsy hills of Australia were like a new world, and the frail *inconspicuousness* of the landscape, that was still so clear and clean, clean of all fogginess or confusion; but the frail, aloof, inconspicuous clarity of the landscape was like a sort of heaven, bungalows, shacks, corrugated iron and all. (346–47)

Lawrence's vision is sharpened by antithetical awareness: Australia is free from the cluttered space and cramped consciousness of Europe; its openness and casualness are valuable antidotes to Europe's used-up, closed-in atmosphere. The temporary quality of human habitations, silhouetted against the sprawling backdrop of land and sky, appears in the image of flimsy "Japanese paper-houses" contrasted with the "huge, pale-grey bulk of . . . an old gothic cathedral" (346). Instantaneity of perception and rapid metonymic shifts are marks of the writer's changed awareness of space and culture.

Each continent has its characteristic tones, and Lawrence has a painter's eye for gradations and combinations. Color is not just an attribute of objects but also a vital element of perception and composition. The changing colors of the sky seem to have a life of their own. Somers's sunset vision (32) is the counterpart of Ursula's dawn awakening on the downs, where "the fountain" of the rising sun spills gold across the land (*Rainbow* 431). Whereas the *Rainbow* passage suggests the power of Van Gogh's sun, the image of sunset in Australia, with its hovering hyphenations and modifications—"star-white," "dusk green," "smoky rose," "flesh-rose," "smoke-blue"—fusing substance or atmosphere with color, and its predominantly blue tonality, parallels the mixed colors and musical harmonies of Gauguin's South Seas.[15]

Lawrence told Brewster that the Australian landscape "needs Japanese treatment." The metonymic "Japanese" style is seen in his treatment of spatial relations and topographical forms; objects are diminished by distance to produce sharply clarified patterns of separate items:

> So it was all round—a far and wide scattering of pale-roofed bungalows at random among grassy, cut-out streets, all along the levels above the sea. . . . There were knolls and pieces of blue creek-hollow, blue of fresh-water in lagoons on the yellow sands. Up the knolls perched more bungalows, on very long front legs and no back legs, caves of dark underneath. And on the skyline, a ridge of wiry trees with dark plume-tufts at the ends of the wires, and those little loose crystals of different-coloured, sharp-angled bungalows cropping out beneath. All in a pale, clear air, clear and yet far off, as it were visionary. (344)

The "visionary" quality of this carefully distributed, decentered composition assimilates Japanese design. Space is divided into a series of planes; scattered roofs are integrated with terrain; organic and geometric forms are contrasted. As Wichmann explains, "depth in Japanese prints and painting is represented by a systematic fragmentation. The eye is directed towards distant or middle ground by the arrangement of foreground objects . . . [and] the fragment [is transformed] into an overwhelming totality" (10). "Instantaneousness, mobility," "a natural, transient posture," plus distinctness, are the aim. In Hokusai's restructuring of space, "[the] different effects of a high- or low-positioned horizon are contrasted. A thin section of empty space, placed high, is reached by a piling-up of landscape elements; the opposite is a soaring sky above a reduced, narrow patch of earth—geological layers being replaced by air, cloud, and atmosphere" (173). In his Australian landscapes and skyscapes, Lawrence uses both the high and low angles of vision, associated with "the tall, narrow format" of Japanese art, which "offers innumerable possibilities for varying the pictorial balance, with weighting to the left, to the right, or centrally" (173). The new metonymic style gives a loosened and liberated sense of space.

The oddly assorted, angular bungalows, perching precariously on the hillside, contrast with the wavelike contours of the land that lead in planar progression past the toylike "colliery steaming among the trees" (that certainly would have caught Lawrence's eye) to an expanse of sunset sky (*Kangaroo* 344). Metonymic eye movements are represented by a series of verbless phrases divided by colons, without other punctuation to modify the staccato scanning. Syntagmatic linking of fragments guides the eye through a succession of planes. Rather than integrating human and natural, as Hiroshige's form tends to do, Lawrence's spatial construction subordinates the human/industrial setting to the apocalyptic drama of sunset—as the human is dwarfed by the natural in Hokusai's *Great Wave Off Kanagawa* or *The Coast of Seven Leagues* (see pl. 20).[16]

In *The Plumed Serpent*, Lawrence further develops the art of the vignette, formalizing human action in a landscape in ways that relate both to Japanese prints and to Gauguin's paintings. In his introduction to the novel, William York Tindall writes: "This glowing landscape, where flat figures move in ritual patterns, is one of the great creations of our time. . . . Comparable in splendor to 'Kubla Khan' or *Salammbô*, or, better perhaps, to the paintings of Gauguin, *The Plumed Serpent* is at once design and vision" (v). Tindall focuses on aesthetic, literary, and mythic dimensions of a novel that has been criticized for its militant phallicism and proto-fascism. "More like a tapestry or a painted window than like the novels we are used to," he observes, "it triumphs by arrangements of shape and color" (ix). In treatment of space, color, and atmosphere, *The Plumed Serpent* is an extraordinary tour de force; although its mythic superstructure is far more ambitious than the political plot of *Kangaroo*, it succeeds best where the Australian novel succeeds, in visually conveying Spirit of Place.

Lawrence's vital art combines "organic description" with spiritual symbolism.[17] and the intensity of his vision transforms Mexico into a mythical landscape. At times, the effect is that of dazzling unreality, hallucination, timelessness, and the drugged expectancy of a world waiting to be born:

> Kate looked at it in wonder, the rather wide stream of soft, full-flowing buff water, that carried little tufts of floating water-hyacinth. Some willow trees stood near the edge, and some pepper trees of most delicate green foliage. Beyond the trees and the level of the shores, big hills rose up to high, blunt points, baked incredibly dry, like biscuit. The blue sky settled against them nakedly, they were leafless and lifeless save for the iron-green shafts of the organ cactus, that glistened blackly, yet atmospherically, in the ochreous aridity. This was Mexico again, stark-dry and luminous with powerful light, cruel and unreal. (*Plumed Serpent* 89–90)

The spellbound, static quality of the land, comparable to Gauguin's dream-atmospheres but with a hard edge that suggests Orozco, has an alienating effect, suggesting the impact of Japanese art with its use of "brilliant color on flat surfaces," "light with no shadows," and clearcut decorative patterns (Wichmann 10).

The transcendent nonhuman landscape is contrasted with the sphere of human activity and evil, where "the flowers seemed to have their roots in spilt blood" and "[the] spirit of place was cruel, down-dragging, destructive" (*Plumed Serpent* 50). During a lull in the gun battle at Jamiltepec the focus switches to the sky, where "[the] clouds had shifted, the sun shone yellowish. In the heavier light, the mountains beyond the parapet showed a fleece of young green, smoky and beautiful" (293). The Mexican landscape has a weird or splendid life of its own that diminishes the life of rootless modern man. Lawrence shows the strangeness of the country chiefly through the eyes of his female protagonist, Kate, who finds the vividness "uncanny" and relates it to (her) swiftly changing moods:

> She saw the hills and lower slopes inland swimming in gold light like lacquer. The black huts of the peons, the lurid leaves of bananas showed up uncannily, the trees green-gold stood up, with boughs of shadow. And away up the road was a puther of dust, then the flash of glass as the automobile turned. (298)

The mood is one of fear. The moving eye affords a cinematic focus, but metonymic form, luminous color, stark contrasts, and spatial dynamics recall Japanese vision and specifically Japanese lacquer work.

Vitalism and organicism pervade atmospheric impressions of the lake:

> It was sunset, with a big level cloud like fur overhead, only the sides of the horizon fairly clear. The sun was not visible. It had gone down in a thick, rose-red fume, behind the wavy ridge of the mountains. Now the hills stood up bluish, all the air was a salmon-red flush, the fawn water had pinkish ripples. Boys and men, bathing a little way along the shore, were the colour of deep flame. (189)

Lawrence's painterly use of adjacent colors and halftones is seen in the choice of nuanced adjectives: "rose-red," "bluish," "salmon-red," "fawn," "pinkish." The exotic beach scene recalls Gauguin's palette and subject matter in *The Day of the Gods* (1894), with its foreground pool of abstract shapes and non-natural colors and its sensuous timelessness. The pure synthesis of colors in Gauguin's canvases is the key to their lyrical, enigmatic moods. Lawrence, similarly, heightens color to make landscape a statement of cosmic energies that irradiate nature.

Some of Lawrence's color effects recall Monet's impressionism, as in a view of the countryside around the lake: "All the air was pinkish, melting to a lavender blue, and the willows on the shore, in the pink light, were apple-green and glowing. The hills behind rose abruptly, like mounds, dry and pinky. Away in the distance, down the lake, the two white obelisk towers of Sayula glinted among the trees . . . " (189). Tentative tones merge here, whereas Gauguin keeps them separate, and the accent is on pinkish air and light, as in Monet's Riviera series.[18] Lake Sayula, home of the old gods, has a magically vital aura: "Earth, air, water were all silent with new light, the last blue of night dissolving like a breath. . . . The great light was stronger than life itself" (90). It is an absorptive, overpowering light, a presence that dissolves colors into sheer radiance. Douglas W. Veitch comments: "In the absence of clearly differentiated objects, the light itself becomes an object in the atmosphere. . . . As in Van Gogh, at the expressionist pole and in the later Monet at the impressionist one, the sun's power is to change objects and even blot them out, or to produce strange visual patterns . . . " (33). The physically dazzling light of "the glaring sun" and "the eternal tremble of pale, earth-coloured water" (*Plumed Serpent* 96) have a numinous quality that eliminates outlines.

Against the changeless background of the lake, with its "sperm-like water," human actions stand out as unchanging rituals. While some of Lawrence's cameos remind one of an Egyptian frieze or a Greek vase, their more direct counterparts are in Japanese art,[19] which arrests motion in gesture and posture and highlights perennial rhythms of life:

> On the wall stood loose little groups of white-clad men, looking into the black belly of the ship. And perched *immobile in silhouette* against the lake, was a black-and-white cow, and a huge *monolithic* black-and-white bull. The whole *silhouette frieze motionless*, against the far water that was coloured brown like turtle doves. . . . Two men were pulling the rope, pressing in the flanks of the *immovable*, passive, spangled monster. Two peons, at the back, with their heads down and their red-sashed, flexible loins thrust out behind, shoved with all their strength in the soft flanks of the mighty creature.
>
> And all was utterly *noiseless and changeless*; against the fulness of the pale lake, this *silent, monumental group of life*. (431–32 [my italics])

While the official ritual of the bullfight in Mexico City is a shambles, a vulgar commercialization, life on the lake continues to follow age-old rhythms linking man with nature. Lawrence's "Japanese" vignettes produce an effect of distance and timelessness, combined with precision and ritual. As random details fall into place, one becomes aware of impersonal rhythms that transcend normal perception and begins "to see into the life of things" (Wordsworth, "Tintern Abbey"). Such tranquil contemplation captures "something of the eternal stillness that lies under all movement, under all life, like a source . . . It is deeper than change, and struggling" (*Letters* 2: 137–38). Lawrence admired this rest and poise in Greek sculpture as Gauguin did in Egyptian reliefs.

The quality of frozen sculpture is less characteristic of Lawrence, however, than of Gauguin, who advised: "[A]void motion in a pose. Each of your figures ought to be in a static position" (*Intimate Journals* 32) and who created decorative, friezelike effects in *Ta Matete* (1892), *The Day of the God* (1894), *Nave nave Mahana* (1896; see pl. 21), *Where Do We Come From? What Are We? Where Are We Going?* (1897), *Faa Iheihe* (1898), and *The Call* (1902).[20] Just as Gauguin, following Egyptian inspiration, imposes a hieratic order on Tahitian life, so Lawrence, following Greek and Japanese sources, imposes a timeless sense of ritual on the casual, chaotic Mexican scene. This is not simply a matter of aesthetic distance but of clarifying archetypal patterns that allow the artist to see one culture more clearly through the prism of another.

The style of *The Plumed Serpent* is heavily symbolic, in keeping with its mythico-religious themes,[21] but metonymic description builds realistic, if selectively arranged, scenes, as in *Sea and Sardinia* and *Mornings in Mexico*. Lawrence Durrell, who seems to assume that mimetic accuracy is Lawrence's aim, overlooks "the trembling instability of the balance" between self and setting that is the writer's opportunity to create. To Durrell, "the mirror he holds up to Mexico . . . is a marvellous triumph of art, [but] the image is often a bit out of focus. He couldn't hold or perhaps wouldn't hold the camera steady enough . . . " ("Landscape and Character" 161). But Lawrence does not hold a mirror or a camera; his pen is more like a brush or a crayon. His response to Spirit of Place leaves room for interaction, modeling, and transmutation. As Tracy puts it, "To charge Lawrence with offering his readers unreal landscapes is as foolish as to chastise Cézanne for not being a photographer" (129).

Metonymic structures are the basis of brilliant swift sketches that catch the atmosphere of the land:

A bright sky, with a bluish shadow on earth. Parched slopes with ragged maize stubble. Then a forlorn hacienda and a man on horseback, in a blanket, driving a silent flock of cows, sheep, bulls, goats, lambs, rippling a bit ghostly in the dawn, from under a tottering archway. A long canal beside the railway . . . paved with bright green leaves from which poked the mauve heads of the *lirio*, the water-hyacinth. The sun was lifting up, red. In a moment, it was the full, dazzling gold of a Mexican morning. (*Plumed Serpent* 87)

Impressions are syntagmatically juxtaposed, with no main verbs in the first three syntactic units focusing on sky, earth, man, and animals. The life of the land emerges from an accumulation of selected visual details.

There is an implied stillness, a reflective depth in these mornings in Mexico, as seen by a foreigner: "Morning was still young on the pale buff river, between the silent earthen banks. There was a blue dimness in the lower air. . . . The blueness and moistness of the dissolved night seemed to linger under the scattered pepper trees of the far shore" (89). As in the Australian novel, there is a recurring emphasis on morning, as Kate feels a new part of her being awaken. In a parallel impression, stark contrasts in the Mexican atmosphere are conjured up without finite verbs:

Morning! Brilliant sun pouring into the patio, on the hibiscus flowers and the fluttering yellow and green rags of the banana trees. Birds swiftly coming and going, with tropical suddenness. In the dense shadow of the mango-grove, white clad Indians going like ghosts. The sense of fierce sun, and almost more impressive, of dark, intense shadow. A twitter of life, yet a certain heavy weight of silence. A dazzling flicker and brilliance of light, yet the feeling of weight. (142)

In the first three sentences a few tenuous rhythms are indicated in present participles; in the next three, even participial movement is snuffed out in the strong sunshine that creates a dazzling chiaroscuro and sense of inertia. Lawrence's impressions of time, place, and season are steeped in changing qualities of light and color. As Veitch says of Kate's journey on the lake, "Phrasal brushstrokes replace connectives and together with the suppression of kinetic verbs give a painterly, often impressionistic, quality to the style. In strong dependence on light as the medium, distances pulse in and out in varying degrees of linear clarity . . . " (29). Yet the style in the "Morning!" passage, with its swift movement contrasted with sultry stillness and brilliant color with brooding darkness, is far too dense and tense for the impressionist ethos. Its resonance is that of Gauguin's tropical mood piece *The Brooding Woman*, also known as *Te Faaturuma (Silence)* (1891; see pl. 22), or the interlocking planes of color in *Tahitian Pastorals* (1892–93).[22]

Some of Lawrence's most memorable writing in *The Plumed Serpent* conveys perceptions of indigenous life through brief cameos linked by motifs of herding, bathing, washing, or fishing. These rituals seem timeless, as if seen from a distance, with all emotion stilled:

> On the flat near the river a peon, perched on the rump of his ass, was slowly driving five luxurious cows towards the water to drink. The big black-and-white animals stepped in a dream-pace past the pepper trees to the bank, like moving pieces of light-and-shade: the dun cows trailed after, in the incredible silence and brilliance of the morning. (90)

Recurring features of such scenes include black/white, light/shade contrasts, hypnotically slow pace, and morning stillness. Timelessness and silence go hand in hand, as if the viewer were content to watch the action in a mindless trance or sensuous dream: "At a water-hole . . . a cluster of women were busily washing clothes. In the shallows of the lake itself two women sat bathing, their shoulders heavy and womanly and of a fine orange-brown colour, their black hair hanging dense and wet" (160)—images that recall Gauguin's tropical nudes in *Tahitian Women Bathing* (1892; see pl. 23) or *Otahi (Alone)* (1893).[23] "A little further along, a man was wading slowly, stopping to throw his round net skilfully upon the water, then slowly stooping and gathering it in, picking out the tiny, glittery fish called charales. Strangely silent and remote everything, in the gleaming morning, as if it were some distant period of time" (160). The becalmed atmosphere recalls Puvis de Chavannes's haunting canvas *The Poor Fisherman* (c. 1879–81), which influenced Gauguin.[24]

Descriptions of market produce, like the baskets of guavas, lemons, mangoes, oranges, and vegetables (230), exploit the decorative sense of color and delight in abundance Lawrence displays so extravagantly in the market scenes of *Sea and Sardinia* and Gauguin in *The Meal or The Bananas* (1891).[25] Kate watches the boats come in: "It pleased her to see the men running along the planks with the dark-green melons, and piling them in a mound on the rough sand, melons dark-green like creatures with pale bellies. To see the tomatoes all poured out into a shallow place in the lake, bobbing about while the women washed them . . . " (229). Other cameos involve cows drinking, women filling jars, fishnets drying, a bird in the sun, and a woman washing "a statuesque pig" (243, 332). The motif of scarlet/yellow/grey/brown cardinal birds "skimming past" (183) shows a playful sense of color in motion, worthy of Henri Rousseau, whose naive art Lawrence knew (*Letters* 6: 62). The text includes dimensions of movement and metamorphosis lacking in painting. There are many colorful descriptions of costumes. The weaving of a serape with a zigzag pattern of red, white, and black is described in loving detail (*Plumed Serpent* 322), as if William Morris's arts and crafts movement had migrated to a Mexican hacienda.

Lawrence's exotic images of brown-skinned, "unconscious" natives are reminiscent of such Gauguin paintings as *Otahi* or *Tahitian Women with Mango Blossoms* (1899).[26] "On the left bank Kate had noticed some men bathing: men whose wet skins flashed with the beautiful brown-rose colour and glitter of the naked natives. . . . Low against the water across-stream she watched the glitter of naked men half-immersed in the river" (90). "Primitive" bodies are readily mythicized: Kate sees the "rich stillness of the morning star" and the "energies of the cosmos" "in the black eyes of the natives, in the sunrise of the man's rich, still body, Indian-warm" (96). The mythic vision recalls Gauguin's depiction of Maori cults in *The Moon and the Earth* (1893),[27] with its grandiose legendary figures. But where Gauguin emphasizes the enigmatic richness of his "savage Eve," Lawrence finds cosmic energy in male bodies. The apotheosis of the "primitive" body is Kate's vision of Cipriano bathing in the lake, "[as] if on fire!" (424). Cipriano, of course, is more than a Mexican general, he is "the living Huitzilopochtli," whom Kate sees as an incarnation of Fire and Blood.

When Lawrence turns from mythopoeic plot to Mexican landscape, his metonymic/impressionist style spans a brilliant sweep of colors and forms.

> Autumn in Mexico, and the coming of the dry season, with the sky going higher and higher, pure pale blue, the sunset arriving with a strange flare of crystal yellow light. With the coffee berries turning red on the straggling bushes under the trees, and bougainvillea in the strong light glowing with a glow of magenta colour so deep you could plunge your arms deep in it. With a few humming-birds in the sunshine, and the fish in the waters gone wild, and the flies, that steamed black in the first rains, now passing away again. (406)

There are no main clauses here; in Jakobson's terms, description is forwarded along the combinative axis by a series of attributive "with" phrases, while participles convey the process of seasonal change ("coming," "going," "arriving," "turning," "passing away again"). The style is painterly and pictorial; illumination suggests Gauguin's sensuous tones and textures, while flaring, glowing color becomes a reified substance, that "*expresses something in itself*," to cite Van Gogh (*Complete Letters* 2: 428). Tindall observes that, "[h]aving passed through his temperament, colors already bright become brighter and assume a mysterious significance. Seeming to reproduce reality, Lawrence creates it" (vii). This is true of the "magenta colour" of the bougainvillea or "the colour of deep flame" of the bathers, but Lawrence also uses subtle nuances of tone to create atmosphere and linguistic devices such as parallelism and metonymy to give a sense of movement and succession. He transmutes what he sees into textures of vision.

The key to landscape moods is found in syntheses of color, form, and space. Layered distances, accentuated by bright touches, show a Japanese sharpness of perception. Kate, caught between conflicting desires to return to Europe and personal life or to stay in Mexico and accept apotheosis, responds to the freshness and fragrance of the season. The "frail green" of the mesquite bushes symbolizes the life-giving powers of the goddess Malintzi, who offers green shoots of renewal and regeneration.

Spirit of Place in Mexico involves brilliant color, subtle gradations, dynamic contrasts, decorative patterning, and Gauguinesque harmonies, all of which are reflected in an atmospheric coda:

> There was a certain autumnal purity and lull on the lake. The moisture still lingered, the bushes on the wild hills were green in puffs. Sunlight lay in a rich gleam on the mountains, and shadows were deep and velvety. The green almost covered the rocks and the pinkish land. Bright green the sugar cane, red the ploughed earth, dark the trees, with white specks of villages here and there. And over the wild places, a sprinkle of bushes, then stark grey rock still coming out. (*Plumed Serpent* 426)

Colors are distributed in clearly delineated zones and color adjectives are inverted to stand out before the nouns they qualify. Various greens, interspersed with touches of pink, white, grey, and complementary red, are the basis of a complex harmony. In *Parahi te Marae* (1892),[28] Gauguin composes a comparable harmony, abruptly juxtaposing mauve, pink, lilac, and orange-red with complementary green, backed by a straw-yellow hillside.

Decorative, painterly effects are part of *The Plumed Serpent*'s visionary design. Objects in a landscape are depicted in bright, flat colors reminiscent of Japanese prints, with their capacity for heightening and ordering perception:

> They had passed the jetty, and rounding the shoal where the willows grew, she could see Sayula: white fluted twin-towers of the church, obelisk shaped above the pepper trees: beyond, a mound of a hill standing alone, dotted with dry bushes, distinct and Japanese looking; beyond this, the corrugated, blue-ribbed, flat-flanked mountains of Mexico. (108)

The syntagmatic sequence, marked off by colons, follows the movement of the boat and of Kate's eye and is a verbal equivalent to the precise arrangement and clarification of space in Japanese prints. The result is harmony: "It looked peaceful, delicate, almost Japanese." Veitch observes that "[the] control of distance, as in Japanese prints, is handled less by optical or mathematical perspective than by juxtaposition, and even the wisps of vague appearing background are delicately etched . . . " (40). Linear and structural elements in Lawrence's Mexican landscapes reflect Japanese design and counterbalance the suffused colors and sumptuous harmonies of Gauguin's palette.

Kate's serial perception of forms, emphasized by syntactic movement, introduces a temporal element into such scenes, accounting for their visual dynamics. Near the end of the novel, her sharply selective way of seeing subordinates sensuous mysticism to patterned perspective. The clarity of her vision relates to a new-found poise in her "soul and womb" as she reorients herself spiritually and physically to Mexico. The changing atmosphere represents a dreamlike transit between the "glacial period" of "old prehistoric humanity" and of her frozen will and the tropical Eden of an unknown future:

> The lake was much fuller and higher up the shore, softer, more mysterious. . . . Distance seemed farther away. The near conical hills were dotted with green bushes, like a Japanese drawing. Bullock wagons with solid wheels came rolling to the village, high with sugar cane, drawn by eight oxen with ponderous heads and slowly swinging horns, while a peon walked in front, with the guiding-stick on the cross-beam of the yoke. So slow, so massive, yet with such slight control! (Plumed Serpent 414)

Lawrence's iconographic reference is precise: rounded hills dotted with bushes and bullock wagons are iconic trademarks in Japanese prints—as in

Hokkei's woodcuts and sketches after Hokusai (see Wichmann 55, 56) and in Hiroshige's Ōtsu: Hashirii Tea House, where a line of heavily laden bullock carts waits at a well. An underlying harmony is the key.[29] The sensuous poise of the oxen, matching strength with delicate control, relates metonymically to the newly won spiritual/physical balance in Kate. What she sees reflects changes in herself: Lawrence's form-language, modulating from Gauguinesque to Japanese keys, is capable of the subtlest adjustments to character psychology.

At a deeper level than that of its convoluted, politically perverse mythos, *The Plumed Serpent* is a record of the writer's quest for wholeness, his desire to come closer to the energies of life through Spirit of Place. To most readers, the Quetzalcoatl myth is ultimately less important than the vitalistic settings of earth and lake, refracted through the brilliant prism of Lawrence's art.

CONCLUSION

Lawrence's genius lies in his penetrating and transformative vision and its inventive and forceful expression. Looking closely at his language one becomes aware of parallels with the visual arts and of imaginative energies that shape both verbal and painterly expression. My aim has been to illustrate the range of Lawrence's styles by drawing parallels with impressionist, expressionist, primitivist, and futurist movements in the arts—specifically with the post-impressionist painting of Van Gogh, Gauguin, and Cézanne, the expressionist painting of Kirchner and Nolde, and the Japanese woodblock prints of Hokusai and Hiroshige—the last being a catalytic source of aesthetic perception Lawrence shared with many modern European artists, including Van Gogh and Gauguin.

In the fifteen years from *The White Peacock* (1911) to *The Plumed Serpent* (1926), Lawrence's vision and expression follow a curve comprising subtle and profound variations. The full span of his percepetual progress is the distance between poles of graphic realism and mythic symbolism, with expressionism and complementary modes of "primitivism" and futurism forming the bulge in the curve, so to speak. In all these changes, Lawrence's eye remains concretely and sensuously on the object and intuitively on its inner life.

The first novel, with its clutter of iconographic references, shows an apprentice novelist assiduously imitating aspects of English landscape painting and Pre-Raphaelite portraiture—in a derivative aesthetic relieved by flashes of pure observation, as in the snowdrop scene—and discovering the relevance of impressionist vision to city life. After an opening phase of pastoral and poetic nostalgia, Lawrence returns to his social roots with the industrial settings and realistic vision of *Sons and Lovers*. In this "autobiographical" novel Lawrence first masters his visual powers, in the process of seeing and shaping his experience, and his creative effort to give form to his life is a case of "art for my sake." Because readers gain an overwhelming sense of lived reality from the novel, there is a tendency to assume that Lawrence's technique is totally realist. But, if examined more closely, the stylistic integrity of *Sons and Lovers* is seen to contain great variety. Lawrence could not achieve the impression of a life unfolding against internal and external pressures without significant use of impressionism, symbolism, and expressionism. These modes of writing enrich the novel in untold ways, and their imaginative effects can most clearly be recognized through the kind of interarts comparison I have practiced here.

The impact of expressionism and futurism on Lawrence, at a time when he was going through challenging personal and cultural experiences, led to the creative ferment of 1912–17. Compared with the realism of *Sons and Lovers*, *The Rainbow* speaks a "foreign language"—a visual and sensory art-speech that articulates "allotropic states of being." The change in Lawrence's style is inconceivable without the impact of European, especially German and Italian, culture on his inherited patterns of thought and expression. If factual objectivity is worth its weight in gold in *Sons and Lovers*, *The Rainbow* is a triumph of subjective vision and innovative expression. While the novel can be read in English cultural terms because of its settings and grip on real historical life, Lawrence's achievement cannot properly be evaluated without recognizing the role that expressionism plays in conveying unconscious states and vital impulses. This previously uncharted territory was accessible to Lawrence only through new structures of vision and expression and the forging of a new stylistic language.

I have devoted a central portion of this study to Lawrence's most complex novel, *Women in Love*, illustrating (a) his innovative uses of expressionism, interrelated with painting, sculpture, and dance, in a series of ritual scenes; (b) the impact of "primitivism," in the form of African sculptures, on the "civilized" self-consciousness of Europe and its desire for change; and (c) Lawrence's use of futurism—Boccioni's sculpture and Marinetti's mechanolatry—in negative, but culturally definitive, contexts. I have found it revealing to compare Lawrence's expressionist affinity with Van Gogh and his elective affinity with Cézanne, which together bring into prominence two main strands of his genius. His interest in the creative struggles of Van Gogh and Cézanne to express their vision in painting bears significant relation to his own writing. Lawrence believes that "every true artist is the salvation of every other" and that "only artists produce for each other the world that is fit to live in" (*Women in Love* 208). That is, vital artists reconstruct or modify the aesthetic perceptions and expressive possibilities of the medium for their contemporaries and successors.

Living in various places around the world and responding to Spirit of Place contributed to the development of Lawrence's visual imagination. This "external vision," inflected by his underlying ontological vision, was further modified by aesthetic perception. In *Kangaroo* and *The Plumed Serpent*, sensory observation combines with images filtered through the pictorial vision of Puvis de Chavannes and Gauguin and the woodblock designs of Hokusai and Hiroshige. Lawrence composed the landscapes of his novels with an almost uncanny power of sensory observation, but his perception grew and changed, incorporating what he learned from the visual arts. Indeed, so keen were his aesthetic responses that (like Birkin) he could penetrate the vision of an artist or a culture through a single iconic work of art—be it a Greek sculpture, an African wood carving, a drawing of Chinese geese, a pair of wagtails in painted wood, a factory frieze, a statuette of a girl on a horse, or a still life of sunflowers or apples. Through empathy he saw into the formative processes—cultural, technical, psychological, aesthetic—that go to the making of a work of art; at the same time he could stand back and criticize the life-values symbolized by the forms.

"All art partakes of the Spirit of Place in which it is produced," says Lawrence, and this maxim can be applied to his own "savage pilgrimage." He is attuned to the "peculiar potentiality" for imaginative and spiritual stimulus in landscapes of Australia and Mexico, and he opens his writing to their "subtle magnetic or vital influence" ("Spirit of Place" 16, 20). In contemplating voyages to the South Pacific, Lawrence must have been thinking of Gauguin's desire to leave Europe behind and look on nature with a serene and sensual "savage eye." But he had also experienced the clarity and conciseness of Japanese art that arranges objects in space in rhythmic and decorative designs. These two orders of seeing might seem to be opposed, but in the vital art of Lawrence's later novels they function as complementary. No longer drawing on English pictorial traditions,[1] Lawrence after 1913 developed new perceptual modes and strange textures of vision that do not reflect, but actively interpret, new environments. This fusion of inner and outer modes of vision characterizes his fiction after *Sons and Lovers*. He wanted something "a stratum deeper" than realistic "sensation and presentation," something that would allow him "[to come] at the real naked essence of [his] vision"— and that required "another language almost" (*Letters* 1: 526; 2: 132; 1: 519).

Art, as Heidegger affirms, is closer to "the authentic numinous fonts of being" than metaphysics is,[2] yet "[r]eflection on what *art* may be is completely and decidedly determined only in regard to the question of *Being*"

("Origin" 86). For Heidegger (as for Vivante), art and being converge: "The work's createdness . . . can obviously be grasped only in terms of the process of creation" ("Origin" 58). If "[the] Being of being(s) is the only proper object of ontological thought," it is also the constant object of Lawrence's vision, albeit in concrete, physical forms. Like Heidegger, he "stands soul- and spirit-deep in immanence" (George Steiner 67, 65). Lawrence's vital art expresses his metaphysic in a critique of beings and a celebration of Being.

Heidegger's ontology has affinities with Lawrence's project of recovering the lost Atlantis of the unconscious through animism. In "Pan in America," he imagines a native hunter participating in the "radiant-cold stillness and enduring presence" of a rock to strengthen his purpose (28). Analogously, "[o]ntology tries to 'think the being of the rock,' tries to experience that which gives it existence or . . . how it is that existence manifests itself in the rock" (George Steiner 67). But Lawrence's vital art denies the separation of being and substance implied by Heidegger, as he denied Fry's theory that Cézanne searched for truth behind the veil of appearances. Lawrence insists on sensory, material presence in art and resists the tendency of language to transmute the being of the rock into "mind content." Daniel Albright observes that "the idea of the thinking body cannot be taken further than Lawrence takes it. . . . The inside of a stone is organized like the inside of the human body; gravity and desire are two names for the same thing" (25–26). Albright cites Lawrence's statement, in a passage on stone worship, that "the phallus itself is but a symbol" (*Phoenix II* 456)—a distinction between means and ends that does not detract from physical reality.

Perception constructs its own reality from sense data. The artist, like the primitive hunter, experiences and expresses the rock as a "tremulation on the ether" that unites material form with living consciousness. The pine tree on Lawrence's New Mexican ranch

> gives out life, as I give out life. Our two lives meet and cross one another, unknowingly: the tree's life penetrates my life, and my life the tree's. . . . Its raw earth-power and its raw sky-power, its resinous erectness and resistance, its sharpness of hissing needles and relentlessness of roots, all that goes to the primitive savageness of a pine tree, goes also to the strength of man. ("Pan in America" 25–26)

Lawrence's art—"a form of supremely delicate awareness and atonement— meaning at-oneness, the state of being at one with the object"[3]—stems from a vital interchange with otherness that expands the subject's being. "And what does life consist in," he asks in "Pan in America," "save a vivid relatedness between [a] man and the living universe that surrounds him?" (27).

Lawrence's vision of the natural world of rock, tree, grass, fox, stallion, fish, mosquito, mountain lion, man, woman and their many-hued relationships, is not simply animistic, blood-conscious, phallic, or sensory, although it is all of these things; ultimately it penetrates to the Being of all that exists. "For man, the vast marvel is to be alive. For man, as for flower and beast and bird, the supreme triumph is to be most vividly, most perfectly alive" (*Apocalypse* 149). Vital art, in text or painting, "communicates a state of being" by doubling and integrating the powers of language: "Art-speech is a use of symbols which are pulsations on the blood and seizures upon the nerves, and at the same time pure percepts of the mind and pure terms of spiritual aspiration" ("Spirit of Place" 19).

Lawrence's vital art responds to the endless variety of phenomena, reawakening readers to visual, tactile, ontological "thereness" and "nowness." The issue for the literary critic is how Lawrence manages to *express* his vision of man's "living unison" with the "incarnate cosmos" (*Apocalypse* 149). In his writing, a "vivid relatedness" links a transforming subjectivity with the object, as it appears to be in itself.[4] Through "acts of attention," Lawrence "immerse[s] himself in the full 'thereness' of things" (to cite George Steiner [67] on Heidegger), combining visual images and verbal rhythms to convey his sense of what *is* to a fully engaged reader. Language is the medium through which the writer discloses his awareness of the living world.

For Rudolf Arnheim, "perception is purposive and selective" and therefore intrinsically "creative"; thinking uses "perceptual and pictorial shapes" so that thought and perception are intertwined (*Visual Thinking* 19, 134, 153). Arnheim contends that real thinking takes place in visual images, whereas verbal language merely handles the structure and relation of concepts. "Seeing comes before words," as Berger says (*Ways of Seeing* 7), and in creative thinking, as Lawrence experienced it, "our mind now definitely moves in images . . . and no longer is there a logical process, but a curious flitting motion from image to image according to some power of attraction, some *sensuous* association between images" (*Apocalypse*, appendix 2: 194). Literary thinking doesn't merely conjure up and associate visual images; a restructuring of the powers of language (*langue*) takes place in the stylistic processing of words and images that forms a style (*parole*). Art-speech operates in "the mysterious zone between the representational and the abstract" (Arnheim, *Visual Thinking* 114), making the reader see as well as think.

Merleau-Ponty (like Arnheim) is concerned with the way the artist's consciousness extends perception. For him, "vision happens among, or is caught in, things. . . . [P]ainting spreads this strange possession to all aspects of Being, which must in some fashion become visible in order to enter into the work of art. . . . This voracious vision, reaching beyond the 'visual givens,' opens upon a texture of Being . . . " ("Eye and Mind" 163, 166). A similar process takes place in Lawrence's novels, where vision is *realized* in the process of writerly expression. Art, in its supra-mimetic function, "makes the invisible visible" and transforms the perception of reality. The artwork "awakens powers dormant in ordinary vision," for the artist's "vision is a mirror or concentration of the universe" (182, 166). Gadamer agrees that the artwork revitalizes or "signifies an increase in being" and maintains that "[the] only relevant thing is whether we encounter a spiritual and ordering energy in the work . . . " (35, 103). Lawrence's verbal art compounds seeing and being; in reading and rereading his work we become aware of the vision that animates it. Communication in his novels is "a tremulation on the ether" that brings language into close contact with expression in the visual arts.

The impact of Lawrence's vital art does not stop with the text but flows through it, refocusing attention on the natural and social worlds and their living relationships. As J. P. Hodin asserts, "it is the warm life of the artist that enables him to strike root directly into existence . . . " ("Problems" 234). Lawrence's fiction is deeply *expressive* of his vision, which may be why he seems so present in his work. Art and ontology merge in that most dynamic of literary forms: "Because a novel is a microcosm," he writes, "and because man in viewing the universe must view it in the light of a theory, therefore every novel must have the background . . . of some theory of being, some metaphysic. *But the metaphysic must always subserve the artistic purpose beyond the artist's conscious aim*" ("Study" 91 [my italics]). Lawrence calls for a trembling balance between art and thought, contemplation and involvement, that constitutes the integrity and vitality of the novel.

Lawrence learned about expression by copying paintings before he ever began to write: "A picture lives with the life you put into it," he says, and vital art can reveal the maker's "concentration of delight or exaltation of visual discovery" ("Making Pictures" 604). Art, like religion, is a way of attuning one's being to the cosmos, of divining its forces, so that the artist has to be a visionary. "The only thing one can look into, stare into, and see only vision, is the vision itself: the visionary image" (605). Here, referring to his own painting, Lawrence is in accord with Gauguin. Vital art discloses the artist's response to Being through vision and expression, and in doing so participates in creative energies beyond the ego. In his novels, stories, and poems, Lawrence expresses this ontological vision in a multiplicity of ways that invite and reward comparison with the visual arts.

Notes

Bibliography

Index

NOTES

INTRODUCTION

1. Michael Bell observes that "Lawrence's presentation of states of being . . . subsumes an ontological understanding every bit as subtle and comprehensive as Heidegger's" (10). Bell's own subtle and penetrating discourse "strictly follow[s] not the ontological *vision* . . . but the development of the ontological *theme*" (11).

2. In Lawrence's view, "The reality of substantial bodies can only be perceived by the imagination, and the imagination is a kindled state of consciousness in which intuitive awareness predominates. The plastic arts are all imagery, and imagery is the body of our imaginative life. . . . In the flow of true imagination we know in full, mentally and physically at once, in a greater, enkindled awareness" ("Introduction to These Paintings" 559).

3. For a study of the process in the converse direction, see Seznec.

4. A pioneering study was Jack Lindsay's "The Impact of Modernism on Lawrence" (1964), which is concerned with Lawrence's painting and touches on his critical responses to Cézanne, futurism, and primitivism. Lindsay emphasizes the visual quality of Lawrence's writing and links his view of the art image with his intuitive sense of Spirit of Place.

5. *Iconography* concerns "subject matter or meaning" and includes references to paintings or sculptures in literary works; *iconology* involves formal or "'symbolical' values" and "underlying principles" and is more concerned with stylistic comparisons (Panofsky 26n31). See also Mitchell.

6. According to Montgomery, "Lawrence's . . . is a 'visionary' tradition, and the fact that [he] chose to cast his vision primarily in the form of the novel is not of the essence. . . . [It is] a vision that can also be described as a philosophical position,

ideal realism" (41). While not beyond philosophy, Montgomery's position is certainly beyond art.

7. Cf. Wendy Steiner.

8. Merleau-Ponty, who has written perceptively on Cézanne and Van Gogh, also links physical consciousness with expression. "My body," he writes,

> is the seat or rather the very actuality of the phenomenon of expression (*Ausdruck*), and there the visual and auditory experiences . . . are pregnant one with the other, and their expressive value is the ground of the antipredicative unity of the perceived world, and, through it, of verbal expression (*Darstellung*) and intellectual signifi- cance (*Bedeutung*). . . . (*Phenomenology* 235)

1. AESTHETICISM AND IMPRESSIONISM IN *THE WHITE PEACOCK*

1. Squires focuses on the "romantic-idyllic-pastoral strain" (178); Ford sees Lawrence's aim as "the loving evocation of a pastoral setting" (47); Herzinger finds "pastoral and anti-pastoral elements" coexisting (81). In a dissenting opinion, Ebbatson sees the novel as "neither pastoral nor anti-pastoral" but as Darwinian and Hardyesque (54).

2. On the earlier iconographic sources, see Stewart, "Landscape Painting."

3. See Weintraub 194.

4. See Wilson, pl. 20.

5. See Wilson, pl. 12.

6. Théophile Gautier, "foremost inspiration in the 'Aesthetic Movement,'" de- clared that "*[u]ne belle forme est une belle idée*" (Beckson xix).

7. See photographs in Sypher 232. Sypher relates the "rococo swirl" of Art Nouveau to the Peacock Room.

8. Both Wilde and Huysmans were inspired by Gustave Moreau's *Salomé* (1876), as Moreau had been by Flaubert's *Tentation de Saint Antoine* (1874). See Robert Ross ix.

9. Kronegger (30) cites the dates from Richard Hamann, *Der Impressionismus in Leben und Kunst* (1923).

10. See Pool, fig. 120; Blunden 119, 120.

11. See Macmillan, pls. 209, 217, 227, 236; *Scottish Painting*, cat. no. 38.

12. See Shikes and Harper 300; Holden, pls. 13, 22.

13. According to Hatzfeld, "[an impressionist] method of seizing the climate of a modern city is to view its silhouette . . . in rain or mist, sunshine or darkness, and thus to evoke, so to speak, its ghost and soul instead of its body . . . " (176).

14. See Seitz 85; Jennings 172.

15. According to Caws, "the city is eternally a source of energy, empowered, empowering, and disempowering, with desire eternally at its center. The high and

continuous erotic charge finds its concrete statement in the latter-day futuristic vision . . . " (10).

16. Kenneth Clark "doubt[s] if a picture could be much truer to a visual impression, with all its implications of light and tone, than the Sisley paintings of Hampton Court, or Pissarro's of Norwood . . . " (170).

17. See Monet's *Boulevard des Capucines* (1873–74; pl. 1), also in *Claude Monet*, pls. 9–11; and Pissarro's *Boulevard Montmartre in Paris* (1897) and *Avénue de l'Opera* (1898) in Jaffé, pls. 104, 105.

18. See Monet's *Westminster Bridge* (1871; pl. 2), also in Seitz 89; *Waterloo Bridge, Sun in the Fog, Charing Cross Bridge* (1903) in Gordon and Forge 182; and *London, The Houses of Parliament: Sun Breaking through the Fog* (1904) and *London, The Houses of Parliament: Stormy Sky* (1904) in Stuckey, pls. 100, 101. See also Lassaigne 54–59.

19. Lawrence's poem "Parliament Hill in the Evening" (*Complete Poems* 142) adds macabre, Baudelairean overtones of corruption to impressionist imagery matching Monet's.

20. Cf. Faris.

21. See Varnedoe, pl. 63. Emily Braun writes: "The oppressive blue interior is a metaphor of Munch's psychological insularity. . . . Munch also referred to the painting as *Symphony in Blue*, attesting to the influence of James McNeill Whistler . . . " (qtd. in Varnedoe 186).

2. FORMS OF EXPRESSION IN *SONS AND LOVERS*

1. Kushigian traces the growth of Paul's vision from "a nineteenth-century naturalistic consciousness through the stages of Pre-Raphaelitism, art nouveau and early Expressionism . . . " (71).

2. See Daiches 167–68; Sanders 23.

3. See Weiss. Kushigian claims that "the paintings of Vincent Van Gogh, Edvard Munch, Egon Schiele and other early expressionist painters provided pictorial images that the writer was able to use effectively to characterize a psychological state in Paul Morel . . . " (37).

4. See Barlach's *Russian Beggarwoman II* (1907; plaster, under dark shellac) and *The Beggar* (1930; bronze), Lehmbruck's *The Fallen Man* (1915–16; bronze), and Kollwitz's *Pietà* (1937–38; bronze) and *The Mothers: The War* (1922–23; woodcut) in *German Expressionist Sculpture*, cat. nos. 7, 22, 91, 85, 82.

5. Cf. Bryson, *Word and Image* 8.

6. According to Jakobson, "the realist author metonymically digresses from the plot to the atmosphere and from the characters to the setting in space and time" (90).

7. See Gordon and Forge 160–62.

8. See animistic images of the mine in Zola 21, 28, 37, 39, 40, 44, 452.

9. Impressionist and post-impressionist painters were among the first to depict industrial landscapes. See Armand Guillaumin's *Sunset at Ivry* (1873) in Courthion, 137; and Van Gogh's *The Factory at Asnières* (1887) in de la Faille, cat. no. F318.

10. Cf. Bowness 9.

11. In Rosenberg's words, "[the] expressionist still used the elements of the visual world to convey his visions, but he took the liberty of distorting them in the interests of a more powerful expressiveness" (301).

12. Rewald observes: "Like Cézanne, Renoir achieved in his last years the synthesis of his lifelong experience. Impressionism lay far behind him. . . . [T]he shimmering surface of pigment he used now not to render atmospheric effects but to build with brilliant and strong colors an image of life in almost supernatural intensity" (584).

13. According to Van Ghent, "[the] most valid symbols are the most concrete realities. Lawrence's great gift for the symbolic image was a function of his sensitivity to and passion for the meaning of real things—for the individual expression that real forms have" (531). As the imagist William Carlos Williams puts it, "No ideas but in things."

14. Watt distinguishes between *homeophoric* images, "[whose] symbolic meaning [is arrived at by] an imaginative extension of the *same* or *similar* properties as are normally possessed by the object," and *heterophoric* images, "[whose] symbolic meaning is carried by *something else* . . . [for instance] another body of knowledge [such as the mythic]" (42).

15. The symbol of a cruel, indifferent life-force putting its mark of pollination on the woman was anticipated by Hardy in the sensuous imagery of *Tess of the d'Urbervilles* (e.g., 104).

16. Joyce Carol Oates remarks: "Such [apocalyptic] art must be violent, it must be outlandish and diabolic at its core because it is revolutionary. . . . [But] its primary concerns are prophetic, even religious" (100).

17. Dube writes: "[In] the landscapes of the Baltic island of Fehmarn [Kirchner] achieved the complete fusion of man and nature. Landscapes and figures unite in a rhythmic structure, a cosmic hieroglyph" ("Ernst Ludwig Kirchner" 10).

18. See Schapiro, *Vincent Van Gogh* 101. Moore also notes the affinity with Van Gogh's painting (249).

19. Apocalyptic elements in *The Starry Night* include the "attempt to unite sun and moon into one figure [and] the tremendous flame-formed cypresses, the dark earthly vertical counterpart of the dragon nebula . . . " (Schapiro, *Van Gogh* 100).

3. VISION AND EXPRESSION IN *THE RAINBOW*

1. See Donald E. Gordon, *Modern Art Exhibitions*, vol. 2. Lawrence's letter to Collings is evidence that he saw expressionist painting in its heyday and was im-

pressed by it, even though, characteristically, he adds: "[T]he real feeling is not there. . . . "

2. See the paintings *Candle Dancers* (1912), in glowing reds, oranges, and golds and flowing greens and blues, and *Tropical Sun* (1914), in resonant reds and greens, in Haftmann, pls. 12 and 14.

3. As Ulrich Weisstein puts it: "Breaking through the individual shell or mask (*persona*), Expressionist art (paradoxically) fuses the extremely subjective with the starkly objective" (Introduction 25).

4. Weisstein similarly claims that "Expressionist art seeks to render visible . . . soul states and the violent emotions welling up from the innermost recesses of the subconscious. . . . What is caught here, on the canvas or in the poem, are extreme moods, such as numinous fear or ecstatic joy, externalized by means of projection and outwardly manifesting themselves as distortions of color, shape, syntax, vocabulary or tonal relationships . . . " (Introduction 23).

5. Pinkney compares the symbolism of "The Rainbow" with that of "The Bridge," the theme with *Die Brücke*'s ideology of growth and liberation, and the medieval inspiration of Will Brangwen's carving with that of expressionist woodcuts.

6. See Green 58–74; and Turner et al.

7. Worthen, in his introduction, observes that the novel is "always moving . . . [toward] its idea of a reality beyond realism" (32).

8. Balbert examines the "interrelationship . . . of 'discourse' and 'form,'" psychology and rhythm, in the novel (13).

9. Max Beckmann refers to the famous cabalist who once said: "If you wish to get hold of the invisible you must penetrate as deeply as possible into the visible." His own aim is "to make the invisible visible through reality" (Chipp 187–88). Similarly, Paul Klee observes, "Art does not reproduce the visible but makes visible" (76).

10. See Timm, pls. 25, 67.

11. Earl Wasserman borrows the term from Kenneth Burke and applies it to the "mystic interfusion of . . . contraries" in Keats's "Ode on a Grecian Urn" (15).

12. See Meyers, "Fra Angelico."

13. Van Gogh writes of his portrait of Eugène Bock: "Behind the head, instead of painting the ordinary wall of the mean room, I paint infinity, a plain background of the richest, intensest blue that I can contrive, and by this simple combination of the bright head against the rich blue background, I get a mysterious effect, like a star in the depths of an azure sky" (*Complete Letters* 3: 6).

14. Weisstein writes of expressionism: "This thrust, this plunging into depth, i.e., into a realm forbidden to the senses, presupposes a quasi-religious fervor, an urge to bring about a total *Vergeistigung* (spiritualization) of life and art" ("Expressionism" 33).

15. For Kandinsky, "[colors] produce a corresponding spiritual vibration, and it

is only as a step towards this spiritual vibration that the elementary physical impression is of importance" (24).

16. Cf. Brandabur.

17. Lippincott, fig. 42.

18. See Schapiro, *Van Gogh* 101; Hammacher, *Genius* 135.

19. Cf. Munch's *Man's Head in Woman's Hair* in *Edvard Munch*, pl. 35.

20. The Russian painter Kasimir Malewich says of Van Gogh's kinetic form: "He saw that everything trembles as the result of a simple, universal movement. . . . [It] was as if a current passed through every growth. . . . Van Gogh separated the textural waves from the object, the latter being for him only form, saturated with a maximum of dynamic power" (quoted in Hammacher, "Van Gogh and the Words" 23).

21. See Lippincott, figs. 33, 42.

22. Charles Ross finds "a linguistic analogue of Futurist painting . . . [in the dazzling ferocity]" of such scenes (62).

23. Sokel finds "the Dionysian roots of vitalism" in expressionism (87).

24. Cf. Munch, *Ashes II* in Timm, pl. 76.

25. See Timm, pls. 35, 47, 80.

26. "Is everything material—or *everything* spiritual?" asks Kandinsky (29). Neither, Lawrence would reply, for the rainbow symbolizes a fusion of physical and spiritual in a new form of being.

27. In *Fantasia of the Unconscious*, Lawrence writes: "The sun's quick is polarized in dynamic relation with the quick of life in all living things. . . . [As] the sun is the great fiery, vivifying pole of the inanimate universe, the moon is the other pole, cold and keen and vivifying . . . " (184).

28. Cf. Henry Fuseli's *The Nightmare* (First Version 1781 and Second Version 1790–91; in Tomory, pl. 1 and fig. 83), an early, dramatic example of symbolist art; and Franz Marc's apocalyptic *Tower of the Blue Horses* (1913; Kuchling 120)—which shows a rainbow in the background.

29. Kushigian sees the surrounding landscape as "an expressionistic reflection of [Ursula's] inner turbulence" but takes the image of the hooves "[in] its emphasis on dynamic motion, flashing light, and electrical energy, [as] a Futurist image" (144, 146).

30. Cf. McLaughlin, who links "the horses' meaning [with] power and frustration" (185).

4. EXPRESSIONISM IN *WOMEN IN LOVE*

1. Lodge notes the homology of Gerald : mare :: colliery : countryside, and the link between "soft white magnetic domination" and "soft black dust" (161–63).

2. For illustrations see (in order of reference) Dube, *Expressionists and Expres-*

sionism 19; Vogt 71, 65; Dube, *Expressionists and Expressionism* 26; Vogt 63, 69. Vogt points to "the elementary tensions [in Kirchner's *Fränzi*] between colors that are overly sharp and have an intensified hue, thereby . . . setting the pictorial surface into expressive vibration" (70).

3. Levine identifies "regression" and "apocalypse" as key themes of early expressionism (3).

4. Wigman recounts how Nolde came to her dance concerts and Kirchner attended daily rehearsals in Dresden, "drawing, sketching, painting as a silent partner" (Sorrell 55, 99). Kirchner's numerous studies of dancers in motion include the early woodcuts *Nude Dancers* (1905), *Dance Hall* (1907), and *Dancer with Lifted Skirt* (1908), and the oil paintings *Russian Dancer* (1909), *Dancing Girl* (1913), *Dancers* (1913), and *Two Red Dancers* (1914; see Grohmann 22, 18, 12, 19, 113, 124, 122). Kinkead-Weekes draws a parallel between Gudrun's eurythmics and Wigman's expressionist "Witch Dance," adding that Lawrence "[may] have known about Wigman" through Frieda (55, 61n7). Wigman's "dance poem" *The Seven Dances of Life* "is a good example of the tormented tone of German Expressionism in which the artist, in his frantic search for the deeper meaning of life and his impatience with the world and himself, escapes into explosive forms of expression . . . " (Sorrell 71).

5. Paul Vogt writes:

The so-called Expressive (Modern) Dance, whose foremost interpreter was Mary Wigman, was one of the typical art forms of the Expressionist decades. As in the visual arts, it aimed at aesthetic mediation of *a state of utter tautness*, and what it expressed was unrestrained passion and primal abandon, at one and the same time Dionysiac and Orphic. As in painting, dancing signified for its artists *the direct transposition of ecstatic excitement into expressive gesture*, reflecting that latent stimulation whose impulses directed the entire body.

Vogt adds: "When [Nolde] painted the dance, it signified a primeval state of divine transport and total abandon . . . " (58 [my italics]).

6. As Sandra Horton Fraleigh observes,

[D]ance takes us to the bodily-lived source for language. It is preverbal expression. . . . The body formulates that which it expresses, taking on the shape of its thought and feeling. Dance captures the first glimmer of our movement toward language. . . . [It has] power to reflect our inmost lived substance. That is . . . it signifies our embodiment, our life as a whole. All dance carries this signifying power . . . and is never divorced from a lived ground. (331–32)

7. Rudolf Laban claims: "The dancer saturates his living self, his human body, with forces otherwise perceptible only separately from it . . . " (179). Thus the expressionist language of dance, like that of painting, "makes the invisible visible."

8. "In front of a Futurist painting the involvement will be more mechanical,

because it is conditioned by the dynamism of the lines of force and the vibration of colors. . . . An Expressionist painting, on the other hand, might take such a receptivity as a possible point of departure, but it goes further by inducing us to identify with a more intentional course, distorting reality in proportion to the subjective emotion contained in it . . . " (Hadermann 136).

9. See Stewart, "Expressionism."

10. See Hodin, *Oskar Kokoschka* 69–71.

11. Ingersoll observes (of another scene) that "[the] reader cannot help feeling the strong impact of powerful forces in the characters' unconscious released, for good or ill, through the agency of their looking at and being looked at by each other" (272).

12. Daleski quotes Oskar Seyffert's *A Dictionary of Classical Antiquities* (1959) and Frazer's *The Golden Bough* on the cult of Cybele (167–68n1).

13. The vortex that dissolves the wrestlers' egos differs in kind from the purely destructive "vortex in which [Gerald's and Gudrun's] love dissolves" (Charles Ross 67).

14. See Leavis 177; Hough 101; Daleski 178; Pritchard 101; Bickerton 58; Miko 273; Sanders 103. An exception to this trend is Vitoux.

15. Jaques-Dalcroze calls such energy "a force analogous to electricity . . . a radio-active agent whose influence restores us to ourselves . . . " (57).

16. Sheppard observes that "the Expressionists sought to rid themselves of the notion that words were known quantities which intellect could synthesize into an elegant, mimetic surface, and to see them as charged reservoirs of energy awaiting release by the visionary writer" (278).

17. See Cowan, "Lawrence and Touch."

18. See Michael Bell, "'Worlds'"; and Stewart, "Dialectics."

19. As Sepčić writes, Lawrence "[finds] concrete embodiment in daring imaginative forms for intangible psychic realities, and this is what all Expressionist art was striving for in the visual arts, in poetry and in drama" ("'Women in Love' [I]" 441). Lawrence's style "exemplif[ies] to perfection the fundamental postulate of Expressionist art: to exteriorize by means of imaginative stylization (abstraction) the hidden soul states (*Seelenstände*), the invisible spiritual realities" ("'Women in Love' [II]" 7).

5. "PRIMITIVISM" IN *WOMEN IN LOVE*

1. See Abrams.

2. Cf. Fagg 43; McCall xi.

3. Cf. Vogel 10, 16.

4. Cf. Wingert 7.

5. Lawrence responds to drumming around the campfire with a mixture of

attraction to "this old tribal experience" and resistance to regressive impulses ("Indians and an Englishman" 99).

6. Heckel woodcuts in Dube, *Expressionists and Expressionism* 20, 27, and Kuchling 40; Kirchner in Selz, figs. 11, 32, Dube, *Expressionists and Expressionism* 10, and Whitford, fig. 35; Schmidt-Rottluff in Kuchling 32.

7. Kirchner's chief source was John Griffiths, *The Paintings in the Buddhist Cave-Temples of Ajanta, Khandesh, India*. 2 vols. (London, 1896); see also Gordon, "Kirchner in Dresden" 357. Lawrence's source was *The Ajanta Frescoes* (Oxford, 1915), a folio that he gave to Lady Ottoline Morrell in December 1915.

8. White defines a fetish as "any natural object believed to possess magical or spiritual power," but he distinguishes this "ethnological meaning" from "figurative" and "psychological" senses. Fetishism, "a mistaking of the form of a thing for its content or the taking of a part of a thing for the whole," is linked, in White's discourse theory, with synecdoche (184, 194).

9. According to Simpson, "[F]etishism occurs when the mind ceases to realize that it has itself created the outward images or things to which it subsequently posits itself as in some sort of subservient relation" (xiii). In the "confusion of product with process, or matter with spirit," sign replaces signified (12). Charles de Brosses (1760) regards "fetishism [as] a step further down the ladder [than idolatry] in that it worships things as and for themselves" (cited in Simpson 13).

10. The following critics also consider various aspects of Lawrence's "primitivism": Widmer, Chamberlain, Ford (184–207), Ruthven, Moody, Heywood, Morris, Atkinson, and Charles Ross (64–66).

11. Frazer speaks of "the slow evolution of civilization out of savagery" (1: 295).

12. Cf. Lou Witt's "vision of evil" in Lawrence's "St. Mawr" 78–80.

13. As a note in the Cambridge edition says, "African carvings of single figures in childbirth are apparently unknown. . . . DHL may be confusing the 'bands' he describes with the unnaturally elongated breasts, held in both hands, common on Yoruba figures . . . " (538n). Examples might include a *Maternity Group Figure* of the Afo peoples, Nigeria (nineteenth century, wood; Sieber and Walker, fig. 8), and an Afo "Mother and child in blackened wood with tribal scarifications" (Meauzé 185). However, tribal carvings of women "with protruding bellies" are "common" (*Women in Love* 538n), as witness *Maternity Figure*, Yoruba peoples, Nigeria (nineteenth to twentieth century, wood; Sieber and Walker, fig. 7), and Senufo and Lulua *Female Figure[s]* (Baldwin 90, 169). (Morris [26–27] cites Baulé and Bambara figures that bear no direct resemblance to those in *Women in Love*.)

14. Torgovnick offers a scathing critique of Fry's unconscious racism in his essays on African art (*Gone Primitive* 94).

15. As Ruthven puts it: "Savage primitivism . . . is a destructive hatred of civilization; the savage primitivist envisages destruction as the only solution to the prob-

lems of a hypercivilized Europe, and . . . generally takes a compensatory interest in primitive peoples, particularly in primitive Africans" (39).

16. Aldrich notes that the *totem* "acts as a focus for the interest, the libido, of both consciousness and the unconscious" (93), just as the "fetish" does for Birkin.

17. For Lovejoy and Boas, "[c]ultural primitivism . . . is the belief of men living in a relatively highly evolved and complex cultural condition that a life far simpler and less sophisticated . . . is a more desirable life" (7). Harrison succinctly states an even more negative view: "The cult of savagery, and even of simplicity, in every form, simply spells complex civilization and diminished vitality" (235). For Levin "[the] positive thrust of this [primitivist] attitude has been provoked by a negativistic re- coil" (5). Among the severest critics of modern primitivism is Kessler, who sees it as an atavistic impulse for destruction that "attacks the historical sense and mani- fests concomitantly a terrific urge toward psychological regression" (470). Similarly, Caudwell, from a Freudian-Marxist perspective, harshly reduces Lawrence's primi- tivism to regression-to-the-womb and repression of history (44, 72).

18. Chamberlain observes that "Birkin's task . . . includes the leashing of delir- ium . . . and the revitalizing of analysis. He must reconcile man's darkness and his light" (414).

19. Felix Speiser's term for "the category of undifferentiated and truly primitive objects" (cited in Leuzinger 19).

20. Robbins and Nooter connect "the quality of dynamism, or what might be called captive energy, found in African sculpture" with "the widespread African be- lief that all objects—inanimate as well as animate—embody a certain 'life-force'" (13).

21. Lawrence may have seen West African sculptures in the collections of Philip Heseltine and Mark Gertler, as well as in the British Museum (see *Women in Love* 538n). Heseltine mentions "a West African carving" in a letter to Frederick Delius (22 April 1916), and Gertler tells Carrington (February 1915): "The other day I picked up a piece of African sculpture wood. . . . It gives me great delight and is like my work" (85).

22. Lawrence uses the terms "totem" and "fetish" loosely, as the change in title of chapter 7 indicates. Frazer defines totem as "a class of material objects which a savage regards with superstitious respect, believing that there exists between him and every member of the class an intimate and altogether special relation. . . . As distin- guished from a fetich [sic], a totem is never an isolated individual" (*Totemism* 1: 3–4).

23. According to the Cambridge editors, "The 'collars' suggest that the piece comes from the Temne or Mende of Sierra Leone, the Asante or Fante of Ghana, or the Baulé of the Ivory Coast: a Mende figure in the British Museum, c. 1900, with collars and 'melon-shaped' head . . . is characteristic" (559–60n). Examples of the elongated neck with "quoits" include *Woman Holding Object* and *Female Figure* (Mende wood carvings; Robbins, fig. 54; Bascom, fig. 24).

24. Cf. Torgovnick's concept of *insinuation*, which "refers to a character's conscious or unconscious dwelling on an art object or pictorial image over a period of time, with a gradual clarification of meaning" (*The Visual Arts* 199).

25. Cf. Jung's metaphors: "[M]odern man is thrown back on himself, his energies flow towards their source, and the collision washes to the surface those psychic contents which are at all times there, but lie hidden in the silt so long as the stream flows smoothly in its course" (81).

26. Hermione's body language displays an almost schizophrenic lack of spontaneity; cf. Laing.

27. See Stewart, "Myth of the Fall." Frye (68–69) offers an existential and psychological analysis of the Fall.

28. Freud, while recognizing the dangers of repression, sees sublimation, from the standpoint of the super-ego, as the motive force of civilization; Róheim, on the contrary, regards culture from the standpoint of the id as "neurosis" (79).

29. Lévi-Strauss regards "civilization, taken as a whole . . . as an extraordinarily complex mechanism, which we might be tempted to see as offering an opportunity of survival for the human world, if its function were not to produce what physicists call entropy, that is inertia" (413).

30. See *Movements in European History*, begun in July 1918 and finished in November 1920 while Lawrence was correcting proofs of *Women in Love*.

6. FUTURISM AND MECHANISM IN *WOMEN IN LOVE*

1. The most detailed and perceptive studies of Lawrence and futurism are those by Giovanni Cianci, who sees futurism as a creative stimulus that was "intense and decisive in the maturation of Lawrence's poetic" (while his reactions to vorticism were largely negative) and Emile Delavenay, who stresses the significance of the futurists to Lawrence's own "process of self-discovery" and shows how "he used futurism as an anvil on which to hammer into shape his own idiosyncratic idea of art" ("Lawrence and the Futurists" 161, 160). See also Alldritt (148), Lindsay (40, 52), Herzinger (127), and Torgovnick, *Visual Arts* (54, 245n5).

2. Delavenay maintains that Marinetti "coined the words" *fisicologia* and *physicologie* (in the French version) and that *psicologia* [psychology], in the reprint, "makes total nonsense of the passage . . . " ("Lawrence and the Futurists" 145). Marinetti, advocating that physiology replace psychology, apparently meant to fuse the two terms.

3. Boccioni's *Development of a Bottle in Space* (1912) is reproduced in Taylor 92.

4. See *Women in Love* 567nn. Charles Ross has shown how Lawrence's manuscript revisions accentuate futurism, substituting chemical/metallurgical imagery for the mythic apple in some passages, so that Gudrun becomes "a futuristic Eve" (63).

5. See Gertler, pl. 10.

6. For Kushigian, the futurist dynamism of the frieze and the primitivist stasis of the African statues represent irreconcilable cultural forces (153).

7. The Cambridge editors rightly see "[one] of the tenets of Futurism" in Loerke's celebration of mechanism (*Women in Love* 578n); an additional reference to Freud's *Essays on the Theory of Sexuality* (1905) implies that such "mechanical agitation" is basically infantile or masturbatory.

8. Freeman comments: "This dwarfing of mankind in the service of machines reinforced the futurist's amorality toward men and exaggerated his drive toward sensuous stimulation to the point of self-destruction" (80).

9. In Taylor 84; see also Carlo Carrà's *Forze centrifughe* in Soffici n.p.

10. Cianci quotes this statement to support his thesis that Loerke is a vorticist who "has been incorrectly identified by critics as a Futurist." Loerke, he argues, "shares the ideals of Vorticism (austere 'nordic' severity, cold detachment etc.). . . . Since [Vorticism] exalted English primacy in the industrial and technological revolution, and emphasised rationalization and abstraction, it was bound to be condemned, in Lawrence's terms, to 'dark dissolution'" (41).

11. As futurist or vorticist, Loerke represents continuing tendencies of the European avant-garde: Perloff cites Howard Fox's statement in *Metaphor: New Projects by Contemporary Sculptors* (1982) that "theatricality may be the single most pervasive property of post-Modern art" (110–11).

7. VITALISM IN LAWRENCE AND VAN GOGH

1. This expressionist intensity has struck generations of critics, four of whom I quote from Bogomila Welsh-Ovcharov's anthology. Julius Meier-Graefe (1906) writes: "Beneath the scorching heavens his pictures erupt into flames. . . . He was not aware of his actions and felt himself united with the subjects he painted. He painted himself in the form of glowing clouds, in the thousand suns . . . " (73). Henri Focillon (1928) comments on Van Gogh's "solar romanticism" and adds: "For him, everything has expression, urgency, and magnetism" (97). Sven Hedenberg (1937) observes: "Everything he reproduces, deeply rooted trees as well as the sun and the hills, is depicted with a great sense of life and rhythm. This is directed by a spiritual life which alternates between despair and ecstasy, between intensity and calmness" (109). And Fritz Novotny (1953) states, in terms that underline the affinity of Lawrence's writing with Van Gogh's painting: "His pantheistic intoxication with color and movement was the aspect of van Gogh's painting by which he plunged furthest into the new perceptual world of Post-Impressionist art" (118).

2. Applying the notion of "imaginative context" to Lawrence and the economist Max Weber, Martin Green notes that it "offers the extra stimulation that each of the

figures represents a different field of knowledge and a different mode of imagination" (371). When two artists practice the same mode of expression, such as letters, the grounds for comparison may be all the firmer, as Mark Roskill notes in his introduction to Van Gogh's letters: "If we want an analogy nearer our own day to Van Gogh's total personality—its strength of character, powers of insight, and rough-hewn forcefulness of language—we may find it in the correspondence of D. H. Lawrence. . . . [O]ne can equally say of the letters of Van Gogh what was written very recently about those of Lawrence: 'no-one halfway alive could be untouched by the joy of living that breathes in the slightest of them'" (11; quotation from *Times Literary Supplement*, 27 April 1962).

3. Van Gogh's stern *Self-Portrait with Gray Felt Hat: Full Face* (Paris 1887; de la Faille F296; also reproduced as frontispiece to *Complete Letters*, vol. 2) has an amazing resemblance to Jan Juta's flamelike portrait of red-bearded Lawrence (1920; see Sagar, *Life of D. H. Lawrence*, illus. 3 and jacket cover). Juta may have conflated a memory of Van Gogh's self-portraits with the image of his sitter, painting Lawrence *as* Van Gogh or as sharing his aura.

4. The Cambridge editors of Lawrence's *Letters* "identify the volume that he was reading as *The Letters of a Post-Impressionist, being the Familiar Correspondence of Vincent Van Gogh* (Constable, 1912)," but they also say that "DHL's sketch clearly refers to Van Gogh's ('with colour directions') in Letter IX, reproduced in *Lettres de Vincent Van Gogh à Emile Bernard* (Paris, 1911)" (2: 296n5; 303n3). The letter (no. II, and not IX as stated), with Van Gogh's sketch at the head of it, is reproduced in an appendix entitled "Cent Reproductions de Dessins et Tableaux" (IV–V). Van Gogh's sketch appears in *Complete Letters* (3: 447—not vol. 1, as stated in Lawrence's *Letters* [2: 303 n. 3]; Lawrence's copy of the sketch is not included in the edition of his *Letters*. Cf. Van Gogh's painting of the motif, *The Drawbridge* (May 1888), in Schapiro, *Van Gogh* 55.

5. In "Making Pictures," Lawrence writes: "A picture lives with the life you put into it. . . . Even if you only copy a purely banal reproduction of an old bridge, some sort of keen, delighted awareness of the old bridge or of its atmosphere, or the image it has kindled inside you, can go over on to the paper and give a certain touch of life . . . " (604).

6. Van Gogh's color is vitalist expression in itself, as some of his contemporaries recognized. In his trail-blazing article (January 1890), Albert Aurier writes:

> [His color] is unbelievably dazzling. He is, as far as I know, the only painter who perceives the chromatism of things with this intensity, with this metallic, jewellike quality. His researches into the coloration of shadows, into the influences of colors on colors, of full sunlight are of the most inquisitive. . . . His brush operates by enormous impasto touches of very pure colors, by curved trails broken by rectilinear strokes . . . by accumulations, sometimes clumsy, of a very glowing ma-

sonry, and all this gives to some of his canvases the solid appearance of dazzling walls made of crystals and sun. (314)

In the Welsh-Ovcharav collection, Frederik van Eeden (1890) says of his "strong, vivid coloring" that he uses "only violently sparkling [hues:] glaring green, pure vermilion, intense violet purple, strong cobalt blue, and above all yellow, a fierce yellow, a brutal chrome yellow. . . . This inclination towards bright colors is a primitive inclination" (58–59). Johan de Meester (1891) writes: "van Gogh was enraptured with strong colors. Golden yellow crowfoots and sunflowers and dark fiery irises were placed before a golden yellow backdrop" (61). Two decades later, Pierre Godet (1911) adds: "*Color* . . . was for van Gogh the great liberator. It was the incendiary of his internal flame. It provided his unsatisfied passion for creation with an instrument of expression which knew no bounds" (89).

   7. Phrases in this paragraph are cited from Eliot 17, 18; Joyce 205, 213, 215; and Lawrence, *Lady Chatterley's Lover* 101.

   8. Other critics who touch briefly on Lawrence's affinity with Van Gogh are Lindsay 53, Sanders 66, and Meyers, *D. H. Lawrence* 141.

   9. See Stewart, "Primordial Affinities."

   10. See Schapiro, *Paul Cézanne* 39.

   11. Cf. Stewart, "Metaphor and Metonymy."

   12. Van Gogh writes Bernard from Arles (June 1888) of his experiments with "simplification of color in the Japanese manner," explaining that "the Japanese artist ignores reflected colors, and puts the flat tones side by side, with characteristic lines marking off the movements and the forms." He concludes: "*There is no blue without yellow and without orange*, and if you put in blue, then you must put in yellow, and orange too" (*Complete Letters* 3: 490, 491).

   13. With the help of Delavenay, Janik, and Zoll, along with Michaels-Tonks, Scott, and Ulmer, one may summarize Lawrence's system of polarities as follows: The north is associated with *water*, ice, cold, grayness, gloom; the Gothic, the blue-eyed Teutons, English, Germans; Apollo, light, spirit, intellect, mental consciousness, introspection, abstraction, the infinite, science, industry, and modern civilization with its neutralizing conformity, permanence, and sterility. The south, by contrast, is associated with *fire*, sun, warmth, clarity, "vivid colours"; classicism, the dark-eyed Etruscans, Italians, Mediterranean peoples; Dionysus, darkness, the body, sensuality, blood-consciousness, spontaneity, empathy, earthiness; primitive agrarian life with its "wild singleness," growth, change, fruitfulness, and vitality. Although integration of opposites was the original ideal, Lawrence consciously oriented himself toward south and west as life-saving directions (see *Letters* 3: 524). The dialectic of north and south becomes a matter of life and death.

   14. See Schapiro, *Van Gogh* 65.

   15. See *The World of Van Gogh* 101, 102.

16. Albert Aurier compares the Sower with Van Gogh himself and sees the image as a symbol of "the coming of a man, a messiah, a sower of truth, who will regenerate our decadent and perhaps imbecilic industrialist society" (313).

17. See *Sunflowers* (August 1888) in Schapiro, *Van Gogh* 69, and *World of Van Gogh* 103. Roger Fry (1923) recognizes the "triumphant success" of *The Sunflowers*: "It has supreme exuberance, vitality, and vehemence of attack. . . . Van Gogh had a predilection for harmonies in which positive notes of yellow predominated. . . . Here he has chosen a pale lemon-yellow background to set off the blazing golden glow of the petals of his sunflowers, which tell against it as dusky masses of burnished gold" (Welsh-Ovcharov 93).

18. Aldous Huxley also recognized this genius for empathy in Lawrence: "He seemed to know by personal experience, what it was like to be a tree or a daisy or a breaking wave or the mysterious moon itself. He could get inside the skin of an animal . . . " (Introduction xxx). Conversely, Nordenfalk says of Van Gogh's landscapes: "[It] is as though the artist had penetrated into the *motif*, filling it with his own mind, his own restlessness, his own agony" (176).

19. The two paintings are reproduced in Schapiro, *Van Gogh* 107 and 109. Lawrence realizes, oddly enough in relation to Cézanne's late landscapes rather than Van Gogh's more dynamic ones, "how intuitively *true* this is of landscape. It is *not* still. It has its own weird anima, and to our wide-eyed perception it changes like a living animal under our gaze" ("Introduction to These Paintings" 580–81). L. D. Clark points out that, in Lawrence's landscapes, "the 'weird anima' of place seldom fails to emerge, in a 'curious rolling flood of vision' . . . " ("Immediacy" 122).

20. See Hammacher, *Genius* 149.

21. Cf. Cowan, "D. H. Lawrence's Dualism."

22. See Tralbaut 236, 302.

23. According to Cirlot, the spiral is "[a] schematic image of the evolution of the universe . . . and a symbol for growth. . . . In the Egyptian system of hieroglyphs . . . [it] denotes cosmic forms in motion . . . " (290–91).

24. Van Gogh tells Bernard that "the southern sky and the blue Mediterranean provoke an orange tint that gets more intense as the scale of blue colors gets a more vigorous tone"; he adds: "What I should like to find out is the effect of an intenser blue in the sky" (*Complete Letters* 3: 490, 491).

25. See Varnedoe, pl. 66 and cover (detail).

26. See Pickvance, fig. 34.

27. Lawrence expounds animism and vitalism in celebrating the life and culture of the Etruscans:

> [All] was alive: the whole universe lived: and the business of man was himself to live amid it all. He had to draw life into himself, out of the wandering huge vitalities of the world. The cosmos was alive, like a vast creature. . . . [It] had a great soul, or

anima. . . . The cosmos was one, and its anima was one. . . . [There was] one underlying religious idea: the conception of the vitality of the cosmos . . . and man, amid all the glowing welter, adventuring, struggling, striving for one thing, life, vitality, more vitality: to get into himself more and more of the gleaming vitality of the cosmos. (*Sketches of Etruscan Places* 56–57)

Lawrence traces this flamelike, spontaneous vitalism in Etruscan art.

28. Lawrence writes:

I think New Mexico was the greatest experience from the outside world that I have ever had. It certainly changed me for ever. . . . [The] moment I saw the brilliant, proud morning shine high up over the deserts of Santa Fé, something stood still in my soul, and I started to attend. . . . In the magnificent fierce morning of New Mexico one sprang awake, a new part of the soul woke up suddenly, and the old world gave way to a new. ("New Mexico" 142)

29. In one panorama, Lawrence builds a spatial image of the landscape with recession of planes and contrasts of light and tone, until his viewer becomes aware of the visionary quality standing alongside the reality:

The desert swept its great fawn-coloured circle around, away beyond and below like a beach, with a long mountain-side of pure blue shadow closing in the near corner, and strange bluish hummocks of mountains rising like wet rock from a vast strand, away in the middle distance, and beyond, in the farthest distance, pale blue crests of mountains looking over the horizon, from the west, as if peering in from another world altogether. (145)

30. See Pickvance, pls. 83, 85 (270–71, 274–75).

31. See Schapiro (illustrations) 97, 99. Van Gogh's verbal descriptions also make colors vibrate against each other, as when he describes "a red vineyard, all red like red wine. In the distance it turned to yellow, and then a green sky with the sun, the earth after the rain violet, sparkling yellow here and there where it caught the reflection of the setting sun" (*Complete Letters* 3: 101).

32. Darwinism is a substratum to Lawrence's way of seeing here. According to Krasner, "Lawrence's material world continually fluxes between energy and matter, form and formlessness" in a way that relates it to "field theory." He observes that "Lawrence makes motion and color more visually determining than form" (155, 157).

33. See *Olive Orchard* or *Road with Cypress and Star* (see pl. 15; both 1889) in Pickvance, pls. 41, 55. Of *Landscape with Olive Trees*, Schapiro writes: "[In] the common movement that seems to issue from an underlying force, overwhelming all objects, these retain their individuality, their unique rhythms" (*Van Gogh* 108).

8. LAWRENCE, VAN GOGH, AND CÉZANNE

1. *The Letters of a Post-Impressionist, being the Familiar Correspondence of Vincent Van Gogh* (1912), which Lawrence had been reading, includes some of Van Gogh's best letters on color, nature, and the Japanese.

2. See Schapiro, *Van Gogh* 101 and frontispiece. One can only surmise what Lawrence knew of Van Gogh's art in 1915; Van Gogh, Cézanne, Matisse, Derain, and Picasso had been introduced to the British public by Roger Fry's Post-Impressionist Exhibitions of 1910 and 1912. Lawrence saw a major exhibition of modern art in Munich in 1913; in Lady Ottoline's circle, he knew the painters Mark Gertler, Carrington, and Duncan Grant, all of whom had ties with post-impressionism.

3. See Schapiro, *Van Gogh* 69.

4. See Ouspensky; also Langer, chapter 5, "Virtual Space," and chapter 6, "The Modes of Virtual Space" (69–103). According to Langer, "The purpose of all plastic art is to articulate visual form, and to present that form—so immediately expressive of human feeling that it seems to be charged with feeling—as the sole, or at least paramount, object of perception. This means that for the beholder the work of art must be not only a shape in space, but a shaping *of* space . . . " (71).

5. See "Poetry of the Present" (1918), in which Lawrence writes: "Give me the still, white seething, the incandescence and the coldness of the incarnate moment: the moment, the quick of all change and haste and opposition. . . . The source, the issue, the creative quick." Of Whitman he adds: "The clue to all his utterance lies in the sheer appreciation of the instant moment, life surging itself into utterance at its very well-head. . . . This is the immanence" (183).

6. According to M. Elizabeth Wallace, "Lawrence's developing epistemology closely parallels [Michael] Polanyi's three claims—that knowledge is personal, is based on unexamined assumptions, and is an unspecifiable skill involving risk and commitment, the extension of our bodies into the world. Like Polanyi, Lawrence emphasized the bodily roots of knowledge . . . " (108).

7. Lawrence writes: "It was part of his desire: to make the human form, the *life* form, come to rest. . . . And at the same time he set the unmoving material world into motion. Walls twitch and slide, chairs bend or rear up a little, cloths curl like burning paper. Cézanne did this partly to satisfy his intuitive feeling that nothing is really *statically* at rest . . . " ("Introduction to These Paintings" 580).

8. See Schapiro, *Van Gogh* 131.

9. See Schapiro, *Cézanne* 67, 75, 125.

10. See Hirsh et al. 158–59, 164, 162, 163.

11. Van Gogh describes one of his landscapes at Arles as "plowed fields; a scenery with nothing but lumps of earth, the furrows the color of an old wooden shoe under a forget-me-not blue sky . . . " (*Complete Letters* 3: 83). A striking example of

Van Gogh's "surging earth" is the spatially dynamic *Landscape with Ploughed Fields* (Saint-Rémy, 1889; see Schapiro, *Van Gogh* 115).

12. Lindsay remarks on the "affinity [Lawrence] found between his own aims and [Cézanne's] effort to create structures . . . " (39); Alldritt sees Cézanne's painting "serv[ing] as the best . . . metaphor for [Lawrence's] own art and concerns" (201). The key to this mutuality is the expression of visual thinking in painting.

13. Lawrence writes: "With Cézanne, landscape 'crystallized,' to use one of the favourite terms of the critics, and it has gone on crystallizing into cubes, cones, pyramids, and so forth ever since" ("Introduction to These Paintings" 565).

14. See Schapiro, *Cézanne* 101. See also *Still Life with Basket of Apples* (1890–94) and *Still Life with Apples and Oranges* (1895–1900) 91, 103. Lawrence himself painted a watercolor still life, *Two Apples* (1910; *Paintings*, fig. 6), in which he exaggerates the rotundity and three-dimensionality of the apples by contrasting highlights and shadows.

15. Lawrence parodies Fry's "jargon about the pure world of reality existing behind the veil of this vulgar world of accepted appearances, and of the entry of the elect through the doorway of visual art" ("Introduction to These Paintings" 566). Cf. his brilliant parody of formal aesthetic concepts of plane, edge, mass, pattern, texture, centering, spotting, color, atmosphere, etc. in the same essay (582–83).

16. Fernihough attempts to dismantle the binary clichés of Lawrence versus Bloomsbury and life versus art. Comparing "Introduction to These Paintings" with Fry's *Cézanne*, she concludes that Lawrence virtually plagiarized Fry's ideas (117) while slamming his formalism. But if Lawrence borrowed freely from Fry, it was to turn the critic's ideas inside out. He ignores areas of agreement between himself and Fry, in order to emphasize a radical divergence of opinion.

17. Remsbury maintains that Lawrence's "capacity for engagement in the vision of the artist" makes him more of a professional art critic than Fry: "[Lawrence's] biographical sketch of Cézanne is much more inward with the creative process, in its presentation of a conflict between the artist's mind and his feelings, or old and new ways of seeing the object" (133, 131).

18. According to Schapiro, the *Portrait of Geffroy* "is a rare union of the realistic vision of a piece of space . . . with a powerful, probing, rigorous effort to adjust all that is seen in a coherent balanced structure with its own vitality and attraction" (*Cézanne* 94; [illustration] 95).

19. This principle applies to Cézanne, "[who] thought that the processes at work in the artist's mind, when he contemplates, through the *transparency* of the hillside, the germinating work of art, were but an extension of those at work in ordinary perception . . . " (Remsbury 129). John and Ann Remsbury find "virtually a point-by-point resemblance between [Lawrence's and Merleau-Ponty's] commentaries on Cézanne" (201).

20. Cf. Bryson, *Vision and Painting*, chapters 3 and 4, 37–86.

21. See Remsbury; Richardson and Ades; Janik, "Toward Thingness."

22. Merleau-Ponty insists that expression of the "primordial world" cannot be "the translation of a clearly defined thought, since such clear thoughts are those which have already been uttered by ourselves or others" ("Cézanne's Doubt" 19, qtd. in Jones 104).

23. Lawrence records his experience of solipsism ("when everything was me") in "New Heaven and New Earth," *Complete Poems* 257.

24. Gauguin maintains that all real values in art are subjective, for the object is always more or less transformed by the artist's vision: "Art is an abstraction, draw this abstraction forth from nature by dreaming before it and thinking about the work that will result from it; the only way to climb up to God is to . . . create" (qtd. in Cachin 63).

25. For a review of painters and styles that attracted both artists, see Stewart, "Common Art Interests."

26. Lawrence, *Paintings*, figs. 11, 18; pl. 12.

27. Lawrence, *Paintings*, figs. 12, 14, 25; pls. 10, 13; fig. 28.

28. To readjust the balance somewhat, it should be noted that Fry, at the end of his study of Cézanne, drops his intellectualism and reminds the reader "that such analysis halts before the ultimate concrete reality of the work of art . . . " (*Cézanne* 88).

29. Lawrence, *Paintings*, pls. 7, 9; fig. 28.

30. Richardson and Ades, however, base the affinity between Lawrence and Cézanne on "correspondences in the life histories and artistry of two geniuses whose works are normally thought of as divergent" (451), while Lindsay maintains that "[in] analysing the art-crisis revealed in Cézanne, Lawrence was, in fact, analysing his own deep creative conflicts . . . " (36).

9. LAWRENCE, GAUGUIN, AND JAPANESE ART IN *KANGAROO* AND *THE PLUMED SERPENT*

1. See Lawrence's essay "The Spirit of Place," in which he affirms: "All art partakes of the Spirit of Place in which it is produced," and "Art communicates a state of being . . . " (16, 19).

2. The classic statement of expansive, energized vision and being is his essay "New Mexico," which subsumes a long perceptual pilgrimage in a moment of vital awareness.

3. L. D. Clark links this fear of the bush with Lawrence's "agarophobia" (*Minoan Distance* 257), but Somers seems more liable to social claustrophobia.

4. Cf. Berger, "Courbet" 135. Berger shows how landscape affects the artist's

vision and calls the Jura "a place where the visible is discontinuous . . . where [it] cannot always be assumed and has to be grasped when it does make its appearance."

5. See Aldous Huxley, "Wordsworth in the Tropics."

6. Cf. Kant; and Weiskel 38–48.

7. Lawrence's claim that "keen, delighted awareness" of another artist's motif and way of seeing can give a "touch of life" to copying ("Making Pictures" 604) is raised to a higher power in Van Gogh's paintings after Japanese woodcuts by Hokusai and Hiroshige, which, with their resplendent color, "appear more Japanese than their Japanese models" (Wichmann 42). By way of illustration, Wichmann (41) juxta-poses Hiroshige's *Flowering Plum Tree in the Kameido Garden* (1856–58) with Van Gogh's *Japonaiserie: The Flowering Plum Tree* (Paris, 1886–88; see pl. 17).

8. See Strange, pls. D and P.

9. The print, *Mannen Bridge, Fukagawa* (1857), in Hiroshige, pl. 56, shows a giant tortoise suspended as if from the bridge, just above a view of Mt. Fuji.

10. Wichmann singles out the Japanese predilection for "a light with no shadows" and the unusual spatial concepts, with "new and astonishing angles of vision—from below, from above—and the separation of planes by a strong diago-nal . . . " (10).

11. See Strange, pl. I.

12. See Haftmann, pl. 13.

13. See Haftmann, pl. 2.

14. "Japanese" is used here to indicate a way of seeing associated with nine-teenth-century Japanese art, particularly of the "Ukiyo-e" school.

15. Goldwater points to "Gauguin's palette of non-primary hues" and "his color harmonies [based] upon the juxtaposition of allied rather than contrasting colors" (*Gauguin* 38).

16. See Narazaki, *Hokusai*, pl. 4; Hillier, pl. 10.

17. For Lawrence, "the art-symbol . . . stands for a pure experience, emotional and passional, spiritual and perceptual, all at once" ("The Spirit of Place" 19). L. D. Clark calls the atmospheric imagery of Lake Sayula "[o]rganic description . . . in-clud[ing] the body and spirit of the principal character . . . and the spirit of religious awareness embodied in the landscape—in 'nature' . . . " (*Dark Night* 56).

18. See Monet's paintings of Antibes (1888) in Gordon and Forge 120; and House, figs. 206, 207.

19. Gauguin's eclectic use of all three sources is well known. Cachin notes that "some of his canvases show a sharp Japanese influence in the decorative handling and style of their composition . . . " (165).

20. See Goldwater, *Paul Gauguin* 111, 127, 131; Cachin 226–27; Goldwater, *Paul Gauguin* 150, 156. Goldwater notes the influence of Puvis de Chavannes on *Nave nave Mahana* but adds: "Puvis views his classic landscapes through a telescope from

some distant Olympus, while Gauguin brings his tropical version close and warm before us" (*Paul Gauguin* 130).

21. On the Quetzalcoatl myth, see Séjourné 24–28, 53–79.

22. See Cachin 151, 186–87.

23. See Cachin 182, 183.

24. See d'Argencourt, cat. no. 138; and Wattenmaker 115–28.

25. See Cachin 156–57.

26. See Goldwater, *Paul Gauguin* 153.

27. See Goldwater, *Paul Gauguin* 123.

28. See Cachin 166–67.

29. According to the *Tung-yin hua-chüeh* painter's manual, "[the] artist must make the dots [depicting moss] in part consciously and in part completely at random, with the spirit concentrated and the mind relaxed"; Van Gogh admired the skill of the Japanese artists: "Their work is as simple as breathing, and they do a figure in a few sure strokes" (quoted in Wichmann 54, 56). The Ōtsu color print is in Narazaki, *Hiroshige*, fig. 70 (series dated 1848–54).

CONCLUSION

1. Alldritt (216) applies a kind of cultural determinism to Lawrence's vision that would arrest it in English "traditions of visualisation"—traditions that Lawrence was absorbing and beginning to supersede in his passage from Pre-Raphaelitism to impressionism in *The White Peacock*. Lawrence's vision and expression, although formed in what he later called "the country of [his] heart," were not unalterably tied to their English origins; it is insufficient, therefore, to compare his vision with Ruskin's, despite his early admiration for the philosopher-critic. As he came in contact with other cultures and the landscapes, Lawrence's visual imagination proved capable of new creative responses and development.

2. George Steiner 61.

3. Lawrence, "Making Pictures" 605.

4. Creative perception involves subtle transactions. Gadamer notes that "we both elicit the image from things and imaginatively project the image into things in one and the same process" (17).

BIBLIOGRAPHY

Abrams, M. H. "Primitivism and Progress." *A Glossary of Literary Terms*. 6th ed. New York: Harcourt, 1993. 169–71.

Albright, Daniel. *Personality and Impersonality: Lawrence, Woolf, and Mann*. Chicago: U of Chicago P, 1978.

Alcorn, John. *The Nature Novel from Hardy to Lawrence*. London: Macmillan, 1978.

Aldrich, C. R. *The Primitive Mind and Modern Civilization*. London: Paul, 1931.

Alldritt, Keith. *The Visual Imagination of D. H. Lawrence*. London: Arnold, 1971.

Apollonio, Umbro, ed. *Futurist Manifestos*. London: Thames, 1973.

Arnheim, Rudolf. *Art and Visual Perception: A Psychology of the Creative Eye*. Berkeley: U of California P, 1974.

———. *Visual Thinking*. Berkeley: U of California P, 1969.

Artaud, Antonin. "Van Gogh, the Man Suicided by Society." 1947. Trans. Helen Weaver. *Antonin Artaud: Selected Writings*. Ed. Susan Sontag. New York: Abrams, n.d.

Atkinson, William. "Africa: A Common Topos in Lawrence and Eliot." *Twentieth Century Literature* 37 (1991): 22–37.

Aurier, G. Albert. "Les Isolés: Vincent van Gogh." Pickvance appendix 3, 310–15.

Ba, Amadou Hampate. "African Art: Where the Hand Has Ears." Foreword. Robbins and Nooter 7–9.

Balbert, Peter. *D. H. Lawrence and the Psychology of Rhythm: The Meaning of Form in The Rainbow*. The Hague: Mouton, 1974.

Baldwin, James, et al. *Perspectives: Angles on African Art*. Interviewed by Michael John Weber. New York: Center for African Art/Abrams, 1987.

Banham, Reyner. *Theory and Design in the First Machine Age*. London: Architectural, 1960.

Bascom, William. *African Art in Cultural Perspective*. New York: Norton, 1973.

Beckmann, Max. "On My Painting." 1938. Chipp 187–92.

Beckson, Karl, ed. *Aesthetes and Decadents of the 1890s: An Anthology of British Poetry and Prose*. New York: Vintage, 1966.

——. Introduction. Beckson xvii–xi.

Bell, Clive. *Art*. 1914. New ed. London: Chatto, 1949.

Bell, Michael. *D. H. Lawrence: Language and Being*. Cambridge: Cambridge UP, 1992.

——. *Primitivism*. London: Methuen, 1972.

——. "The 'Worlds' of *Women in Love*." *D. H. Lawrence: Language and Being* 97–132.

Ben-Ephraim, Gavriel. *The Moon's Dominion: Narrative Dichotomy and Female Dominance in Lawrence's Earlier Novels*. London: Associated UP, 1981.

Benjamin, Walter. "The Work of Art in the Age of Mechanical Reproduction." Trans. Harry Zohn. *Illuminations*. Ed. Hannah Arendt. New York: Schocken, 1969. 217–51.

Benn, Gottfried. *Primal Vision*. Ed. E. B. Ashton. Norfolk, CT: New Directions, n.d.

——. *Selected Writings*. Ed. E. B. Ashton. London: Bodley Head, 1961.

Berger, John. "Courbet and the Jura." *About Looking*. New York: Pantheon, 1980. 134–41.

——. *Ways of Seeing*. London: BBC-Penguin, 1972.

Bickerton, Derek. "The Language of '*Women in Love*.'" *Review of English Literature* 8 (1967): 56–67.

Biebuyck, Daniel P., ed. *Tradition and Creativity in Tribal Art*. Berkeley: U of California P, 1969.

Blackmur, R. P. "D. H. Lawrence and Expressive Form." 1935. *Form and Value in Modern Poetry*. New York: Anchor-Doubleday, 1957. 253–67.

Bloom, Harold. *The Anxiety of Influence*. New York: Oxford UP, 1975.

Blunden, Maria, and Godfrey Blunden. *Impressionists and Impressionism*. New York: Rizzoli, 1980.

Bodkin, Maud. *Archetypal Patterns in Poetry: Psychological Studies of Imagination*. London: Oxford UP, 1963.

Bowness, Alan, ed. *Impressionists and Post-Impressionists*. New York: Grolier, 1965.

Brandabur, A. M. "The Ritual Corn Harvest Scene in *The Rainbow*." *D. H. Lawrence Review* 6 (1973): 284–302.

Brown, Norman O. *Life Against Death*. New York: Vintage, 1959.

Bryson, Norman. *Vision and Painting: The Logic of the Gaze*. New Haven: Yale UP, 1983.

——. *Word and Image: French Painting of the Ancien Regime*. Cambridge: Cambridge UP, 1981.

Buchheim, Lothar-Günther. *The Graphic Art of German Expressionism*. New York: Universe, 1960.

Cachin, Françoise. *Gauguin*. Trans. Bambi Ballard. Paris: Flammarion, 1990.

Carrieri, Raffaele. *Futurism*. Trans. Leslie van Rensselaer White. Milano: Edizioni del Milione, n.d.

Carswell, Catherine. *The Savage Pilgrimage: A Narrative of D. H. Lawrence*. 1932. Cambridge: Cambridge UP, 1981.

Caudwell, Christopher. *Studies in a Dying Culture*. 1938. London: Bodley Head, 1949.

Caws, Mary Ann. *City Images: Perspectives from Literature, Philosophy, and Film*. Langhorne, PA: Gordon, 1991.

Cézanne, Paul. *Letters*. Ed. John Rewald. Trans. Seymour Hacker. Rev. ed. New York: Hacker, 1984.

Chamberlain, Robert L. "Pussum, Minette, and the Africo-Nordic Symbol in Lawrence's *Women in Love*." *PMLA* 78 (1963): 407–16.

Chambers, Jessie. *D. H. Lawrence: A Personal Record*. 1935. Cambridge: Cambridge UP, 1980.

Cheney, Sheldon. *Expressionism in Art*. Rev. ed. New York: Liveright, 1958.

Chipp, Herschel B., ed. *Theories of Modern Art: A Source Book by Artists and Critics*. Berkeley: U of California P, 1968.

Cianci, Giovanni. "D. H. Lawrence and Futurism/Vorticism." *Arbeiten aus Anglistik und Amerikanistik* 8 (1983): 41–53.

Cirlot, J. E. *A Dictionary of Symbols*. Trans. Jack Sage. New York: Philosophical Library, 1962.

Clark, Kenneth. *Landscape into Art*. New ed. New York: Harper, 1976.

Clark, L. D. *Dark Night of the Body: D. H. Lawrence's* The Plumed Serpent. Austin: U of Texas P, 1964.

———. "Immediacy and Recollection: The Rhythm of the Visual in D. H. Lawrence." Partlow and Moore 121–35.

———. *The Minoan Distance: The Symbolism of Travel in D. H. Lawrence*. Tucson: U of Arizona P, 1980.

Claude Monet: Paintings in Soviet Museums. Trans. Hugh Aplin and Ruslan Smirnov. Leningrad: Aurora, 1990.

Clough, Rosa Trillo. *Futurism: The Story of a Modern Art Movement: A New Appraisal*. New York: Greenwood, 1969.

Cogniat, Raymond. *Sisley*. Trans. Alice Sachs. New York: Crown, 1978.

Conrad, Joseph. Heart of Darkness: *An Authoritative Text; Backgrounds and Sources; Criticism*. Ed. Robert Kimbrough. 3rd ed. Norton Critical Edition. New York: Norton, 1988.

Courthion, Pierre. *Impressionism* Trans. John Shepley. New York: Abrams, n.d.

Cowan, James C. "D. H. Lawrence's Dualism: The Apollonian-Dionysian Polarity and *The Ladybird.*" *Forms of Modern British Fiction.* Ed. Allan Warren Friedman. Austin: U of Texas P, 1975. 173–99.

——. "Lawrence and Touch." *D. H. Lawrence and the Trembling Balance.* University Park: Pennsylvania State UP, 1990. 135–55.

Daiches, David. "Lawrence and the Form of the Novel." Salgādo 164–70.

Daleski, H. M. *The Forked Flame: A Study of D. H. Lawrence.* London: Faber, 1965.

d'Argencourt, Louise, et al. *Puvis de Chavannes, 1824–1898.* Ottawa: National Gallery of Canada, 1977.

de la Faille, J.-B. *The Works of Vincent van Gogh: His Paintings and Drawings.* New York: Reynal, 1970.

Delavenay, Emile. *D. H. Lawrence: The Man and His Work.* Trans. Katharine M. Delavenay. Carbondale: Southern Illinois UP, 1980.

——. "Lawrence and the Futurists." *The Modernists: Studies in a Literary Dimension.* Ed. Lawrence B. Gamache and Ian S. MacNiven. Rutherford, NJ: Farleigh Dickinson UP, 1987. 140–62.

——. "Lawrence's Major Work." Partlow and Moore 139–42.

Dube, Wolf-Dieter. "Ernst Ludwig Kirchner." *Kirchner 1880–1938: Oils, Watercolours, Drawings and Graphics.* Catalogue of First London Exhibition, June–July 1969. London: Marlborough Fine Art, 1969. 8–11.

——. *The Expressionists.* Trans. Mary Whittall. London: Thames, 1972.

——. *Expressionists and Expressionism.* Trans. James Emmons. Geneva: Skira, 1983.

Durrell, Lawrence. "Landscape and Character." *Spirit of Place: Letters and Essays on Travel.* Ed. Alan G. Thomas. New York: Dutton, 1969. 156–63.

Durrell, Lawrence, and Henry Miller. *A Private Correspondence.* Ed. George Wickes. New York: Dutton, 1964.

Ebbatson, Roger. *Lawrence and the Nature Tradition: A Theme in English Fiction, 1859–1914.* Sussex: Harvester, 1980.

Edvard Munch: The Major Graphic. Oslo: Munch Museum, n.d.

Elgar, Frank. *Van Gogh: A Study of His Life and Work.* Trans. James Cleugh. New York: Praeger, 1966.

Eliot, T. S. "Tradition and the Individual Talent." *Selected Essays.* 1932. London: Faber, 1986. 13–22.

Fagg, William. "The African Artist." Biebuyck 42–57.

Fagg, William, and Margaret Plass. *African Sculpture: An Anthology.* London: Studio Vista, 1964.

Faris, Wendy B. "The Labyrinth as Sign of City, Text, and Thought." Caws 33–41.

Farr, Judith. Introduction. Farr 1–23.

———, ed. *Twentieth Century Interpretations of* Sons and Lovers : *A Collection of Critical Essays.* Englewood Cliffs, NJ: Prentice-Hall, 1970.

Fernihough, Ann. *D. H. Lawrence: Aesthetics and Ideology.* Oxford: Clarendon, 1993.

Ford, George H. *Double Measure: A Study of the Novels and Stories of D. H. Lawrence.* New York: Holt, 1975.

Fraleigh, Sandra Horton. "Poetic Body." *Word and Image* 2 (1986): 331–32.

Frazer, James G. *The Golden Bough.* 3rd ed. 12 vols. London: Macmillan, 1911.

———. *Totemism and Exogamy.* 4 vols. London: Macmillan, 1910.

Freeman, Mary. "Lawrence and Futurism." *D. H. Lawrence: A Basic Study of His Ideas.* Gainesville: U of Florida P, 1955. 70–81.

Freud, Sigmund. *Civilization and Its Discontents.* 1930. Trans. James Strachey. New York: Norton, 1962.

Friedman, Alan. "The Other Lawrence." *Partisan Review* 37 (1970): 239–53.

Frobenius, Leo. *The Voice of Africa.* Trans. Rudolf Blind. 2 vols. London: Murray, 1920.

Fry, Roger. *Cézanne: A Study of His Development.* 1927. New York: Noonday, 1958.

———. *Vision and Design.* 1920. Harmondsworth, Middlesex: Penguin, 1961.

Frye, Northrop. *The Return of Eden: Five Essays on Milton's Epics.* Toronto: U of Toronto P, 1964.

Gadamer, Hans-Georg. *The Relevance of the Beautiful and Other Essays.* Trans. Nicholas Walker. Ed. Robert Bernasconi. Cambridge: Cambridge UP, 1986.

Garnett, Edward. "From *Friday Nights.*" Farr 95.

Gauguin, Paul. *The Intimate Journals.* Trans. Van Wyck Brooks. 1923. London: Heinemann, 1953.

———. *Noa Noa: The Tahiti Journal of Paul Gauguin.* Trans. O. F. Theis. Océanie ed. San Francisco: Chronicle, 1994.

———. *The Writings of a Savage.* Ed. Daniel Guérin. Trans. Eleanor Levieux. New York: Viking, 1978.

Gaunt, William. *The Impressionists.* London: Thames, 1970.

German Expressionist Sculpture. Los Angeles: Los Angeles County Museum of Art, 1984.

Gertler, Mark. *Mark Gertler: Selected Letters.* Ed. Noel Carrington. London: Hart-Davis, 1965.

Goldwater, Robert. "Judgments of Primitive Art, 1905–1965." Biebuyck 24–41.

———. *Paul Gauguin.* New York: Abrams, n.d.

———. *Primitivism in Modern Art.* 1938. Rev. ed. New York: Vintage, 1967.

Gordon, Donald E. *Ernst Ludwig Kirchner.* Cambridge: Harvard UP, 1969.

———. *Ernst Ludwig Kirchner: A Retrospective Exhibition.* Boston: Museum of Fine Arts, 1968.

———. "Kirchner in Dresden." *Art Bulletin* 48 (1966): 335–69.

——. *Modern Art Exhibitions, 1900–1916: Selected Catalogue Documentation*. 2 vols. Munich: Prestel, 1974.

Gordon, Robert, and Andrew Forge. *Monet*. New York: Abrams, 1983.

Graetz, H. R. *The Symbolic Language of Vincent Van Gogh*. New York: McGraw-Hill, 1963.

Grant, Damian. *Realism*. London: Methuen, 1970.

Green, Martin. *The Von Richthofen Sisters: The Triumphant and the Tragic Modes of Love*. New York: Basic Books, 1974.

Grohmann, Will. *Ernst Ludwig Kirchner*. Trans. Ilse Falk. New York: Arts, 1961.

Grottanelli, Vinigi L. "The Lugard Lecture of 1961." McCall and Bay 3–22.

Hadermann, Paul. "Expressionist Literature and Painting." Weisstein 111–39.

Haftmann, Werner. *Emil Nolde*. Trans. Norbert Guterman. New York: Abrams, n.d.

Hammacher, A. M. *Genius and Disaster: The Ten Creative Years of Vincent Van Gogh*. New York: Abrams, n.d.

——. "Van Gogh and the Words." de la Faille 9–37.

Hardy, Thomas. Tess of the d'Urbervilles : *An Authoritative Text; Hardy and the Novel; Criticism*. 2nd ed. Ed. Scott Elledge. Norton Critical Edition. New York : Norton, 1979.

Harrison, Jane Ellen. *Ancient Art and Ritual*. 1913. Home University Library. London: Butterworth, 1927.

Hatzfeld, Helmut A. *Literature Through Art: A New Approach to French Literature*. Chapel Hill: U of North Carolina P, 1969.

Hauser, Arnold. *The Social History of Art*. 2 vols. London: Routledge, 1951.

H.D. [Hilda Doolittle]. *Bid Me to Live: A Madrigal*. 1960. Redding Ridge, CT: Black Swan, 1983.

Heidegger, Martin. *Being and Time*. Trans. John Macquarrie and Edward Robinson. New York: Harper, 1962.

——. "The Nature of Language." *On the Way to Language*. Trans. Peter D. Herz. San Francisco: Harper, 1971. 57–108.

——. "The Origin of the Work of Art." *Poetry, Language, Thought*. Trans. Albert Hofstadter. New York: Harper Colophon, 1975. 17–87.

Herzinger, Kim A. *D. H. Lawrence in His Time : 1908–1915*. Lewisburg: Bucknell UP, 1982.

Heyd, Milly. *Aubrey Beardsley: Symbol, Mask and Self-Irony*. American University Studies. Series 4. Vol. 35. New York: Lang, 1986.

Heywood, Christopher. "African Art and the Work of Roger Fry and D. H. Lawrence." *Sheffield Papers on Literature and Society* 1 (1976): 102–13.

Hillier, J. *Hokusai: Paintings, Drawings and Woodcuts*. Oxford: Phaidon, 1978.

Hiroshige, Ando. *One Hundred Famous Views of Edo*. New York: Braziller, 1986.

Hirsh, Diana, et al. *The World of Turner, 1775–1851*. New York: Time-Life, 1969.

Hodin, J. P. *Oskar Kokoschka: The Artist and His Time*. Greenwich, CT: New York Graphic Soc., 1966.

———. "Problems of Living Art Criticism." *The Dilemma of Being Modern: Essays on Art and Literature*. London: Routledge, 1956. 220–40.

Holden, Donald. *Whistler Landscapes and Seascapes*. New York: Watson-Guptill, 1976.

Holderness, Graham. *D. H. Lawrence: History, Ideology and Fiction*. Dublin: Gill, 1982.

Hough, Graham. *The Dark Sun: A Study of D. H. Lawrence*. 1956. Harmondsworth, Middlesex: Penguin, 1961.

House, John. *Monet: Nature into Art*. New Haven: Yale UP, 1986.

Humma, John B. *Metaphor and Meaning in D. H. Lawrence's Later Novels*. Columbia: U of Missouri P, 1990.

Huxley, Aldous. Introduction. *The Letters of D. H. Lawrence*. Ed. Huxley. ix–xxxiv.

———, ed. *The Letters of D. H. Lawrence*. London: Heinemann, 1932.

———. "Wordsworth in the Tropics." *Collected Essays*. London: Chatto, 1959. 1–9.

Ingersoll, Earl. "Staging the Gaze in D. H. Lawrence's *Women in Love*." *Studies in the Novel* 26 (1994): 268–80.

Jaffé, Hans L. C. *The World of the Impressionists*. Maplewood, NJ: Hammond, 1969.

Jakobson, Roman. "The Metaphoric and Metonymic Poles." *Modern Criticism and Theory*. Ed. David Lodge. London: Longman, 1988. 57–61.

Janik, Del Ivan. *The Curve of Return: D. H. Lawrence's Travel Books*. English Literary Studies No. 22. Victoria, B.C.: U of Victoria P, 1981.

———. "Toward Thingness: Cézanne's Painting and Lawrence's Poetry." *Twentieth Century Literature* 19 (1973): 119–28.

Jaques-Dalcroze, Emile. *Eurythmics, Art and Education*. Trans. Frederick Rothwell. Ed. Cynthia Cox. New York: Arno, 1980.

Jauss, Hans Robert. *Toward an Aesthetic of Reception*. Trans. Timothy Bahti. Theory and History of Literature. Vol. 2. Minneapolis: U of Minnesota P, 1982.

Jennings, Guy. *Impressionist Painters*. Twickenham, Middlesex: Hamlyn, 1986.

Jones, Edwin. "The Book of Nature Read by Cézanne." *Reading the Book of Nature: A Phenomenological Study of Creative Expression in Science and Painting*. Athens: Ohio UP, 1989. 90–112.

Joyce, James. *A Portrait of the Artist as a Young Man: Text, Criticism, and Notes*. Ed. Chester G. Anderson. Viking Critical Library. New York: Viking, 1968.

Jung, Carl G. "The Spiritual Problem of Modern Man." 1931. *Civilization in Transition. The Collected Works of C. G. Jung*. Trans. R. F. C. Hull. Vol. 10. Bollingen Series 20. New York: Pantheon-Bollingen, 1964. 74–94.

Kandinsky, Wassily. *Concerning the Spiritual in Art*. 1911. Trans. M. T. H. Sadler. New York: Dover, 1977.

Kant, Immanuel. "On the Dynamically Sublime in Nature." *Critique of Judgment*. 1790. Trans. Werner S. Pluhar. Indianapolis: Hackett, 1987. 119–40.

Kazin, Alfred. "Sons, Lovers and Mothers." Moynahan 597–610.

Keats, John. *The Letters of John Keats*. Ed. Maurice Bundon Forman. 3rd ed. London: Oxford UP, 1947.

Kessler, Jascha. "D. H. Lawrence's Primitivism." *Texas Studies in Literature and Language* 5 (1964): 467–88.

Kinkead-Weekes, Mark. "D. H. Lawrence and the Dance." *Journal of the D. H. Lawrence Society* (1992–93): 45–62.

Kirchner 1880–1938: Oils, Watercolours, Drawings. June–July 1969. London: Marlborough Fine Art, 1969.

Klee, Paul. *The Thinking Eye*. Ed. Jürg Spiller. Trans. Ralph Manheim. 2nd rev. ed. New York: Wittenborn, 1964.

Kockelmans, Joseph J. *Heidegger on Art and Art Works*. Dordrecht: Nijhoff, 1985.

Kooistra, Lorraine Janzen. "Beardsley's Reading of Malory's *Morte Darthur*: Images of a Decadent World." *Mosaic* 23 (1990): 55–72.

Kozloff, Max. *Cubism/Futurism*. New York: Charterhouse, 1973.

Krasner, James. *The Entangled Eye: Visual Perception and the Representation of Nature in Post-Darwinian Narrative*. New York: Oxford UP, 1992.

Kronegger, Maria Elisabeth. *Literary Impressionism*. New Haven, CT: College and University, 1973.

Kuchling, Heimo. *Expressionism*. Trans. Stephen Gorman. Bristol: Artlines, 1985.

Kushigian, Nancy. *Pictures and Fictions: Visual Modernism and the Pre-War Novels of D. H. Lawrence*. New York: Lang, 1990.

Kwant, Remy C. *Phenomenology of Expression*. Pittsburgh: Duquesne UP, 1969.

Laban, Rudolf. *A Life for Dance: Reminiscences*. New York: Theatre Arts, 1975.

Laing, R. D. "The Case of Peter." *The Divided Self*. Harmondsworth, Middlesex: Penguin, 1970. 94–105.

Langer, Susanne. *Feeling and Form*. New York: Scribner's, 1953.

Lassaigne, Jacques. *Impressionism*. Trans. Paul Eve. New York: Funk, 1969.

Laude, Jean. *The Arts of Black Africa*. Trans. Jean Decock. Berkeley: U of California P, 1971.

Lawrence, D. H. *Apocalypse and the Writings on Revelation*. Ed. Mara Kalnins. Cambridge: Cambridge UP, 1980.

———. "Art and Morality." 1925. *Study of Thomas Hardy* 163–68.

———. *The Complete Poems of D. H. Lawrence*. Ed. Vivian de Sola Pinto and Warren Roberts. Harmondsworth, Middlesex: Penguin, 1977.

———. *The Complete Short Stories of D. H. Lawrence*. 3 vols. New York: Viking, 1961.

———. "The Crown." *Reflections on the Death of a Porcupine and Other Essays*. Ed. Michael Herbert. Cambridge: Cambridge UP, 1988. 251–306.

———. "Daughters of the Vicar." 1914. *The Prussian Officer* 40–87.

———. *England, My England and Other Stories.* Ed. Bruce Steele. Cambridge: Cambridge UP, 1990.

———. *The Escaped Cock.* 1928. Ed. Gerald M. Lacy. Los Angeles: Black Sparrow, 1973.

———. "Fantasia of the Unconscious." 1922. *Psychoanalysis and the Unconscious* and *Fantasia of the Unconscious.* New York: Viking, 1960.

———. "Flowery Tuscany." 1927. *Sketches of Etruscan Places.* 223–43.

———. "Foreword to *Women in Love*." *Women in Love.* Appendix 1. 485–86.

———. "Herman Melville's *Typee* and *Omoo*." *The Symbolic Meaning* 217–29.

———. "The Hopi Snake Dance." 1924. *Mornings in Mexico* 139–79.

———. "The Horse Dealer's Daughter." 1922. *England, My England* 137–52.

———. "Indians and an Englishman." 1923. *Phoenix* 92–99.

———. "Introduction to These Paintings." 1929. *Phoenix* 551–84.

———. *Kangaroo.* 1923. Ed. Bruce Steele. Cambridge: Cambridge UP, 1994.

———. *Lady Chatterley's Lover; À Propos of* Lady Chatterley's Lover. 1929, 1930. Ed. Michael Squires. Cambridge: Cambridge UP, 1993.

———. *The Letters of D. H. Lawrence: Vol. 1: September 1901–May 1913.* Ed. James T. Boulton. Cambridge: Cambridge UP, 1979.

———. *The Letters of D. H. Lawrence: Vol. 2: June 1913–October 1916.* Ed. George J. Zytaruk and James T. Boulton. Cambridge: Cambridge UP, 1981.

———. *The Letters of D. H. Lawrence: Vol. 3: October 1916–June 1921.* Ed. James T. Boulton and Andrew Robertson. Cambridge: Cambridge UP, 1984.

———. *The Letters of D. H. Lawrence: Vol. 4: June 1921–March 1924.* Ed. Warren Roberts, James T. Boulton, and Elizabeth Mansfield. Cambridge: Cambridge UP, 1987.

———. *The Letters of D. H. Lawrence: Vol. 5: March 1924–March 1927.* Ed. James T. Boulton and Lindeth Vasey. Cambridge: Cambridge UP, 1989.

———. *The Letters of D. H. Lawrence: Vol. 6: March 1927–November 1928.* Ed. James T. Boulton and Margaret H. Boulton, with Gerald M. Lacy. Cambridge: Cambridge UP, 1991.

———. *The Letters of D. H. Lawrence: Vol. 7: November 1928–February 1930.* Ed. Keith Sagar and James T. Boulton. Cambridge: Cambridge UP, 1993.

———. *The Lost Girl.* 1920. Ed. John Worthen. Cambridge: Cambridge UP, 1981.

———. "Making Pictures." 1929. *Phoenix II* 602–7.

———. "Morality and the Novel." 1925. *Study of Thomas Hardy* 169–76.

———. *Mornings in Mexico.* 1927. Salt Lake City: Smith, 1982.

———. *Movements in European History.* 1921. Ed. Philip Crumpton. Cambridge: Cambridge UP, 1989.

———. "New Mexico." 1931. *Phoenix* 141–47.

——. "Nottingham and the Mining Countryside." 1930. *Phoenix* 133–40.

——. "The Novel." 1925. *Study of Thomas Hardy* 177–90.

——. "Odour of Chrysanthemums." 1911. *The Prussian Officer* 181–99.

——. *Paintings of D. H. Lawrence.* Ed. Mervyn Levy. London: Cory, 1964.

——. "Pan in America." *Phoenix* 22–31.

——. *Phoenix: The Posthumous Papers of D. H. Lawrence.* Ed. Edward D. McDonald. 1936. New York: Viking, 1964.

——. *Phoenix II: Uncollected, Unpublished, and Other Prose Works by D. H. Lawrence.* Ed. Warren Roberts and Harry T. Moore. New York: Viking, 1970.

——. *The Plumed Serpent (Quetzalcoatl).* 1926. Ed. L. D. Clark. Cambridge: Cambridge UP, 1987.

——. "Poetry of the Present." 1919. *Complete Poems.* 181–86.

——. "The Prussian Officer [Honour and Arms]." *The Prussian Officer* 1–21.

——. *The Prussian Officer and Other Stories.* 1914. Ed. John Worthen. Cambridge: Cambridge UP, 1983.

——. *The Rainbow.* 1915. Ed. Mark Kinkead-Weekes. Cambridge: Cambridge UP, 1989.

——. "Reflections on the Death of a Porcupine." *Reflections on the Death of a Porcupine and Other Essays.* 1925. Ed. Michael Herbert. Cambridge: Cambridge UP, 1988. 347–63.

——. *Sea and Sardinia.* 1921. Harmondsworth, Middlesex: Penguin, 1976.

——. *Sketches of Etruscan Places and Other Italian Essays.* Ed. Simonetta de Filippis. Cambridge: Cambridge UP, 1992.

——. *Sons and Lovers.* 1913. Ed. Helen Baron and Carl Baron. Cambridge: Cambridge UP, 1992.

——. "The Spirit of Place." 1918. *The Symbolic Meaning* 16–31.

——. "St. Mawr." 1925. *St. Mawr and Other Stories.* Ed. Brian Finney. Cambridge: Cambridge UP, 1983.

——. "Study of Thomas Hardy." *Study of Thomas Hardy and Other Essays* 3–128.

——. *Study of Thomas Hardy and Other Essays.* Ed. Bruce Steele. Cambridge: Cambridge UP, 1985.

——. *The Symbolic Meaning: The Uncollected Versions of* Studies in Classic American Literature. Ed. Armin Arnold. Fontwell, Arundel: Centaur, 1962.

——. *The Trespasser.* 1912. Ed. Elizabeth Mansfield. Cambridge: Cambridge UP, 1981.

——. "Twilight in Italy." 1916. *Twilight in Italy and Other Essays.* Ed. Paul Eggert. Cambridge: Cambridge UP, 1994. 85–226.

——. "The Two Principles." 1919. *The Symbolic Meaning* 175–89.

——. *The White Peacock.* 1911. Ed. Andrew Robertson. Cambridge: Cambridge UP, 1983.

——. "Why the Novel Matters." 1925. *Study of Thomas Hardy* 191–98.

——. "The Woman Who Rode Away." *The Complete Short Stories.* Vol. 2. 546–81.

——. *Women in Love.* 1920. Ed. David Farmer, Lindeth Vasey, and John Worthen. Cambridge: Cambridge UP, 1987.

Leavis, F. R. *D. H. Lawrence: Novelist.* 1955. Harmondsworth, Middlesex: Penguin, 1976.

Leiris, Michel, and Jacqueline Delange. *African Art.* Trans. Michael Ross. London: Thames, 1968.

Lerner, Laurence. "Blood and Mind: The Father in *Sons and Lovers.*" Salgādo 216–20.

Leuzinger, Elsy. *The Art of Black Africa.* Trans. R. A. Wilson. London: Studio Vista, 1972.

Levin, Harry. *The Myth of the Golden Age in the Renaissance.* London: Faber, 1970.

Levine, Frederick S. *The Apocalyptic Vision: The Art of Franz Marc as German Expressionism.* New York: Harper, 1979.

Lévi-Strauss, Claude. *Tristes Tropiques.* Trans. John and Doreen Weightman. New York: Atheneum, 1974.

Lindsay, Jack. "The Impact of Modernism on Lawrence." *Paintings of D. H. Lawrence* 35–53.

Lippincott, Louise. *Edvard Munch: "Starry Night."* Malibu, CA.: Getty Museum, 1988.

Lodge, David. *The Modes of Modern Writing: Metaphor, Metonymy, and the Typology of Modern Literature.* London: Arnold, 1977.

Lovejoy, Arthur O., and George Boas. *Primitivism and Related Ideas in Antiquity.* New York: Octagon, 1965.

Lucie-Smith, Edward. "The Poetry of D. H. Lawrence—with a Glance at Shelley." Spender 224–33.

Lukács, Georg. *Studies in European Realism.* The Universal Library. New York: Grosset, 1964.

Macke, August. "Masks." *The "Blaue Reiter" Almanac.* Ed. Wassily Kandinsky and Franz Marc. New Documentary ed. Ed. Klaus Lankheit. New York: Viking, 1974. 83–89.

Macmillan, Duncan. *Scottish Art, 1460–1990.* Edinburgh: Mainstream, 1990.

Malraux, André. *The Voices of Silence.* Trans. Stuart Gilbert. St. Albans, Herts.: Paladin, 1974.

Marinetti, F. T. *I Poeti Futuristi.* Milano: Edizioni Futuriste di "Poesia," 1912.

Mark Gertler: The Early and Late Years. Catalogue, 30 March–27 May 1982. London: Ben Uri Art Gallery, 1982.

Martin, Marianne. *Futurist Art and Theory, 1909–1915.* New York: Hacker, 1978.

Masheck, Joseph. "Raw Art: 'Primitive' Authenticity and German Expressionism." *Res* 4 (1982): 92–117.

McCall, Daniel F. "Introduction: Art, History, and Art History." McCall and Bay ix–xiii.

McCall, Daniel F., and Edna G. Bay, eds. *African Images: Essays in African Iconology*. Boston University Papers on Africa. Vol. 6. New York: Africana/Boston U, 1975.

McLaughlin, Ann L. "The Clenched and Knotted Horses in *The Rainbow*." *D. H. Lawrence Review* 13 (1980): 179–86.

Meauzé, Pierre. *African Art: Sculpture*. Cleveland: World, 1978.

Meier-Graefe, Julius. *Vincent Van Gogh: A Biographical Study*. Trans. John Holroyd-Reece. New York: Literary Guild, 1933.

Merleau-Ponty, Maurice. "Cézanne's Doubt." *Sense and Non-Sense*. Trans. Hubert L. Dreyfus and Patricia Allen Dreyfus. N.p.: Northwestern UP, 1964. 9–25.

———. "Eye and Mind." Trans. Carleton Dallery. *The Primacy of Perception*. Ed. James M. Edie. N.p.: Northwestern University Press, 1964. 159–90.

———. *Phenomenology of Perception*. Trans. Colin Smith. London: Routledge, 1962.

Meyers, Jeffrey. *D. H. Lawrence and the Experience of Italy*. Philadelphia: U of Pennsylvania P, 1982.

———. "Fra Angelico and *The Rainbow*." *Painting and the Novel* 53–64.

———. *Painting and the Novel*. Manchester: Manchester UP, 1975.

Michaels-Tonks, Jennifer. *D. H. Lawrence: The Polarity of North and South—Germany and Italy in His Prose Works*. Bonn: Grundmann, 1976.

Miko, Stephen J. *Toward* Women in Love: *The Emergence of a Lawrentian Aesthetic*. New Haven: Yale UP, 1971.

Miles, Thomas H. "Birkin's Electro-Mystical Body of Reality: D. H. Lawrence's Use of Kundalini." *D. H. Lawrence Review* 9 (1976): 194–212.

Miller, Henry. *The World of Lawrence*. Ed. Evelyn J. Hinz and John J. Teunissen. Santa Barbara, CA: Capra, 1980.

Milton, Colin. *Lawrence and Nietzsche: A Study in Influence*. Aberdeen: Aberdeen UP, 1987.

Mitchell, W. J. T. *Iconology: Image, Text, Ideology*. Chicago: U of Chicago P, 1986.

Montgomery, Robert E. *The Visionary D. H. Lawrence: Beyond Philosophy and Art*. Cambridge: Cambridge UP, 1994.

Moody, H. L. B. "African Sculpture Symbols in a Novel by D. H. Lawrence." *Ibadan* 26 (1969): 73–77.

Moore, Harry T. "The Prose of D. H. Lawrence." Partlow and Moore 245–57.

Morris, Inez R. "African Sculpture Symbols in *Women in Love*." *D. H. Lawrence Review* 16 (1983): 25–43.

Morrison, Kristin. "Lawrence, Beardsley, Wilde: *The White Peacock* and Sexual Ambiguity." *Western Humanities Review* 30 (1976): 241–48.

Moynahan, Julian. "*Sons and Lovers*: The Search for Form." Moynahan 560–76.

——, ed. Sons and Lovers: *Text, Background and Criticism*. Viking Critical Library. Harmondsworth, Middlesex: Penguin, 1977.

Murry, J. M. "Review of *Women in Love*." *D. H. Lawrence: A Critical Anthology*. Ed. H. Coombes. Harmondsworth, Middlesex: Penguin, 1973. 138–43.

Myers, Bernard S. *The German Expressionists: A Generation in Revolt*. Concise ed. New York: McGraw-Hill, n.d.

Narazaki, Muneshige. *Hiroshige: The 53 Stations of the Tōkaidō*. Adapted by Gordon Sager. Tokyo: Kodansha, 1969.

——. *Hokusai: "The Thirty-Six Views of Mt. Fuji."* Adapted by John Bester. Tokyo: Kodansha, 1968.

Nehls, Edward. *D. H. Lawrence: A Composite Biography: Vol. 1, 1885–1919*. Madison: U of Wisconsin P, 1957.

Neumann, Erich. "Creative Man and Transformation." *Art and the Creative Unconscious: Four Essays*. Trans. Ralph Manheim. Bollingen Series 61. Princeton: Princeton UP, 1971. 149–205.

Nordenfalk, Carl. *The Life and Work of Van Gogh*. Trans. Lawrence Wolfe. London: Elek, 1953.

Oates, Joyce Carol. "Lawrence's Götterdämmerung: The Apocalyptic Vision of *Women in Love*." *Critical Essays on D. H. Lawrence*. Ed. Dennis Jackson and Fleda Brown Jackson. Boston: Hall, 1988. 92–110.

Ortega y Gasset, José. *The Dehumanization of Art and Other Writings on Art and Culture*. New York: Anchor-Doubleday, n.d.

Ouspensky, P. D. *Tertium Organum*. Trans. Nicholas Bessaraboff and Claude Brangdon. New York: Vintage, 1970.

Panofsky, Erwin. "Iconography and Iconology: An Introduction to the Study of Renaissance Art." *Meaning in the Visual Arts: Papers in and on Art History*. New York: Anchor-Doubleday, 1955. 26–54.

Partlow, Robert B., Jr., and Harry T. Moore, eds. *D. H. Lawrence: The Man Who Lived*. Carbondale: Southern Illinois UP, 1980.

Paudrat, Jean-Louis. "From Africa." Trans. John Shepley. Rubin Vol. 1. 125–75.

Perloff, Marjorie. *The Futurist Moment: Avant-Garde, Avant Guerre, and the Language of Rupture*. Chicago: U of Chicago P, 1986.

Pickvance, Ronald. *Van Gogh in Saint-Rémy and Auvers*. New York: Metropolitan Museum of Art-Abrams, 1986.

Pinkney, Tony. *D. H. Lawrence and Modernism*. Iowa City: U of Iowa P, 1990.

Poggioli, Renato. *The Theory of the Avant-Garde*. Trans. Gerald Fitzgerald. Cambridge: Harvard UP, 1968.

Pool, Phoebe. *Impressionism*. New York: Oxford UP, 1967.

Pratt, William, ed. *The Imagist Poem*. New York: Dutton, 1936.

Price, Sally. *Primitive Art in Civilized Places*. Chicago: U of Chicago P, 1989.

Pritchard, R. E. *D. H. Lawrence: Body of Darkness*. London: Hutchinson U Library, 1971.

Read, Herbert. "Lawrence as a Painter." *Paintings of D. H. Lawrence* 55–65.

Remsbury, John. "'Real Thinking': Lawrence and Cézanne." *Cambridge Quarterly* 2 (1967): 117–47.

Remsbury, John, and Ann Remsbury. "Lawrence and Art." *D. H. Lawrence: A Critical Study of the Major Novels and Other Writings*. Ed. A. H. Gomme. Sussex: Harvester, 1978. 190–218.

Rewald, John. *The History of Impressionism*. 4th rev. ed. New York: Museum of Modern Art, 1973.

Richardson, John Adkins, and John I. Ades. "D. H. Lawrence on Cézanne: A Study in the Psychology of Critical Intuition." *Journal of Aesthetics and Art Criticism* 28 (1970): 441–53.

Robbins, Warren M. *African Art in American Collections/L'Art Africain dans les Collections Americaines*. Trans. Richard Walters. New York: Praeger, 1966.

Robbins, Warren M., and Nancy Ingram Nooter. *African Art in American Collections: Survey 1989*. Washington: Smithsonian Institution, 1989.

Róheim, Géza. *The Origin and Function of Culture*. New York: Nervous and Mental Disease Monographs, 1943.

Rosenberg, Jakob. "German Expressionist Printmakers." *Magazine of Art* 38 (1945): 300–305.

Roskill, Mark. "Introduction." *The Letters of Vincent Van Gogh*. Ed. Roskill. Glasgow: Fontana/Collins, 1963. 11–31.

Ross, Charles L. Women in Love: *A Novel of Mythic Realism*. Boston: Twayne, 1991.

Ross, Robert. "A Note on Salomé." *Salomé: A Tragedy in One Act Translated from the French of Oscar Wilde with Sixteen Drawings by Aubrey Beardsley*. London: Lane, 1912. vii–xxiii.

Rothschild, Edward F. *The Meaning of Unintelligibility in Modern Art*. Chicago: U of Chicago P, 1934.

Rubin, William, ed. *"Primitivism" in 20th Century Art: Affinity of the Tribal and the Modern*. 2 vols. New York: Museum of Modern Art, 1984.

Ruthven, K. K. "The Savage God: Conrad and Lawrence." *Critical Quarterly* 10 (1968): 39–54.

Sagar, Keith. *D. H. Lawrence: Life into Art*. Harmondsworth, Middlesex: Penguin, 1985.

———. *The Life of D. H. Lawrence: An Illustrated Biography*. London: Eyre Methuen, 1980.

Salgādo, Gāmini, ed. Sons and Lovers: *A Casebook*. London: Macmillan, 1969.

Sanders, Scott. *D. H. Lawrence: The World of the Five Major Novels*. New York: Viking, 1974.

Schapiro, Meyer. *Paul Cézanne*. New York: Abrams., n.d.

———. *Vincent Van Gogh*. New York: Abrams, n.d.

Schvey, Henry. "Lawrence and Expressionism." *D. H. Lawrence: New Studies*. Ed. Christopher Heywood. London: Macmillan, 1987. 124–36.

Scott, James F. "D. H. Lawrence's Germania: Ethnic Psychology and Cultural Crisis in the Shorter Fiction." *D. H. Lawrence Review* 10 (1977): 142–64.

Scottish Painting, 1880–1930. Glasgow: Glasgow Art Gallery and Museum, 1973.

Seitz, William C. *Claude Monet*. New York: Abrams, n.d.

Sejourné, Laurette. *Burning Water: Thought and Religion in Ancient Mexico*. Berkeley: Shambhala, 1976.

Selz, Peter. *German Expressionist Painting*. Berkeley: U of California P, 1974.

Sepčić, V. "'Women in Love' and Expressionism (I)." *Studia Romanica et Anglica Zagrabiensia* 26 (1981): 397–442.

———. "'Women in Love' and Expressionism (II)." *Studia Romanica et Anglica Zagrabiensia* 27 (1982): 3–64.

Seznec, Jean. "Literary Inspiration in Van Gogh." *Magazine of Art* 43 (1950): 282–83, 306–7.

Sheppard, Richard. "German Expressionism." *Modernism 1890–1930*. Ed. Malcolm Bradbury and James McFarlane. Harmondsworth, Middlesex: Penguin, 1976. 274–91.

Shikes, Ralph E., and Paula Harper. *Pissarro: His Life and Work*. New York: Horizon, 1980.

Sieber, Roy, and Roslyn Walker. *African Art in the Cycle of Life*. Catalogue, 28 September 1987–20 March 1988. Washington, DC: National Museum of African Art/Smithsonian Institution, 1987.

Simpson, David. *Fetishism and Imagination: Dickens, Melville, Conrad*. Baltimore: Johns Hopkins UP, 1982.

Soffici, Ardengo. *Cubismo e Futurismo*. 2nd ed. Firenze: Libreria della Voce, 1914.

Sokel, Walter H. *The Writer in Extremis: Expressionism in Twentieth-Century German Literature*. 1959. New York: McGraw-Hill, 1964.

Sorrell, Walter. *The Mary Wigman Book: Her Writings Edited and Translated*. Middletown, CT: Wesleyan UP, 1975.

Sotriffer, Kristian. *Expressionism and Fauvism*. Trans. Richard Rickett. New York: McGraw-Hill, 1972.

Spender, Stephen, ed. *D. H. Lawrence: Novelist, Poet, Prophet*. New York: Harper, 1973.

Squires, Michael. *The Pastoral Novel: Studies in George Eliot, Thomas Hardy, and D. H. Lawrence*. Charlottesville: UP of Virginia, 1974.

Steiner, George. *Martin Heidegger*. Chicago: U of Chicago P, 1987.

Steiner, Wendy. "The Painting-Literature Analogy." *The Colors of Rhetoric: Problems in the Relation Between Modern Literature and Painting*. Chicago: U of Chicago P, 1982. 1–18.

Stewart, Jack F. "Common Art Interests of Van Gogh and Lawrence." *Studies in the Humanities* 11 (1984): 18–32 (illus.).

———. "Dialectics of Knowing in *Women in Love*." *Twentieth Century Literature* 37 (1991): 59–75.

———. "Expressionism in 'The Prussian Officer.'" *D. H. Lawrence Review* 18 (1985–86): 275–89 (illus.).

———. "Landscape Painting and Pre-Raphaelitism in *The White Peacock*." *D. H. Lawrence Review* 27 (1997–98): 3–25 (illus.).

———. "Metaphor and Metonymy, Color and Space in *Sea and Sardinia*." *Twentieth Century Literature* 41 (1995): 208–23.

———. "The Myth of the Fall in *Women in Love*." *Philological Quarterly* 75 (1996): 443–63.

———. "Primordial Affinities: Lawrence, Van Gogh and the Miners." *Mosaic* 24 (1991): 93–113 (illus.).

Strange, Edward F. *Hiroshige's Woodblock Prints: A Guide*. New York: Dover, 1983.

Stuckey, Charles F. *Monet: A Retrospective*. New York: Levin, 1985.

Sweeney, James Johnson. *Plastic Redirections in 20th Century Painting*. Chicago: U of Chicago P, 1934.

Sypher, Wylie. *Rococo to Cubism in Art and Literature*. New York: Vintage, 1960.

Taylor, Joshua C. *Futurism*. New York: Museum of Modern Art, 1961.

Timm, Werner. *The Graphic Art of Edvard Munch*. Trans. Ruth Michaelis-Jena, with Patrick Murray. Greenwich, CT: New York Graphic Soc., 1969.

Tindall, William York. Introduction. *The Plumed Serpent (Quetzalcoatl)*. By D. H. Lawrence. New York: Vintage, 1955. v–xv.

Tomory, Peter. *The Life and Art of Henry Fuseli*. London: Thames, 1972.

Torgovnick, Marianna. *Gone Primitive: Savage Intellects, Modern Lives*. Chicago: U of Chicago P, 1990.

———. *The Visual Arts, Pictorialism, and the Novel: James, Lawrence, and Woolf*. Princeton: Princeton UP, 1985.

Tracy, Billy T., Jr. *D. H. Lawrence and the Literature of Travel*. Studies in Modern Literature, No. 18. Ann Arbor: UMI, 1983.

Tralbaut, Marc Edo. *Vincent Van Gogh*. New York: Alpine, 1969.

Tuchman, Maurice. *Van Gogh and Expressionism*. New York: Guggenheim, 1964.

Turner, John, with Cornelia Rumpf-Worthen and Ruth Jenkins. "The Otto Gross-Frieda Weekley Correspondence: Transcribed, Translated, and Annotated." *D. H. Lawrence Review* 22 (1990): 137–225.

Tylor, Edward B. *Primitive Culture*. 1871. 6th ed. 2 vols. London: Murray, 1920.

Ulmer, Gregory L. "D. H. Lawrence, Wilhelm Worringer, and the Aesthetics of Modernism." *D. H. Lawrence Review* 10 (1977): 165–81.

Vajda, György M. "Outline of the Philosophic Backgrounds to Expressionism." Weisstein 45–58.

Van Ghent, Dorothy. "On *Sons and Lovers*." Moynahan 527–46.

Van Gogh, Vincent. *The Complete Letters of Vincent Van Gogh*. 2nd ed. 3 vols. Boston: New York Graphic Soc., 1978.

———. *Lettres de Vincent Van Gogh à Emile Bernard*. Paris: Vollard, 1911.

Varnedoe, Kirk, ed. *Northern Light: Realism and Symbolism in Scandinavian Painting 1880–1910*. New York: Brooklyn Museum, 1982.

Veitch, Douglas W. *Lawrence, Greene and Lowry: The Fictional Landscape of Mexico*. Waterloo, Ontario: Wilfrid Laurier UP, 1978.

Vitoux, Pierre. "The Chapter 'Excurse' in *Women in Love*: Its Genesis and the Critical Problem." *Texas Studies in Literature and Language* 17 (1976): 821–36.

Vivante, Leone. *Essays on Art and Ontology*. Trans. Arturo Vivante. Salt Lake City: U of Utah P, 1980.

———. *A Philosophy of Potentiality*. London: Routledge, 1955.

Vogel, Susan. Introduction. *Perspectives: Angles on African Art*. Baldwin et al. 10–17.

Vogt, Paul. *Expressionism: German Painting 1905–1920*. Trans. Antony Vivis and Robert Erich Wolf. New York: Abrams, 1980.

Walker, John A. "Art History Versus Philosophy: The Enigma of the 'Old Shoes.'" *Van Gogh Studies: Five Critical Essays*. London: Jaw, 1981. 61–71.

Wallace, M. Elizabeth. "The Circling Hawk: Philosophy of Knowledge in Polanyi and Lawrence." *The Challenge of D. H. Lawrence*. Ed. Michael Squires and Keith Cushman. Madison: U of Wisconsin P, 1990. 103–20.

Wasserman, Earl R. *The Finer Tone: Keats's Major Poems*. Baltimore: Johns Hopkins P, 1967.

Watt, Ian. "Impressionism and Symbolism in *Heart of Darkness*." *Joseph Conrad: A Commemoration*. Ed. Norman Sherry. London: Macmillan, 1976. 37–53.

Wattenmaker, Richard J. *Puvis de Chavannes and the Modern Tradition*. Catalogue of Exhibition, October 24–November 30, 1975. Rev. ed. Toronto: Art Gallery of Ontario, 1976.

Weintraub, Stanley. *Aubrey Beardsley: Imp of the Perverse*. University Park: Pennsylvania UP, 1976.

Weiskel, Thomas. *The Romantic Sublime: Studies in the Structure and Psychology of Transcendence*. Baltimore: Johns Hopkins UP, 1976.

Weiss, Daniel A. *Oedipus in Nottingham: D. H. Lawrence*. Seattle: U of Washington P, 1962.

Weisstein, Ulrich, ed. *Expressionism as an International Literary Phenomenon*. Paris: Didier, 1973.

———. "Expressionism: Style or 'Weltanschauung'?" Weisstein 29–44.

——. Introduction. Weisstein 15–28.

Welsh-Ovcharov, Bogomila, ed. *Van Gogh in Perspective*. Englewood Cliffs, NJ: Prentice-Hall, 1974.

White, Hayden. "The Noble Savage Theme as Fetish." *Tropics of Discourse: Essays in Cultural Criticism*. Baltimore: Johns Hopkins UP, 1978. 183–96.

Whitford, Frank. *Expressionism*. London: Hamlyn, 1970.

Wichmann, Siegfried. *Japonisme: The Japanese Influence on Western Art in the 19th and 20th Centuries*. Trans. Mary Whittall et al. New York: Harmony, 1980.

Widmer, Kingsley. "The Primitivistic Aesthetic: D. H. Lawrence." *Journal of Aesthetics and Art History* 17 (1959): 344–53.

Wigman, Mary. *The Language of Dance*. Trans. Walter Sorrell. Middletown, CT: Wesleyan UP, 1966.

Wilde, Oscar. Preface. *The Picture of Dorian Gray*. Ed. Isobel Murray. Oxford: Oxford UP, 1974. xxxiii–xxxiv.

Wildi, Max. "The Birth of Expressionism in D. H. Lawrence." *English Studies* 19 (1937): 241–59.

Willett, Frank. *African Art: An Introduction*. London: Thames, 1971.

Wilson, Simon. *Beardsley*. Oxford: Phaidon, 1976.

Wingert, Paul S. *Primitive Art: Its Traditions and Styles*. New York: Oxford UP, 1962.

Wordsworth, William. The Prelude *with a Selection from the Shorter Poems, the Sonnets, "The Recluse," and "The Excursion."* Ed. Carlos Baker. New York: Holt, 1964.

The World of Van Gogh 1853–1890. By Robert Wallace and the Editors of Time-Life Books. Time-Life Library of Art. New York: Time-Life, 1969.

Worthen, John. Introduction. *The Rainbow*. By D. H. Lawrence. Ed. Worthen. London: Penguin, 1981. 11–33.

Zatlin, Linda Gertner. *Aubrey Beardsley and Victorian Sexual Politics*. Clarendon Studies in the History of Art. Oxford: Clarendon, 1990.

Zola, Emile. *Germinal*. Trans. Leonard Tancock. London: Penguin, 1954.

Zoll, Allan R. "Vitalism and the Metaphysics of Love: D. H. Lawrence and Schopenhauer." *D. H. Lawrence Review* 11 (1978): 1–20.

INDEX

Jack Stewart is a professor of English at the University of British Columbia, specializing in the interrelations of literature and painting in the modern period. He is the author of *The Incandescent Word: The Poetic Vision of Michael Bullock* and of numerous articles on D. H. Lawrence and Virginia Woolf. A frequent contributor to the *D. H. Lawrence Review* and a member of its editorial board, he has also published articles in *Twentieth Century Literature*, *Journal of Modern Literature*, *Modern Fiction Studies*, *Novel*, *Studies in the Novel*, *Studies in the Humanities*, *Canadian Literature*, *Mosaic*, *Style*, *Philological Quarterly*, and other journals.